Development-Induced Dis
and Resettlement

Every year millions of people are displaced from their homes, livelihoods and communities due to land-based development projects. There is no limit to what can be called a 'development project'. They can range from small-scale infrastructure or mining projects to mega hydropower plants; can be public or private, well-planned or rushed into. Knowledge of development-induced displacement and resettlement (DIDR) remains limited even after decades of experience and research. Many questions are yet unanswered: What is 'success' in resettlement? Is development without displacement possible or can resettlement be developmental? Is there a global safeguard policy or do we need an international right 'not to be displaced'?

This book revisits what we think we know about DIDR. Starting with case studies that challenge some of the most widespread preconceptions, it goes on to discuss the ethical aspects of DIDR. The book assesses the current laws, policies and rights governing the sector, and provides a glimpse of how the displaced people defend themselves in the absence of effective governance and safeguard mechanisms.

This book is a valuable resource for students, researchers, practitioners and policy makers working on international development, forced migration and population movements.

Irge Satiroglu, PhD, is an International Social Impact Assessment and Resettlement Specialist. She joined the Refugee Studies Centre, Department of International Development, University of Oxford as a Visiting Research Fellow in 2011–2012.

Narae Choi, DPhil, is a Social and Urban Development Specialist at the World Bank. She obtained her doctoral degree in International Development at the University of Oxford.

Routledge Studies in Development, Displacement and Resettlement

Land Solutions for Climate Displacement
Scott Leckie

Development-Induced Displacement and Resettlement
New perspectives on persisting problems
Edited by Irge Satiroglu and Narae Choi

'Theory meets experience in this volume of essays. It is about what actually happens to people and to communities when they become the development-induced-displaced. In querying the (im)probabilities of rehabilitation, it produces evidence from the ground that demands to be acknowledged while thinking about development, risk and loss.'

Usha Ramanathan, research fellow at the Centre for the Study of Developing Societies

'Forced population displacement and resettlement is among today's most complex and controversial development problems globally. Despite advanced planning, displacement is virtually always a mess and a breeding ground for unanticipated consequences and impoverishment risks. This book's co-authors invite the readers to a candid exploration of many questions seldom asked about development: Is success possible in recovery post-displacement? Are there adequate national and global safeguards against impoverishing the resettlers? Can powerless displaced people be empowered to stand up for their human rights? Yet despite big hurdles, the book contends that realistic and innovative solutions to the difficult – but not intractable – problems of displacement and resettlement do exist. But how can enough political will be mobilised for applying the known solutions? Professors, students, and development practitioners, specialists in building the infrastructures that require displacement, sociologists and lawyers, economists, political scientists, and philosophers, can understand better the contradictions of the world we live in due to the perspectives, research, and findings reported in this book.'

Professor Michael M. Cernea, NR Senior Fellow, Brookings Institution, Washington, DC

'This aptly titled volume of edited essays provides state-of-the-art analysis of current thinking and case study evidence on the continuing challenges of development-induced displacement and resettlement. Deploying an innovative, cross-cutting structure that covers assumptions, ethics, policy, and voice and power, the book will be of immense value to academics, policy makers and activists alike.'

Professor Roger Zetter, Professor Emeritus in Refugee Studies, University of Oxford

'Development-induced resettlement is one of the most important issues associated with large-scale infrastructure construction, urbanization and industrialization globally. The impoverishment risks caused by resettlement have been recognized by affected people, international organizations, governments, developers, consultants and civil society. Successful resettlement is a result of multiple factors such as policy, compensation, patterns of rehabilitation and reconstruction, planning, databases and management. China has the largest scale resettlement population in the word. Since the 1980s a number of excellent practices have been created but have received little attention. This book presents an excellent opportunity to examine both the successes and the lessons learnt from development-induced resettlement and will be an excellent asset for all researchers, policy-makers and practitioners from China and all over the world.'

Professor SHI Guoqing, Professor and Director of National Research Center for Resettlement, Hohai University, China

Development-Induced Displacement and Resettlement

New perspectives on persisting problems

Edited by Irge Satiroglu and Narae Choi

Routledge
Taylor & Francis Group
LONDON AND NEW YORK

First published 2015
by Routledge
2 Park Square, Milton Park, Abingdon, Oxon OX14 4RN

and by Routledge
711 Third Avenue, New York, NY 10017

Routledge is an imprint of the Taylor & Francis Group, an informa business

British Library Cataloguing-in-Publication Data
A catalogue record for this book is available from the British Library

Library of Congress Cataloging-in-Publication Data
Development-induced displacement and resettlement / edited by Irge Satiroglu and Narae Choi.
pages cm
1. Forced migration--Developing countries. 2. Internally displaced persons--Rehabilitation--Developing countries. I. Satiroglu, Irge, editor. II. Choi, Narae, 1981- editor.
HB2160.D48 2015
307.2--dc23
2014040254

ISBN: 978-1-138-79415-3 (hbk)
ISBN: 978-1-315-76052-0 (ebk)

Typeset in Goudy
by GreenGate Publishing Services, Tonbridge, Kent

Contents

Figures

Tables

Contributors

Yue Cao, MSPH, PhD, holds the Assistant Professor position in the Department of Health Science and Research at the Medical University of South Carolina. His research interests focus on migration and health studies, health disparities and psychosocial perspectives of rehabilitation among people with disability. In the past four years, he has published 15 articles in peer-reviewed journals.

Dawn Chatty is Professor in Anthropology and Forced Migration and former Director of the Refugee Studies Centre, Department of International Development, University of Oxford, UK. Her academic experience encompasses forced migration issues caused by development and conservation projects as well as conflicts and violence. She has authored ten books, more than 30 book chapters and more than 40 journal articles.

Narae Choi is a Social and Urban Development Specialist at the World Bank. She obtained her Master's and Doctoral degrees in International Development at the University of Oxford, UK. For over seven years, she conducted extensive research on direct and indirect impacts of development-induced displacement in Southeast Asia and elsewhere.

Chris de Wet, formerly Professor of Anthropology, is now at the Institute of Water Research, Rhodes University, South Africa. He specialises in the field of development-induced resettlement, having conducted research in southern Africa and India. He has consulted for a number of international agencies, and his fields of interest are the theory of resettlement, policy and ethics relating to resettlement.

Jay Drydyk is Professor of Philosophy at Carleton University, Canada, where he is also Director of the Centre on Values and Ethics. He is Past President of the International Development Ethics Association and a continuing Fellow of the Human Development and Capabilities Association.

Christine Gilmore, BA (Oxon), MA (York), MA (Manchester), is a PhD candidate at the Institute for Colonial and Postcolonial Studies at the University of Leeds, UK. Her research into the impact of DIDR on the Nubian Community in Egypt combines insights from the fields of literary and cultural studies, political ecology and critical development studies.

Pierre Gouws holds a Master's degree in Research Psychology from the University of Pretoria, South Africa and is a senior social scientist for Golder Associates Africa. His project experience spans ten years across Africa, conducting socio-economic impact assessments and developing resettlement plans in the extractive industries. He also serves as guest lecturer at the University of Pretoria in psychology and at the University of Johannesburg in socio-economic impact assessment.

Sean-Shong Hwang is Professor Emeritus in the Department of Sociology, University of Alabama, Birmingham, UK. His publications cover topics including involuntary migration in China's Three Gorges, causes and effects of English proficiency among immigrants to the US, interracial marriage and residential segregation in the US.

Jill Kavanagh, BA Law (Oxon), MSc (LSE), currently Myanmar Project Manager for Geneva-based PeaceNexus Foundation, has worked in Southeast Asia for five years and has direct experience advising public sector and corporate actors on conflict risks associated with displacement and resettlement, human rights impacts, social responsibility and stakeholder engagement. She was previously Senior Associate at Vriens & Partners corporate advisory firm. She speaks French and Myanmar.

Dolores Koenig, Professor of Anthropology, American University, Washington, DC, USA, has written on rural resettlement in West Africa, including its effects on those forced to move by Mali's Manantali Dam. She now works and publishes on the effects of development-caused forced resettlement in the growing cities of Africa and India.

Michèle Morel is legal advisor at the Brussels-based consultancy Milieu Ltd, department of Justice and Fundamental Rights. Before joining Milieu Ltd, she worked as legal advisor at Caritas International in the area of asylum and migration. She obtained her doctoral degree in law in 2012 at Ghent University, Belgium, and has been a visiting researcher at Oxford University, UK. Her main expertise is in the field of forced migration and human rights law.

Priti Narayan has been doing research on slum policy and implementation in Chennai, India, for over three years, with specific focus on resettlement practices. She has a Masters degree in Sociology from Columbia University and a year's experience as a journalist. She is currently a PhD student in Geography at Rutgers University, USA.

Susanna Price, currently Research Associate in the College of Asia and the Pacific at the Australian National University, has worked at the Asian Development Bank (ADB) and AusAID (Australia's former bilateral aid agency). International prizes include the Praxis Award, Washington Association of Professional Anthropologists (2003) for resettlement policy enhancement in the Asia Pacific region.

Irge Satiroglu is an International Social Impact Assessment and Resettlement Specialist with 15 years of experience in Eastern Europe, Middle East, Africa and Asia. She has double Master's in Development Studies (University of Reading, UK) and Social Sciences (Ankara University, Turkey) and completed her Doctoral degree in the latter. She joined the Refugee Studies Centre, Department of International Development, University of Oxford as a Visiting Research Fellow in 2011–2012.

Margarita Serje is Doctor in Social Anthropology (École des Hautes Études en Sciences Sociales, Paris, France) and has a BSc in architecture (Universidad de los Andes, Bogotá), Colombia. She specialises in problems related to development and the anthropology of space.

Indrani Sigamany is a senior international development consultant working with social justice. Her present doctoral research explores legal responses to the displacement of indigenous peoples from their ancestral lands in India. She is affiliated to the Centre for Applied Human Rights, York Law School, University of York, UK.

Juan Xi is Associate Professor in the Department of Sociology at University of Akron, USA. Her research focuses on migratory processes and their effects on the health and adaptation of immigrants. She has published one book and 20 articles in some of the leading journals in social and biomedical sciences such as *Social Science and Medicine*, *Social Science Research*, *Social Forces*, *Society and Mental Health*, *Ethnic and Racial Studies*, and *Medical Care*.

Foreword

Dawn Chatty

This volume emerges from several years' engagement among faculty, doctoral students and visiting fellows at the Refugee Studies Centre and the Department for International Development at the University of Oxford. It is, in some ways, the culmination of 20 years of research and advocacy in this area of forced migration that began with the publication of Chris McDowell's edited proceedings of the first Development-Induced Displacement and Resettlement (DIDR) conference at Oxford in 1995 (McDowell, 1996). The story, however, goes back much further and could be said to have started with Elizabeth Colson and Thayer Schudder's now classic, long-term study of the consequences of forced resettlement after dam-induced displacement among the Tonga of the Gwembe Valley in Zambia and Zimbabwe (Colson, 1995).

Forced migration is as long as history itself. Development-induced displacement is a post-World War Two phenomenon. It is an outcome of development and development aid that has tended to prioritise the greater good for a nation's people or economy over the specific needs or consequences to the subaltern, the marginal and often the indigenous. Every year 15 million people are displaced from their homes, their livelihoods shattered and their communities destroyed as a result of development projects (Terminski, 2012; Oliver-Smith, 2009; Cernea, 2006). These estimates suggest that now, in the twenty-first century, after nearly 50 years of organised development aid, we may have more than 500 million people who have suffered forced migration – as well as forced settlement – all this in the name of development.

Some of the displaced, particularly by large-scale urban redevelopment, road building and dam construction financed internationally through both public and private lending agencies, do have access to some forms of compensation, with resettlement planned and carried out by the state. Despite these plans, few of these resettlement projects are recorded as success stories and popular opposition continues across the world. Other development projects, particularly those involving multinational extractive industry companies – such as oil and mining – are not necessarily bound by the policy guidelines of international lending institutions. They generally refer to internal 'social corporate responsibility' guidelines. While it may be the case that positive examples are underreported in the media, the rhetoric is often stronger than visible action. The populations affected by this kind of development activity are generally poor, marginal traditional or indigenous communities. Resettlement is infrequently an option, and compensation or restitution are rarely adequate. Protection of nature through conservation projects is a more recent form of DIDR. It emerged in the late twentieth century as an outcome of the 1987 Brundtland Commission report *Our Common Future*. This Commission set up long-term strategies to protect our environment, resulting, not unexpectedly, in the dispossession and displacement of millions of mobile peoples (hunters and gatherers, pastoralists and other non-settled peoples) in order to create areas of 'pristine' nature nomads. By the beginning of the twenty-first century more than 11 per cent of the earth's surface has been declared protected. At the same time, local inhabitants in these areas have been displaced and sometimes forcibly settled, thus losing connection with centuries-old sustainable patterns of land use and livelihoods.

This volume revisits what we know today about development-induced displacement and reveals as well what we do not know. Unlike other volumes that have addressed DIDR, the editors have been careful to explore new territory. Their volume is divided into five sections. After a brief introduction, the first section challenges some of the most established notions in resettlement and reveals how a 'one size fits all' formula simply does not work. The second section engages in rethinking the ethics of DIDR. The next section covers the current laws, policies and rights governing development and the resultant displacement of people, and explores current protection perspectives in international law with regard to the situation of forced evictions of people. Issues of eminent domain, the shifting responsibly of the private sector, as well as the rights of mobile peoples are explored. The fourth section of the book examines how people claim for and achieve some rights in the absence of sufficient 'rights-based' governing systems in DIDR. The book ends with a concluding chapter that invites us to reconsider what we know about DIDR. The book's 16 chapters are a much needed and long awaited body of work on a topic that has not received the attention it deserves. It contributes admirably to emphasising the (ethical and political) importance of giving more voice to the displaced, increasing their stake in development decision-making and recognising their agency and, furthermore, their right to not be displaced arbitrarily.

References

Cernea, M. (2006) 'Development-induced and conflict-induced IDPs: bridging the research divide'. *Forced Migration Review*, Special Issue (December): 25–27.

Colson, E. (1995) *The Social Organization of the Gwembe Tonga*. Oxford: Berg.

McDowell, C. (1996) *Understanding Impoverishment: The Consequences of Development-Induced Displacement*. Oxford: Berghahn.

Oliver-Smith, A. (ed.) (2009) *Development and Displacement: The Crisis of Forced Migration and Resettlement*. Santa Fe, NM: School for Advanced Research Press.

Terminski, B. (2012) *Environmentally-Induced Displacement: Theoretical Frameworks and Current Challenges*. Liege: CEDEM. Accessed at www.cedem.ulg.ac.be/wp-content/uploads/2012/09/Environmentally-Induced-Displacement-Terminski-1.pdf

Acknowledgements

This book has emerged from a desire to share the discussions and views expressed at the International Conference on Development-Induced Displacement and Resettlement (DIDR) that was held at the Refugee Studies Centre (RSC), University of Oxford on 22–23 March 2013. While this event started as a volunteer student initiative, we are deeply thankful to the enthusiastic response and participation from all over the world that turned it into a major international conference and facilitated an inter-disciplinary information exchange and communication between the civil, private and government sectors.

We would like to express our deepest gratitude to those who have supported us throughout the organisation of the Conference and publication of this book. First of all, we would like to thank Professor Dawn Chatty, the former director of the Refugee Studies Centre, who shared our passion and supported us strongly in these initiatives. Professor Roger Zetter and Dr David Turton, earlier directors of the RSC, contributed greatly to the Conference by providing their precious views for the selection of papers. Professor Michael M. Cernea offered the keynote address of the Conference and continued to encourage and inspire us throughout the entire process of preparing this book for publication. We would also like to thank to Susan Tamandong, Michael M. Cernea, Ted Downing, Inga-Lill Aronsson, Patrick Giraud, Anthony Oliver-Smith and Thayer Scudder who shared their experience and wisdom through an interactive closing panel at the Conference, which unfortunately could not be reflected in this book. The University of Oxford Department of International Development generously provided financial and logistical assistance without which the Conference could not have taken place.

We would like to thank all our authors for their contribution, collaboration and kindness in the face of our shortfalls as first-time editors. Professor Chris de Wet, Professor Jay Drydyk and Susanne Price have committed extra time to help us with their valuable remarks. We are also thankful to the Routledge publication team who have been very kind in guiding and supporting us through the publication process.

We, as researchers, had the opportunity to research, record and interpret the DIDR findings presented in this book. Yet, we would not have been able to do this without the collaboration of relevant institutions and particularly the displaced people. Therefore, we would like to thank the displaced people who have taken their time to participate in our research and answered our questions patiently. We would also like to extend our gratitude to all institutions that have been supporting DIDR research by providing information, data or financial means.

We would also like to thank our families and friends who have been very tolerant at times when we had to enclose ourselves to work on the book. Without their understanding and backing, life would not be as easy or joyful during those busy times of hard work.

Lastly, we would like to thank our readers who are concerned about learning or researching about DIDR with a hope to see improvements in the policies and implementations. We are pleased to have had the opportunity to edit such a dynamic book covering a wide range of aspects with authors from diverse backgrounds and we hope that it will add to the existing knowledge and discussions and contribute to moving the DIDR studies forward.

Abbreviations

ACHPR	African Charter on Human and Peoples' Rights
ACHR	American Convention on Human Rights
ACmHPR	African Commission on Human and Peoples' Rights
ADB	Asian Development Bank
AfDB	African Development Bank
AHCR	Asian Human Rights Commission
BRAC	Bangladesh Rural Advancement Committee
CBA	cost–benefit analysis
CERD	Convention on the Elimination of Racial Discrimination
CESCR	Committee on Economic, Social and Cultural Rights
CFR-LA	Community Forest Rights Learning and Advocacy
CID	conflict-induced displacement
CMDA	Chennai Metropolitan Development Authority
CMRL	Chenai Metro Rail Limited
CRF	Citizens' Rights Forum
CSD	Council for Social Development
DAC	Development Assistance Committee
DFDR	development-*forced* displacement and resettlement
DID	development-induced displacement
DIDR	development-induced displacement and resettlement
DKBA	Democratic Karen Buddhist Army
EBRD	European Bank for Reconstruction and Development
ECHR	European Convention on Human Rights
ECmHR	European Commission on Human Rights
ECtHR	European Court of Human Rights
EIA	environmental impact assessment
EIB	European Investment Bank
FDI	Foreign Direct Investment
FLLRC	Forum for Securing Land and Livelihood Rights of Coastal Communities
FPIC	free and prior informed consent
FRA	Forest Rights Act
HRC	Human Rights Committee

HRW	Human Rights Watch
IACmHR	Inter-American Commission on Human Rights
IACtHR	Inter-American Court of Human Rights
IADB	Inter-American Development Bank Group
IBLF	International Business Leaders Forum
ICCPR	International Covenant on Civil and Political Rights
ICESCR	International Covenant on Economic, Social and Cultural Rights
ICMM	International Council on Mining and Metals
IDMC	Internal Displacement Monitoring Centre
IDP	internally displaced person
IFC	International Finance Corporation
IFI	international financial institution
IHA	International Hydrosector Association
ILO	International Labour Organisation
IRR	Impoverishment Risks and Reconstruction
IsDB	Islamic Development Bank
ITD	Italian-Thai Development
JCDP	Jamuna Char Integrated Development Project
JMBA	Jamuna Multi-purpose Bridge Authority
KHRG	Karen Human Rights Group
KNLA	Karen National Liberation Army
KNU	Karen National Union
₺	symbol of the new Turkish lira which dropped six zeros in 2005
LARR	Land Acquisition, Resettlement and Rehabilitation Act
MDB	Multilateral Development Bank
MoEF-MoTA	Ministry of Environment and Forests and Ministry of Tribal Affairs
MRTS	Chennai Mass Rapid Transit System
MUTP	Mumbai Urban Transport Project
NGO	non-governmental organizations
NHA	National Housing Authority
NID	natural disaster-induced displacement
NIRP	National Involuntary Resettlement Policy
NLD	National League for Democracy
NSAG	non-state armed groups
OECD	Organisation for Economic Co-operation and Development
OHCHR	Office of the [UN] High Commissioner for Human Rights
OP	Operational Policy (of the World Bank)
PNR	Philippine National Railway
PRC	People's Republic of China
PUCL	People's Union for Civil Liberties
PUKAR	Partners for Urban Knowledge, Action and Research
R&R	relief and rehabilitation
RAP	Resettlement Action Plan

RAY	Rajiv Awas Yojana
RSC	Refugee Studies Centre, University of Oxford, Department of International Development
SEMS	social and environmental management systems
SIA	social impact assessment
SPARC	Society for the Promotion of Area Resource Centers
TBC	The Border Consortium
TGP	Three Gorges Project
TL	old Turkish lira before dropping of six zeros in 2005
TNSCB	Tamil Nadu Slum Clearance Board
UN	United Nations
UNDP	United Nations Development Programme
UN-HABITAT	United Nations Human Settlement Programme
USDP	Union Solidarity and Development Party
WCD	World Commission on Dams
WRDR	Wanxian Relocation and Development Region

Editors' introduction

Reflections on development-induced displacement and resettlement research and practice for renewed engagement

Irge Satiroglu and Narae Choi

Background of the book

Land-based development initiatives may and often do cause physical and economic displacement that results in impoverishment and disempowerment of affected populations. Despite the decades of experience and study on development-induced displacement and resettlement (DIDR), the severity of the problem persists, with its adverse impacts not yet being effectively addressed.

For the current decade (2010–2019), around 15 million people are estimated to be displaced due to development projects every year around the globe (Cernea, 2008, p. 20), although the exact figures are not known. Given the vast amount of details required for the planning and implementation of each 'development' project, this is inexplicable. In addition to lack of data and information, even the discussions on the subject have become scant in recent years with different interests and ethical considerations pulling the academia, private and civil sectors apart. This disconnection manifests in the knowledge gaps whereby controversies in policymaking and implementation remain understudied, while academic findings have not been incorporated as basis for practice.

Addressing these gaps was the main thinking and motivation behind the organisation of a conference at the University of Oxford in 2013, from which this book has emerged. Back then, Irge was a Visiting Research Fellow at the Refugee Studies Centre (RSC) and Narae was a DPhil student at the Department of International Development at the University of Oxford. Our research in DIDR brought us together and led us to the idea of organising a specialised gathering dedicated to DIDR that had long been absent in academia.

It was remarkable to hold the conference at the RSC which has played a central role in establishing and advancing the study of DIDR. The first global conferences of DIDR were held at the RSC in 1995 and 1996. They paved the way for the publication of several edited volumes that have become invaluable in the DIDR literature, notably, *Understanding Impoverishment: The Consequences of Development-Induced Displacement* (McDowell, 1996) and *Risks and Reconstruction: Experiences of Resettlers and Refugees* (Cernea and McDowell, 2000). The RSC has also accommodated many researchers and research projects on DIDR, contributing to continuous knowledge production in the field with the most recent volume being edited by de Wet (2006).

With the enthusiastic responses and over 150 papers received from all over the world, the event soon grew from a volunteer student initiative into an international conference of two days that took place on 22–23 March 2013. The final participant list was impressive with a representation of more than 30 countries and in terms of the diversity of the background, with 60 per cent joining from academia, 8 per cent from governmental and intra-governmental organisations, 12 per cent from NGOs and 20 per cent from the private sector. We were proud to facilitate such cross-communication between different disciplines and perspectives, which also formed the basis of the diverse views presented in this book.

This book has emerged from a desire to share the discussions at the conference with a wider audience. However, out of 52 papers presented at the conference, only one-quarter could be accommodated in the book. This entailed an inevitable selection process, primarily conducted on a merit basis, through which the book has evolved into an entity of its own with more clarity and focus. We are pleased to note that, although we have not specifically aimed for this, the selection represents a balanced mix of papers from professors and students, private and civil sectors, and different disciplines, which generates dynamism to the book.

Review of the DIDR literature

There is virtually no limit to what can be called a development project. It can range from a small-scale mining project to a hydropower plant construction or the building of a highway, harbour or railway; can be public or private; well planned or rushed into. The question 'what is development?' is fundamental to the discussion on DIDR but providing a comprehensive answer to the question is beyond the scope of this book. We adopt the 'descriptive' definition suggested by Penz *et al.* (2011, pp. 40–42):[1] 'enhanced production or distribution of perceived public or private goods'. The contested nature of development and its alternative or normative interpretations are suggested later in this chapter and by others in this volume (see Drydyk, Chapter 6). As long as development initiatives require land acquisition or incur changes in the existing use of land, they often do cause physical and economic displacement.

An overview of the DIDR landscape through terminologies

A range of terminologies have been employed to depict a situation where people are displaced by projects from their homes, livelihoods and communities, each with subtle differences in their emphasis. 'Development-induced displacement and resettlement (DIDR)' is the most widely recognised term and also the term that we adopt in this book. Given that DIDR can be optimistic in its orientation with an implicit assumption that there is a provision of resettlement (de Wet, 2006), it needs to be differentiated from development-induced displacement (DID), which refers to a broader context where displacement takes place, regardless of whether or not a resettlement programme is in place.

'Resettlement and rehabilitation', which appears predominantly in the Indian context,[2] has faced a similar critique. Although conveying the importance of rehabilitation that goes beyond mere physical relocation, the term also disguises the contested nature of the situation by avoiding negatively connoted words such as 'displacement' or 'involuntary'. As compared to 'resettlement', which embodies the policy ideal of reconstructing the lives of displaced people, 'relocation' appears to be used more widely on the ground and to capture the reality whereby displaced people are often merely transferred from one place to another.

'Involuntary resettlement', which was initially used by Colson and Scudder as a counterpart to voluntary resettlement such as a planned settlement programme (Partridge, 1989), has been widely used within the policy circle, particularly in reference to the involuntary resettlement policies of the Multilateral Development Banks (MDBs). While 'involuntary' implies the forced nature of resettlement, its focus has moved to 'resettlement' taking displacement as being given.

More recently, 'development-*forced* displacement and resettlement (DFDR)' has been suggested with a particular emphasis on its forced nature (Cernea, 2008; Oliver-Smith, 2010). Oliver-Smith (2010, p. 2) notes that 'induced' has a connotation that people may be convinced by arguments or rewards that they would be resettled and thus is not appropriate for a process that is decided and planned in advance. De Wet (Chapter 5) proposes the use of 'initiated' instead of 'forced' on the grounds that the idea of initiation allows us to stay open to the mix of both voluntary and involuntary aspects present in the process.

On the other hand, agencies primarily concerned with human rights issues such as the United Nations Human Settlement Programme (hereafter UN-HABITAT) and Amnesty International use 'forced eviction' to underline the systematic violation of human rights in such forceful movement. They point out that the term 'forced eviction' has been seldom used in the DIDR literature, which has preferred more 'neutral' terms such as 'population displacement' and the aforementioned 'involuntary resettlement' (UN-HABITAT, 2011, p. 29).[3]

Development of DIDR studies

Spearheaded by pioneering studies conducted back in the 1950s (Colson, 1971; Scudder, 1991), a large body of illuminating research has collated experiences of DIDR all over the world for over half a century. DIDR studies have advanced through concerted efforts into theorisation, which have resulted in key models that are aimed to abstract common patterns across myriad cases. The first of the kind is a four-stage model developed by Scudder and Colson (1982) that identifies stages in the long-term process of resettlement: (1) planning and recruitment, (2) adjustment and coping, (3) community formation and economic development, and (4) handing over and incorporation.

While contributing greatly to elevating the level of theoretical abstraction in DIDR studies, the relevance of which still persists (see de Wet, Chapter 5), the model has also been challenged on a number of fronts. Cernea (2000) comments that resettlers steadily moving through the four stages would be an exception rather than a norm. Muggah (2000, p. 141) suggests that even if such a continuum did exist, it would be 'a complex process of negotiation—a process invariably subject to highly politicized interventions'. Similarly, the assumption that all resettlers are part of an open society is questionable, considering that communities are far from being equal and are often controlled by elites at local, provincial and state levels (Partridge, 1989).

Through an extensive surveying of past research, Cernea (2000) discovered a basic pattern of impoverishment in the majority of cases and formulated the Impoverishment Risks and Reconstruction (IRR) model. Instead of dealing with the phases of resettlement, the model categorises the major risks involved in DID into eight impoverishment risks of: landlessness, joblessness, homelessness, marginalisation, food insecurity, increased morbidity, loss of common property resources, and community disarticulation (Cernea, 2000). With the level of conceptual abstraction, the IRR model has stimulated broad discussions in the field. Suggestions have been made to expand the basic model by adding educational loss (Mahapatra, 1999) and the loss of access to basic services (Mathur, 1998).

The model has also given rise to questions of the fundamental nature of DIDR. Muggah (2000, p. 142) notes that the model does not consider vulnerabilities and capabilities of individual displaced persons sufficiently. The model's anticipation of improvements in resettlement planning and implementation is criticised for being rather optimistic, given the complexities inherent in the resettlement process that is characterised by 'non-rational' political motivations and financial and institutional challenges (Horgan, 1999; de Wet, 2001). Alternatively, an open-ended, flexible approach to resettlement planning is proposed, which recognises that projects rarely proceed according to plan (de Wet, 2001 and Chapter 5), perhaps including the institutional risk of failing to implement the resettlement project (Horgan, 1999).

More broadly, the need for a comprehensive, democratic discussion on the distribution of development impacts has been promoted alongside efforts to address some of the detrimental effects such as displacement. The World Commission on Dams (WCD), an independent, international body created in the late 1990s to investigate issues related to dam construction, suggests a framework to evaluate the overall 'development effectiveness' (of dams)[4] and proposes that both the risks and rights of all relevant actors be discussed in a democratic way for making decisions on dams. This is seen as having shifted the dams debate onto a new plane, addressing both procedural and distributional justice (Hoover, 2001; Robinson, 2003; Sneddon and Fox, 2008). It also recognises a series of new entitlements generated by development and seeks mechanisms for sharing the benefits.

For such discussion, the guidelines of the WCD underline the importance of better understanding the broader impacts of a developmental change, including human, environmental, economic, social and cultural impacts, and both direct and indirect impacts. While some of these proposals are incorporated into relevant policies, such as involuntary resettlement policies, the realization of the ideal put forward by the WCD has remained challenging. Notably, it is critical to have a deliberative forum wherein the balancing of the rights and risks of all stakeholders can be discussed and all the available options – including alternative development options – explored.[5] For the forum to be truly democratic, it is imperative that relevant actors are able to participate in key decision points, including needs assessment, selection of alternatives and project preparation, implementation and operation. This relates to the issue of existing power imbalances, which have been challenged by DIDR activists (see sections below).

Evolution of DIDR policies

Based on the accumulated knowledge, a proposition emerged that although DIDR is an extremely challenging situation where affected people often experience negative impacts, such adversarial risks are not necessarily unavoidable and can in fact be prevented through an effective implementation of measures based on careful analysis of risks (McDowell, 1996; Cernea, 2000). In order to channel the existing knowledge on the processes and consequences of displacement into the operational mechanisms of development agencies, Cernea – in his role as the first in-house sociologist at the World Bank – proposed the aforementioned IRR model. In addition to predicting impoverishment risks, the primary function of the IRR model is to map out the ways to prevent them and furthermore to turn them into reconstruction opportunities. Hence, the model suggests a policy action that turns each risk on its head, for example by addressing landlessness through land-based resettlement, joblessness through re-employment and homelessness through house reconstruction.

Attempts to realise the core idea of risk prevention and reconstruction as represented in the IRR model resulted in 'the generation of resettlement guidelines and resettlement policies' over the last three decades (de Wet, 2006, p. 1). This documentation was also largely a result of active international advocacy by affected people, civil society organisations, concerned academics and development practitioners (Muggah, 2008). In 1980, after a series of project fiascos and large-scale protests against displacement, the World Bank accepted its first policy on involuntary resettlement (Operational Policy (OP) 4.12). This was a landmark in the field as no other institution or country had such a multidimensional social policy with an explicit aim to reverse the impacts of DIDR back then. During an interview, Cernea notes that the main achievement of this initial policy was to abolish the previous de-linking of 'resettlement' from 'displacement', which was the root of the ills as it allowed 'the practice of projects using their power for doing systematic displacement but externalizing resettlement to happenstance' (Mathur, 2011, p. 2). After being revised multiple times,[6] the final policy is based on the key principles of (1) avoiding or minimising displacement where possible, (2) establishing resettlement plans to identify and reverse the physical and economic impacts, (3) participatory planning, (4) protection of vulnerable persons, (5) grievance redressing and (6) monitoring and evaluation of the projects.

The World Bank policy has been an influential benchmark for regional development banks and other international financial institutions (IFIs) in adopting their own resettlement policy such as the Asian Development Bank (in 1995), the African Development Bank (in 1995) and the Inter-American Development Bank (in 1998) (Mathur, 2011, p. 3). The Organisation for Economic Co-operation and Development (OECD) also proposed policy guidelines regarding population displacement and relocation to all the member countries' international aid agencies (Cernea and Guggenheim, 1993). In the meantime starting with the United Nations Guiding Principles on Internal Displacement in 1998, a number of soft legislations on human rights came on the scene. More recently, in 2007, the United Nations Special Rapporteur on adequate housing presented to the Human Rights Council a set of 'basic principles and guidelines on development-based evictions and displacement'.[7]

Realities of involuntary resettlement and DIDR movements

Improvements in policy implementation have been noted in available post-project information (e.g. World Bank, 1994; Asian Development Bank, 2000; Picciotto *et al.*, 2001; Asian Development Bank, 2006). Notwithstanding, these improvements, the overall dismal record of resettlement interventions and the continuing sufferings of displaced people, either short term or long term, have raised a number of questions regarding the way in which DIDR is perceived and practised in the broader development arena and, more fundamentally, have initiated the need to revisit the concept of development itself.

DIDR is frequently described and perceived as a 'planned' phenomenon but Turton (2006) suggests, in real terms, it hardly ever is. More often there is a lack of resources, as well as intention, to make adequate plans for displacement and resettlement. In countries where land rights are not well established, people are often simply expelled from their lands. In the Republic of Congo, for example, when the Noubale Ndoki National Park was established in 1993, the Babenzélé pygmies were driven off without any compensation or land allocated for them (Cernea and Schmidt-Soltau, 2003). The report of Forced Migration Organization on Sudan (Verney, 2006) depicts how the Sudan government expulsed tens of thousands of people using armed forces to provide the required lands for the oil industry.

On the other hand, there are certainly better managed projects in which detailed plans are prepared, people are informed and consulted throughout the whole process, adequate compensations are paid, resettlement sites are established and some people end up with better living standards and incomes (Partridge, 1993; Tamandong, 2008; Trembath, 2008).

Given such diversity in implementation outcomes, one of the recurring questions is why and how involuntary resettlement has often failed to achieve its set goals of improving or even restoring the living standard of affected people (de Wet, 2006). A range of factors have been identified from the lack of political will and financial/human resources to the institutional complexity compounded by conflicting interests. They are summarised by two kinds of explanation: one focuses on the 'insufficient inputs' into resettlement projects and the other is concerned with the 'inherent complexities' of forced resettlement (de Wet, 2006, p. 2).

The first approach attributes the poor performance of resettlement policy to insufficiencies in necessary inputs. Many governments lack a legal and policy framework for resettlement at the national level and tend to employ project-based resettlement action plans (if any attempt is made at all), although situations without any plans are known to be much worse (Price, 2007). Not only is the political will of the state to seriously implement resettlement policy weak, its institutional capacity is also limited as resettlement teams are short of expertise or staff (Tamondong-Helin, 1996; Parasuraman, 1999). The cost of resettlement is often underestimated in the project evaluation and thus resettlement suffers from poor financing (Cernea, 2003).

The second approach proposes that forced resettlement is an inherently complex process that is often beyond the control of rational planning (de Wet, 2006). The institution of resettlement policy is comprised of multiple actors from policymakers to 'street-level' officers, who recreate policy as a document by reinterpreting it and making decisions at their discretion as the implementation process unfolds (Rew *et al.*, 2000). While administrators struggle with practical challenges of their own, responsibilities are easily lost amidst poor communication and coordination, leading to implementation deficits (Rew, 1996; Rew *et al.*, 2000). Meanwhile, the resettled people themselves have to develop new sets of socio-economic relationships in unfamiliar sites amidst fierce competition for resources (Koenig, 2002). The challenge of adjustment is further exacerbated by the agenda and timetable of an outside agency, which accelerates the pace of changes and undermines the control of people over their daily life (de Wet, 2006).

Varying interests and multiple tensions revolve around the power to make myriad decisions in the resettlement process. Political challenges to the imbalance in such decision-making power have taken place mostly outside the policy arena, which has been predominantly led by states, donors and private-sector actors (Mathur and Marsden, 1998; Oliver-Smith, 2002). DIDR movements often start from a specific project in a confined local context, thus reflecting the most immediate concerns of local people, and represent a range of positions from advocating avoidance of involuntary resettlement at all costs (thus often resisting a project itself) to having better-quality resettlement; however, in terms of a common thread, they tend to be connected with broader movements or other groups sharing their values and experiences (Oliver-Smith, 2002; Penz *et al.*, 2011). In particular, in the era of globally dynamic activism, DIDR resistance movements often scale up to become connected to global movements promoting an alternative view of development that is people-centred, culturally sensitive and environmentally sustainable (Muggah, 2008). Even though community-level mobilisation may not convey a strong alternative development agenda, displaced people's engagement with the developmental process, either through resistance, negotiation or asserted participation, is valuable in itself as an act of voicing their views on the development process and attempting to enlarge the participatory space (Choi, 2008; Bennett and McDowell, 2012). Through such engagement, people can restore some control over their life and thus overcome the feeling of powerlessness (Oliver-Smith, 1996).

Yet, we are still short of cases where development decisions are made so as not to displace people and undermine natural environments; and likewise of the cases where resettlement may have led to (re)constructive outcomes. Against this background, the current book aims to reinvigorate critical discussions on DIDR by posing thought-provoking questions and refining the understandings of long-lasting as well as emerging issues in DIDR. In particular, we aim to strike a fine balance between (a) maintaining a critical stance in sight of a bigger picture of development contexts where displacement and resettlement take place and (b) continuing to improve our knowledge and practice (including institutional changes) towards achieving better outcomes as long as displacement persists. In doing so, we focus on four major areas: (1) questioning of conventional assumptions, (2) ethical perspectives, (3) international and national DIDR policies, and (4) activism and modes of engagement.

The themes and structure of the book

Introduction: reflections on DIDR research and practice for renewed engagement

The introduction aims to inform the reader about the origin of the book and provide a brief background on the development of the DIDR studies and policies, movements and present challenges.

Part I Challenges to the assumptions of DIDR

Chapter 1 puts forward thought-provoking questions with regards to some of the common assumptions in DIDR. Satiroglu starts with teasing out the fact that whilst we have long worked to improve the DIDR practice, a consensus on what 'success' is and how we should assess it is yet to be reached. Over an ironic case that was deemed successful but demonstrated several failures and in which the quantitative and qualitative research tools generated contradicting results regarding the change in income levels, she professes that the DIDR research is immune to neither methodological nor political bias. Highlighting the importance of accountability and comprehensiveness in project assessments, she advocates conceptualization of 'success' for DIDR.

In the following chapter, Choi brings up the possibility that the stake of DIDR has weakened in the broader development arena where it is treated as the same old problem. She proposes that the strong focus on resettlement issues in the DIDR field tends to limit the room for questioning the necessity of displacement in the first place and rethinking the models of development that are dependent on population displacement. Through a case-study investigating the impacts of DIDR on the people who have stayed in the project area, she reveals the current shortfalls of resettlement policy more evidently and asks for a more thorough assessment of a development project.

Xi *et al.* (Chapter 3) criticise the fact that tools for risk measurement have been developed mainly for the risk evaluation of the planners whereas affected people have been constantly excluded from this information and thus been poorly aware of the potential risks. Over an empirical study using pre- and post-relocation data on a sample of households who were relocated to make way for the Three Gorges Dam Project in China, the authors demonstrate that high-risk perception is beneficial to the mental well-being of the relocated, thereby supporting the transparent sharing of risk information for increasing the coping capacity of affected people.

While a household is a common unit of entitlement that typically forms the base on which resettlement is planned, Gouws (Chapter 4) notes that the very definition of what constitutes a household varies in different societies and is open to debate. He demonstrates the importance of the definitional issue in two case studies where the meaning of a household was disputed and had practical implications for the process of resettlement.

Part II Ethics of DIDR

The second part of the book broadens the discussion to the ethical aspects of DIDR, discussions that have been fundamental to the field. The part starts with de Wet (Chapter 5) who focuses on the inherent complexities in DIDR and argues that it is important to face what we are up 'against' in the attempt to treat people ethically. He suggests ways of grappling with the ethical issues through resettlement diagnostics that pay attention to externally initiated spatial and related social changes involved in a resettlement project, as well as to similarities and locally specific differences emerging across cases. Settlements are socio-spatially embedded ('emplacement') and thus DIDR involves a process of 'de-emplacement' and 're-emplacement' – which can be explained further with the aid of the complexity theory.

In his study, Drydyk (Chapter 6) first identifies entitlements of displaced people as appropriate means of achieving worthwhile development pertaining to just outcomes. In particular, he focuses on the entitlement to empowerment, the critical importance of which is reversely justified by many practices and circumstances that are disempowering and thus lead to inequitable outcomes. He introduces the WCD framework as a way to structure development management and governance to overcome and avoid sources of disempowerment, although noting that the centrality of empowerment for equity is lacking in the WCD framework that treats stakeholders as equal participants.

Based on the ethnographic work carried out on several resettlement projects in Colombia, Serje (Chapter 7) reflects on the politics of resettlement and argues that the practices involved in different stages of most resettlement create a de facto state of exception. While concentration camps – the archetypal spaces of exception – are established outside the juridical order, resettlement projects constitute their exceptionality by strictly abiding by regulations that deny the affected people the right to their customary way of life. In this way, the very specific regulations created and supposedly put in place to avoid the negative effects of resettlement become forms of both symbolic and physical violence.

Part III International and national policies

Building on the ethical and political discussions in the previous part, Part III examines the international and national policies as one mechanism of governing the DIDR field. Price (Chapter 8) explores whether there is a globally effective resettlement safeguard for displaced people. The question is more acute in the changing global aid and investment environments where new financial modalities, non-traditional donors and financiers create new patterns of operation with consequent ambiguities and increased/new risks for DIDR. The need for enhanced state regulation is still pressing, particularly in terms of mobilising DIDR skills, knowledge and practice down to the negotiations with displaced people. To this end, we need to better understand the outcomes of resettlement policies as an evidence basis for building an effective and transparent global safeguard.

Contributing to the discussion on global DIDR governance system, Morel (Chapter 9) sheds light on the fact that development with displacement raises important legal issues as well as ethical questions: do benefits of a project ever outweigh the costs of displacement? If so, what is owed to those displaced? The existing international legal framework for the protection of people against arbitrary forms of DID is well developed. Several well-established human rights guarantee legal protection against unjust displacement. In particular, the right to adequate housing, the freedom of movement and residence, and the right to a private life and home offer significant legal protection and can moreover be said to imply a 'right not to be arbitrarily displaced'. In addition, several guidelines on DID spell out the circumstances under which displacement can be carried out in a lawful way. Nonetheless, this protection could be further reinforced by the explicit recognition of an autonomous human right not to be displaced in a legally binding international instrument.

The following two chapters examine laws and policies at the national and local levels respectively and demonstrate how the DIDR governance system (or its limitations) translates into complex and often inconsistent outcomes in a given context. Sigamany (Chapter 10) examines the land displacement of indigenous peoples, some of whom are nomadic, and whose livelihoods such as hunting and gathering and herding animals are a continuation of ancient lifestyles. They have faced particular problems of displacement by the emergence of the land conservation movement and the development of extractive industries. On the other hand, the evolution of human rights norms has created positive change for indigenous rights, leading to the development of legal architecture based on principles of social justice and human rights. Using two contemporary case studies of land displacement of two groups of forest people in Odisha and in Madhya Pradesh, she examines empirically whether the Forest Rights Act of 2006 offers indigenous peoples a tool with which to advocate for their rights against displacement, or whether in reality it makes this community more vulnerable.

Narayan (Chapter 11) takes us to the dynamic context of Chennai, India, where paradigms of both urban planning and slum intervention have gone through multiple changes. She examines whether a uniform procedure for eviction and resettlement exists in the city, especially in the absence of formal status for many urban poor settlements. Through a comparative study of 14 slum communities, she finds that while eligibility criteria and compensation schemes are marred by inconsistency, the coerciveness of the process and the absences of transparency and accountability were widely observed. Variations across cases are explained by the patterns in which communities are treated during evictions and resettlement.

Part IV Voice and power of people

The last part of the book documents how people have engaged with DIDR through various modes of activism. In the absence of proper governance or a legal system in Myanmar, Kavanagh (Chapter 12) argues that strong community action to navigate local power dynamics and negotiate for unofficial remedies, championed in some cases by an increasingly more active domestic media, is forging new and promising avenues for informal rights claiming. Recent legislative reforms have done little to address the challenges that compound the displacement and resettlement of villagers in rural and remote areas, such as an opaque, corrupt and expensive land registration process, land grabbing and a lack of standard best practice during project implementation. In a number of cases where villagers were forcefully displaced by government and non-state actors, often without compensation, consultation or notification, to make way for *inter alia* eight dams and five coal and gold mines, as well as the Dawei (Tavoy) deep-sea port, strategies such as negotiation, collective action, non-compliance, public protest, complaints to authorities, and reporting to media or external observers have in some cases operated effectively to stem the rule of law shortfall in rural Myanmar. Given the fact that even well-framed legislative reform will reach marginalised ethnic communities last, local rights-claiming strategies can provide viable routes to redress in the meantime.

Gilmore (Chapter 13) finds a potential in literature to develop suitable methodologies to understand the reasons behind their resistance and their strategies to achieve their political objectives. Discursive opposition to DIDR in the form of hidden script or dissenting discourse is rarely articulated openly or publicly for fear of retribution, particularly in contexts where freedom of speech and political association are repressed. However, she argues that when it enters the public domain, it constitutes a powerful form of symbolic resistance against hegemonic political and development discourses. With reference to the literature of the Nubian minority in Egypt who were resettled four times over the course of the twentieth century by dam construction on the Nile (in 1902, 1912, 1933 and 1964), she examines whether and how writer-activists articulate the experiences, concerns and demands of those most affected by development and bring these into the political process.

Similarly, Koenig (Chapter 14) proposes DIDR activism as a political action that calls into question existing power relations and for greater inclusion of the affected, within development as well as resettlement decision making. Focusing on urban activism and using multiple case studies, she identifies major strategies/strategic arenas of activism such as negotiation, urban alliance, media, national courts, international institutions and demonstrations. She then examines the achievements of activism in terms of (a) stopping infrastructure construction (or decreasing its footprints), (b) improving resettlement outcomes and (c) changing policy.

Conclusion: a step forward in theory, methodology and practice in DIDR

The concluding chapter wraps up the presented papers attracting attention to the inherent complexities and injustices, inefficiencies in current policies, means of activism and improvement opportunities in DIDR research and practise. Reiterating some of the thought provoking questions proposed by the contributors, it invites the reader to reconsider what we think we know about DIDR.

Notes

1 They distinguish between the normative definition and descriptive definition of 'development', whereby the latter means a definition before normative judgements such as 'good' or 'bad' development are made.

2 India is a country with abundant cases of DID and also strong resistance movements against DID that has resulted in a body of India-specific DIDR literature. See, for example, Mathur (2006) and Parasuraman (1999).

3 The use of forced eviction is particularly noticeable in urban studies and a few chapters in this volume on urban cases also tend to use DIDR and forced eviction interchangeably.

4 Source: International Rivers (www.internationalrivers.org/node/5565; accessed 14 September 2014).

5 This is different from a call for having measures and procedures in place to increase equity in bearing the burden of loss and in the distribution of benefits (Cernea, 2000, p. 12), in the sense that the forum is open to reconsidering the original development plan itself.

6 We note that the World Bank is currently conducting a major review of its environmental and social safeguards, including its involuntary resettlement policy, as this book is printing. This has generated debates within and outside the institution but the final outcome and its repercussions are yet to be seen.
7 This is contained in Annex I of the report of the Special Rapporteur (A/HRC/4/18) (www.ohchr.org/EN/Issues/Housing/Pages/ForcedEvictions.aspx; accessed 19 December 2012). This is a development of the previous guidelines such as United Nations Comprehensive Human Rights Guidelines on Development-based Displacement (E/CN.4/Sub.2/1997/7, annex).

References

Asian Development Bank (ADB) (2000). *Special Evaluation Study on the Policy Impact of Involuntary Resettlement*. ADB.

Asian Development Bank (ADB) (2006). *Involuntary Resettlement Safeguards: ADB Evaluation Study*. Available online at www.adb.org/documents/involuntary-resettlement-safeguards (accessed 5 September 2014).

Bennett, O. and McDowell, C. (2012). *Displaced: The Human Cost of Development and Resettlement*. Palgrave studies in oral history. New York; Basingstoke: Palgrave Macmillan.

Cernea, M. M. (2000). Risks, safeguards, and reconstruction: A model for population displacement and resettlement. In M. M. Cernea and C. McDowell (eds), *Risks and Reconstruction Experiences of Resettlers and Refugees* (pp. 11–55). Washington, DC: World Bank.

Cernea, M. M. (2003). For a new economics of resettlement: A sociological critique of the compensation principle. *International Social Science Journal*, 55(175), 37–45.

Cernea, M. M. (2008). Compensation and investment in resettlement: Theory, practice, pitfalls, and needed policy reform. In M. M. Cernea, and H. M. Mathur (eds), *Can Compensation Prevent Impoverishment? Reforming Resettlement Through Investments and Benefit-Sharing* (pp. 15–82). Oxford: Oxford University Press.

Cernea, M. M. and Guggenheim, S. E. (1993). *Anthropological Approaches to Resettlement: Policy, Practice, and Theory*. Boulder, CO; Oxford: Westview.

Cernea, M. M. and McDowell, C. (eds) (2000). *Risks and Reconstruction: Experiences of Resettlers and Refugees*. Washington, DC: World Bank.

Cernea, M. M. and Schmidt-Soltau, K. (2003). *Biodiversity Conservation Versus Population Resettlement: Risks to Nature and Risks to People*. International Conference on Rural Livelihoods Forests and Biodiversity, May 19–23, 2003. Bonn, Germany.

Choi, N. (2008). *Putting 'Relationships' into the Impoverishment Risks and Reconstruction (IRR) Model: A Case Study of the Metro Manila Railway Project in the Philippines*. University of Oxford.

Colson, E. (1971). *The Social Consequences of Resettlement: The Impact of the Kariba Resettlement upon the Gwembe Tonga*. University of Zambia. Institute for African Studies. Kariba studies; 4; Manchester: Manchester University Press.

de Wet, C. (2001). Economic development and population displacement: Can everybody win? *Economic and Political Weekly*, 36(50): 4637–4646.

de Wet, C. (ed.) (2006). *Development-induced Displacement: Problems, Policies and People*. Studies in forced migration; vol. 18. New York; Oxford: Berghahn.

Hoover, R. (2001). *Pipe Dreams: The World Bank's Failed Efforts to Restore Lives and Livelihoods of Dam-Affected People in Lesotho*. International Rivers Reports.

Horgan, J. (1999). The Itaparica Dam Project in north-eastern Brazil: Models and reality. *Forced Migration Review*, 9, 25–28.

Koenig, D. (2002). *Toward Local Development and Mitigating Impoverishment in Development-induced Displacement and Resettlement*. Oxford: Refugee Studies Centre, University of Oxford, Working Paper No.8.

Mahapatra, L. K. (1999). Testing the risks and reconstruction model on India's resettlement experiences. In M. M. Cernea (ed.), *The Economics of Involuntary Resettlement: Questions and Challenges* (pp. 189–230). Washington, DC: World Bank.

Mathur, H. M. (1998). The impoverishment risk model and its use as a planning tool. In H. M. Mathur and D. Marsden (eds), *Development Projects and Impoverishment Risks: Resettling Project-affected People in India* (pp. 67–78). Oxford: Oxford University Press.

Mathur, H. M. (2006). Urban development and involuntary resettlement. In H. M. Mathur (ed.), *Managing Resettlement in India: Approaches, Issues, Experiences*. New Delhi; Oxford: Oxford University Press.

Mathur, H. M. (2011). A historic landmark in development: Reflecting on the first resettlementpolicy–aninterviewwithProf.MichaelCernea.*ResettlementNews*.Available at: http://www.brookings.edu/~/media/research/files/interviews/2011/7/resettlement%20cernea/resettlement%20news_2011_mcernea.pdf (accessed 5 September 2014).

Mathur, H. M. and Marsden, D. (1998). *Development Projects and Impoverishment Risks: Resettling Project-affected People in India*. Delhi: Oxford University Press.

McDowell, C. (1996). *Understanding Impoverishment: The Consequences of Development-induced Displacement*. Refugee and forced migration studies; vol. 2; Providence, RI; Oxford: Berghahn.

Muggah, R. (2000). Through the developmentalist's looking glass: Conflict-induced displacement and involuntary resettlement in Colombia. *Journal of Refugee Studies*, 13(2), 133–164.

Muggah, R. (2008). Protection and durable solutions: Regimes for development and conflict-induced internally displaced and resettled populations. In K. Grabska and L. Mehta (eds), *Forced Displacement: Why Rights Matter*. Basingstoke; New York: Palgrave Macmillan.

Oliver-Smith, A. (1996). Fighting for a place: The policy implications of resistance to development-induced resettlement, in C. McDowell (ed.), *Understanding Impoverishment: The Consequences of Development-induced Displacement*. Refugee and forced migration studies; vol. 2; Providence, RI; Oxford: Berghahn.

Oliver-Smith, A. (2002). *Displacement, Resistance and the Critique of Development: From the Grass-roots to the Global*. Oxford: Refugee Studies Centre, University of Oxford, Working Paper No.9.

Oliver-Smith, A. (2010). *Defying Displacement: Grassroots Resistance and the Critique of Development*. Austin, TX: University of Texas Press.

Parasuraman, S. (1999). *The Development Dilemma: Displacement in India*. London: Macmillan; New York: St. Martin's Press.

Partridge, W. L. (1989). Involuntary resettlement in development projects. *Journal of Refugee Studies*, 2(3), 373–384.

Partridge, W. L. (1993). Successful involuntary resettlement: Lessons from the Costa Rican arenal hydroelectric project. In M. M. Cernea and S. E. Guggenheim (eds), *Anthropological Approaches to Resettlement: Policy, Practice, and Theory* (pp. 351–374). Boulder, CO: Westview Press.

Penz, P., Drydyk, J. and Bose, P. S. (2011). *Displacement by Development: Ethics, Rights and Responsibilities*. Cambridge; New York: Cambridge University Press.

Picciotto, R., van Wicklin, W. and Rice, E. (2001). *Involuntary Resettlement: Comparative Perspectives*. Vol. 2, World Bank Series on Evaluation and Development. Washington, DC: World Bank.

Price, S. (2007). Compensation, restoration, and development opportunities: National standards on involuntary resettlement. In M. M. Cernea and H. M. Mathur (eds), *Can Compensation Prevent Impoverishment? Reforming Resettlement Through Investments and Benefit-sharing*. Delhi; Oxford: Oxford University Press.

Qasim, M. K. (2011). *Ash-Shamandoura*. 3rd edn, Cairo, Egypt: Al-Hay'a al-'Ama Lee Qusuwr al-Thaqafa.

Rew, A. (1996). Policy implications of the involuntary ownership of resettlement. In C. McDowell (ed.), *Understanding Impoverishment: The Consequences of Development-induced Displacement*. Refugee and forced migration studies; vol. 2; Providence, RI; Oxford: Berghahn.

Rew, A., Fisher, E. and Pandey, B. (2000). *Addressing Policy Constraints and Improving Outcomes in Development-induced Displacement and Resettlement Projects*. Oxford: Refugee Studies Centre and the Department for International Development.

Robinson, C. (2003). *Risks and Rights: the Causes, Consequences, and Challenges of Development-induced Displacement*. Brookings-SAIS Project on Internal Displacement. Washington, DC: The Brookings Institution-SAIS Project on Internal Displacement.

Scudder, T. (1991). A sociological framework for the analysis of new land settlements. In M. M. Cernea and World Bank (eds), *Putting People First: Sociological Variables in Rural Development* (2nd edn). New York; Oxford: published for the World Bank by Oxford University Press.

Scudder, T. and Colson, E. (1982). From welfare to development: A conceptual framework for the analysis of dislocated people. In A. Hansen and A. Oliver-Smith (eds), *Involuntary Migration and Resettlement: The Problems and Responses of Dislocated People*. Boulder, CO: Westview Press.

Sneddon, C. and Fox, C. (2008). Struggles over dams as struggles for justice: The World Commission on Dams (WCD) and anti-dam campaigns in Thailand and Mozambique. *Society and Natural Resources*, 21, 625–640.

Tamandong, S. (2008). Can improved resettlement reduce poverty? In M. M. Cernea and H. M. Mathur (eds), *Can Compensation Prevent Impoverishment? Reforming Resettlement through Investments and Benefit Sharing* (pp. 394–422). New Delhi: Oxford University Press.

Tamondong-Helin, S. D. (1996). State power as a medium of impoverishment: The case of the Pantabangan dam resettlement in the Philippines. In C. McDowell (ed.), *Understanding Impoverishment: The Consequences of Development-induced Displacement*. Refugee and forced migration studies; vol. 2; Providence, RI; Oxford: Berghahn.

Trembath, B P. (2008). Beyond compensation: Sharing of rents arising from hydropower projects. In M. M. Cernea and H. M. Mathur (eds), *Can Compensation Prevent Impoverishment?* (pp. 375–393). New Delhi: Oxford University Press.

Turton, D. (2006). Who is a forced migrant? In C. de Wet (ed.), *Development-Induced Displacement: Problems, Policies and People* (pp. 13–37). Oxford: Berghahn.

UN-HABITAT (2011). *Losing Your Home: Assessing the Impact of Eviction*. Nairobi: United Nations Human Settlements Programme (UN-HABITAT).

Verney, P. (2006). *Forced Migration Organization Country Guide: Sudan*. Available online at: www.forcedmigration.org/research-resources/expert-guides/sudan/fmo040.pdf/view (accessed 5 September 2014).

World Bank (1994). *Resettlement and Development: The Bankwide Review of Projects Involving Involuntary Resettlement 1986–1993*. Washington, DC: World Bank Environment Department.

Part I

Challenges to the assumptions of development-induced displacement and resettlement

1 Looking for a 'successful' resettlement

Is Tahtali Dam the right address?

Irge Satiroglu

Introduction

With the power of moving hundreds and thousands of people out of their homes, development-induced displacement and resettlement (DIDR) is an immensely multifaceted phenomenon. The ethical, political, economic, social and psychological dimensions of DIDR are put forward by many studies in the literature. Its long-term and complex nature is well documented, impacts and risks are analysed, solutions are suggested and policies are established (de Wet, this volume; World Bank, 1994; Cernea, 1998, 2003, 2004, 2008b; Asian Development Bank (ADB), 2000, 2006; Scudder, 2005; Mathur, 2006). Yet nothing seems to have been enough to reverse its adverse impacts and bad reputation of DIDR (Cernea, 2008a; Scudder, 2005, Mathur, 2006). With a large portfolio of failures, only a handful of successful cases have been reported to date. And even those are not unchallengeable.

What is success in DIDR? What makes it so inaccessible? When accessed, what makes it so disputable? Is it a matter of different stakes and interests? Is this a matter of perspectives? Or is it a question of methodological approaches and research limitations? With such questions in mind, I aimed to find and explore a successful case in DIDR.

In the following sections I will first outline the literature on 'success' in DIDR and reasons identified for its frequent failures. After explaining my research methodology, I will narrate the history of the Tahtali Water Supply Dam which was deemed a successful case in Turkey. Notwithstanding its outward appearance, the research reveals that the misapplications of hitherto inadequate laws had sorted the displacees as state-resettled, cash-compensated and uncompensated households in Tahtali. Looking at the experiences of these groups throughout the 14 years following displacement, I will make a comparison of the quantitative and qualitative findings of the study, which were complementary in many ways but were contradicting with regards to the change in income levels. I will conclude the chapter by emphasizing the limitations and complications in research, the need to conceptualize 'success' and the importance of facilitating accountable and comprehensive studies in order to minimize the potential political and methodological biases in DIDR.

Success and failure in DIDR

There have been a few attempts to define success in DIDR (see Scudder, 1984, p. 14; Horowitz *et al.*, 1993, p. 234) but the most commonly accepted definition belongs to Cernea (2008a, p. 23) who defined it as 'when the resettled people end up better-off, in terms of income and livelihood, or at least restore to the same level as before'. This definition has also found its way to international standards and guidelines. Yet the vagueness in real-life assessments persists as the definition does not clarify what percentage of the society that needs to be equal or better-off for a project to be considered successful or when and how the assessment should be held.

There are not many 'success' cases in the DIDR literature. The few cases that are claimed as successful such as the Arenal Hydroelectric Power Plant (Costa Rica), Shuikou Hydroelectric Power Plant (China) or Dalian Water Supply (China) are referenced and reproduced again and again. In these cases judgements are mainly based on increased income levels, whereas the timing, methodology and sample sizes of the assessments differ (Partridge, 1993; ADB, 2000; Zhu *et al.*, 2000; Tamandong, 2008).[1] Yet, if one is interested in challenging these evaluations, it is not impossible. Those who think resettlement can only be concluded in the second generation (Scudder, 1991; Horowitz *et al.*, 1993, p. 234; Mathur, 2006, p. 78) can ask whether the increased income levels had continued in the long term for example. Or their common focus on 'resettlers' can also be questioned: were there no other affected groups, such as host communities or those who partially lost their lands and were cash-compensated, or were they not included in the assessments?

On the other hand, there are projects that are defined as 'success' by some and 'failure' by others. The Sardar Sarovar Dam Project was praised by the Indian government for its successful policies (Joseph, 1995) whereas it was criticized by many activists, civil organizations and researchers for its implementations (Alvares and Billorey, 1988; Morse and Berger, 1992; Tata Institute of Social Sciences, 1997; Roy, 1999). In fact an official impact assessment had not been conducted and even the number of affected people was not known for the project, let alone mitigating the entire impacts (Morse and Berger, 1992).

While the Sardar Sarovar case shows how success claims can be biased with political interests, Karimi *et al.* (2005) argued that 'failure' claims may also be political, when, for instance, doing so would bring advantage for lawsuits against the government as in the case of Kotapanjang Dam in Indonesia. Pak Mun Dam was another case that remained controversial for which the World Bank report (1998) suggested that the compensation schemes were revised and improved many times upon request from the displaced people, and the livelihoods had improved after the project, whereas the civil organizations and researchers were not totally satisfied (Amornsakchai *et al.*, 2000).

Apart from few cases, the studies in literature generally conclude that DIDR has resulted in impoverishment (Mburugu, 1994; World Bank, 1994; Cernea, 1996; Syagga and Olima, 1996; Cernea, 1997; ADB, 2000, 2006; Nayak, 2000;

Scudder, 2005). In cases of displacement, 'cash' remains as the most commonly used method of compensation (Cernea, 2008a, p. 49). However, experience suggests that cash compensations frequently failed as the assets were undervalued, payments were syphoned-off by corrupt practices, poor people could not manage money well, the prices of surrounding lands tended to inflate and money was spent on other causes than restoring livelihoods (Mburugu, 1994; Syagga and Olima, 1996; Mathur, 2006, p. 55; Cernea, 2008a, pp. 53–54).

Land compensation performed arguably better (World Bank, 1994, p. x), but neither did it come without problems. The difficulties in finding enough and adequate lands, insufficient planning, under-estimation of number of displacees, houses and lands not being ready at the time of displacement, lack of consultation with displaced people, wrong site selections, lack of compensation for loss of common resources and potential conflicts with host communities were documented from various studies (Lassailly-Jacob, 1996; World Bank, 1994, 1998; Eriksen, 1999; Mejia, 1999; Koenig, 2006; Mathur, 2006).

As we were about to believe nothing works in DIDR and the displacees were almost always bound to impoverishment, a systematic bibliographic research by Wescoat (1999) suggested that actually few comprehensive post-project evaluations have been conducted to date and we knew little about the long-term impacts of forced migration. In his attempt to find and compare the displacement impacts of dams, Scudder (2005, p. 57) also attracted attention to the difficulty of gathering sufficient data even for 50 dams out of the more than 40,000 dams worldwide. Lack and weakness of both pre- and post-project data has also been acknowledged by other reports (Cook and Mukendi, 1994, p. 35; World Bank, 1994, pp. x, xiii; ADB, 2000, p. 18; ADB, 2006, p. 65).

Recently, an interesting statistical study emerged from Finland regarding the long-term impacts of forced migration. Finland had ceded one-tenth of its territory to the Soviet Union and resettled the entire population (430,000 people) living in these areas in the remaining parts of the country after the Second World War (Sarvimäki *et al.*, 2009). The studied resettlement policy provided both land and cash compensation for lost property for the rural population and only cash compensation for the urban population. The displaced were free not to take up or sell the lands that were offered to them and to choose where to live (Sarvimäki *et al.*, 2009). Sarvimäki *et al.* (2009) used individual-level official tax records of a randomized sample of more than 20,000 individuals from a displaced and a non-displaced population in order to investigate the changes in income levels. According to the findings, the displaced population did not differ from the rest of the nation before the displacement. However, they became substantially more mobile in the coming years and earned 10 per cent more than the population that had not been displaced in 30 years. Sarvimäki *et al.* (2009) concluded that those whose bonds were cut off from their homelands and communities had gained mobility and were able to seek the best options for themselves and this had had a positive effect on their long-term incomes.

The research of Sarvimäki *et al.* (2009) did not include a qualitative assessment, hence did not reply to questions such as whether there were uncompensated people or vulnerable groups who were affected more adversely than others. However, the overall result of such a large-scale study being positive appears promising for land and cash compensations. One naturally wonders whether this outcome was specific to Finland or whether we could find similar results if only we could replicate the study in other regions. With such questions in mind I decided to undertake research on the long-term impacts of cash and land compensation in Turkey, combining qualitative and quantitative methods.

Selection of case study and research methodology

Turkey has a long history and experience of forced migration (Babus, 2006) with its first Resettlement Law (No. 2510) dating back to 1934 which was amended in 1970 to cover development-induced displacement (DID).[2] However, it is known that the implementations are far from being perfect yet, with hundreds of households waiting to be resettled up to several years after the displacement (Ministry of Environment and Urbanization, 2014). There is much to discuss about the general DIDR policies and implementations in the country but this is beyond the scope of this chapter.

In order to find a case where the people were actually and timely provided with land and cash compensations, I consulted with the State Hydraulic Works (government agency responsible for the dams) and asked for a 'successful' resettlement case. I was proposed the Tahtali Water Supply Dam located in Menderes District of Izmir Province in western Turkey. It was constructed between 1987 and 1997 and was financed by the World Bank as per the policies of which some socio-economic data was collected and a belated Resettlement Action Plan was prepared in 1994. Other than this, upon request from the State Statistical Institute, I was informed that no statistical information was available regarding the socio-economic conditions of the displaced people before or after the project.

During my initial site visit (three weeks in January 2010) it became clear that besides the cash-compensated and state-resettled households, there was also an uncompensated group among the displacees. Hence I decided to cover all three groups. In order to gain an idea about the general socio-economic situation in the region and have a comparison point, I also included a control group (Cileme village) that had not been affected by the displacement. There was no host population as the resettlement site was established on unused state lands.

For research purposes, I lived with the resettled community (Yeni Bulgurca village) for about six months (from September 2010 to February 2011) and conducted a total of 283 household surveys with the Tahtali displacees and the control group. The household surveys questioned various socio-economic data regarding the pre- and post-project conditions and also included open-ended questions to better understand the experiences of the displacees. As the name lists were available for the state-resettled and control groups, simple random sampling was applied to these groups.[3] A name list of contact details was not available for the cash-compensated and uncompensated households and therefore snowball sampling was adopted for these groups. The displacees were identified in the close-by villages (Sancakli, Esen, Malta, Sasal) and urban centres (Menderes, Karabaglar and Gaziemir districts). IBM SPSS statistics software was used for data entry and analysis.

Apart from the household surveys, I have conducted countless informal discussions with the displacees and eight key informant interviews with the officers of the responsible institutions,[4] the village headmen of the resettlement site and the control village and two lawyers who had worked with the displacees.

History of the Tahtali Dam

In 1997, Tahtali Dam submerged eight settlements in Izmir. Three of those villages (Bulgurca, Camkoy, Keler) were displaced entirely whereas the other five (Develi, Kuner, Malta, Sasal, Eski Sasal) were partially affected. According to official information, the dam displaced around 8,000 households (State Hydraulic Works, 1994), however a population census had not been conducted and the World Bank (1994, pp. 5/4) suggests this number could be as high as 13,000 households.[5]

Before the dam

The displacees explain that the affected villages were quite typical in their setting and facilities. They were surrounded with cultivable and pasture lands and the main livelihood sources included agriculture, animal husbandry and forest labour. Apart from this, Bulgurca, the largest of the displaced villages, also benefited from its position on the connection road between inlands and coastal touristic areas, trading goods and services to the passengers especially in the summer.

Extended families typically constructed their houses around a common garden they shared. Almost all houses at the project site had electricity but there was no water supply or sewage system and the common water sources were village fountains. Bulgurca was a lot more flourished as compared to the other villages. With its diverse shops, health care unit, primary school and several public bus facilities, it functioned as a commercial and public service centre and transportation hub for the settlements close by.

Entitlements of the displacees

According to the statements of the displacees, public information meetings were held in 1988 at all the villages. The Resettlement Law[6] (No. 2510) provided that all people who held a legal ownership of any of the properties that were to be submerged were entitled to cash compensation. Furthermore, the households who were to be displaced as a result of losing all or part of their assets could apply for state resettlement. Yet the resettlement entitlement depended on three criteria.

The first criterion was residing at the affected villages for at least three years. As is quite frequent in DIDR situations (International Finance Institution, 2002, p. 37), experience showed in Turkey that these kinds of displacement and resettlement situations could attract opportunist people who wanted to benefit from the compensations offered to the affected populations. Hence this criterion perhaps aimed at preventing such encroachment into the area.[7] While the law required evidence of a long period of settlement, a positive aspect was that it did not require legal ownership and included owners, renters and illegal occupiers alike.

The second criterion was being a family of at least two members (a couple or a parent with a child). According to this criterion the singles or widows without children were not entitled to state resettlement. It is understood that earlier in similar projects it was experienced that married couples divorced to obtain two houses from the government and for this reason the Resettlement Law (No. 2510) had been amended not to entitle widowed or divorced people without children, apparently at the expense of imperilling the real widows.[8]

The third criterion was 'not having social security', which meant working in the informal market or the agricultural sector, as back in those times the farmers did not have social security. While not certain, it is understood from the Resettlement Action Plan (SHW, 1994) that this might have aimed at ensuring only the 'farmers' were compensated with land.

According to the Resettlement Law, the entitlement holders could opt for rural resettlement with house and land or urban resettlement with an apartment in an urban area. Values of the assets of those who were to be resettled would be subtracted from the value of the assets given by the state. Then depending on which value was higher, the difference would either be paid to the displacee by the government or vice versa. The displacees would start paying their debt five years after receiving their houses and would pay fixed amounts for a period of 20 years. Notwithstanding the Law, the displacees were informed that in case they opted for state resettlement, they would have to 'donate' all the cash compensation they would obtain for their assets and would not receive back a difference.[9]

Implementations

The land acquisitions and resettlement assessment started in 1988. According to the Resettlement Action Plan (SHW, 1994) a total of 577 households applied for resettlement, out of which 389 were found to comply with the resettlement criteria. Of these households, 344 had opted for rural and 45 had opted for urban resettlement.

The construction of the rural site was completed in 1997, but the construction of the urban resettlement site had never even started. Therefore, instead of 389 houses, eventually only 344 houses were available. It is likely that for this reason a 'second resettlement assessment' was held through which the officers could assess whether or not the entitlement holders still complied with the resettlement criteria.

Nine years had passed since the first resettlement assessment and people had died, married, widowed, remarried or had entered into jobs with social securities during this time. On the basis that they had lost their 'family' status, around

60 families were disqualified from the Bulgurca village which was scheduled to be resettled first. Examples included people who were widowed as their spouses died, widows whose children got married and left home, or children who had lost both parents.

> During the first assessment [in 1988] my father and mother-in-law were living with my husband who was single then. I married my husband in 1992. My father- and mother-in-law died in 1993, one after the other. In 1997, three months before the evacuation, they told us that we had lost our entitlement. I was pregnant when I heard this. I was constantly thinking 'what am I going to do now, I have to work, we have to buy a plot, we have to build a house'. I panicked and aborted my baby. Now I am so regretful about this.
>
> (Female, 41, Bulgurca)

Around 20 people who had entered jobs that provided social security were also eliminated. Neither the Law, nor the officers, clarified when the applicant should not receive social security, whether it was during the application, while the houses were given, in-between or after.

> I did not have social security during the first assessment [in 1988]. Between 1988 and 1997, I changed jobs six times, but did not work more than a year in total. While the houses were being allocated, I was working at a water bottling factory. I went to the resettlement site to collect my keys. They told me that I would not be given a house. There had been a complaint about me as I was insured. We did not have a place to go; we did not know what to do. We suffered a lot. Within the next two years, the factory was closed and I was jobless and uninsured again.
>
> (Male, 44, Bulgurca)

Furthermore, when they were preparing to receive their keys for the resettlement houses, around 20 forest labour families learned that they had also lost their entitlement due to an earlier investigation that recorded that they were not residing in the villages. They were exasperated as they had been living in temporary forest camps during this time as they were contracted as usual for logging work.

The second assessment and loss of entitlement was undoubtedly a shock for people as they had laid all their hopes on the houses and land they would receive. The families who lost their entitlement were informed that they would receive back the cash compensations they had donated during the applications; however, nine years had passed and the money had lost all its value due to inflation. Hence the eliminated displacees received literally a negligible amount of cash compensation.

> In 1993, they had given my father-in-law 500 million Turkish lira (TL) for his 60 ha of land. That was a lot! He came home with a big bag of money.

> I begged him to buy a house with that money. But he wanted to apply for state resettlement. He said a stray lamb would be prey for the wolves and we should stay with the community. He deposited the money to the resettlement account. Then his wife died. While others were receiving houses, we received a letter stating that he was no longer entitled as he was widowed and there was no child with him. The letter stated that he could get back his money. We received the money in 2000. In 1993, 500 million TL [US$45,500] would buy a three floor apartment in Menderes. In 2000 it became a penny fee [US$800]. We tried so hard, but they did not give a penny of interest.
>
> (Female, 41, Bulgurca)

Obviously, the second assessment only worked in one direction. While many families lost their resettlement rights, no new families (i.e. couples who were newly married) or people who lost their jobs (and social security) were given entitlement. Eventually, as 100 families were disqualified, 55 houses were left empty at the resettlement site. In 1998, to the surprise of the 'local displacees', 36 of these leftover houses were offered to Kurdish families. These families had been displaced by the Ataturk Dam built in south-eastern Turkey in 1992 and had been waiting for resettlement since then.

After the relocation of Kurdish families, the remaining 19 houses were offered to the residents of Keler, located in the upper parts of the dam. Yet, as the number of entitlement holders amounted to 39, the lucky ones to be resettled were identified through a lottery. Those who pulled out an empty paper were promised that their houses would be constructed within a year. They had no clue that, 13 years after this lottery, while this research was conducted, they would still be waiting for their houses.

The protection zone was evacuated later between 1999 and 2004. Camkoy was totally, and Malta, Esen and Sasal were partially evacuated. Except for Camkoy, which received cash compensation but also had their names written on the waiting list for 'resettlement' (together with the 20 villagers from Keler), other displacees were not offered a resettlement option.

As a result, lack of proper planning and misapplication of hitherto inadequate laws, which discriminated against the widows, singles and people with social security, meant that the displacees were effectively sorted into four main groups: (1) state-resettled families with houses and land, (2) cash-compensated persons, (3) uncompensated displacees (including those who were eliminated in the second assessment and those who were entitled but not resettled) and (4) the Kurdish households who had a different long-distance resettlement experience.

Due to space limitations, the experience of Kurdish resettlers is not included in this paper. In the following sections, post-displacement experiences of the state-resettled, cash-compensated and uncompensated groups are summarized and brief information is provided on the socio-economic situation of the control group (Cileme village).

After the dam

The state-resettled households

As the households were required to 'donate' all their cash compensation for state-resettlement, it was mainly the landless and poorer families who preferred the state resettlement (see Tables 1.1 and 1.2). They were provided two options to choose from for the location of the resettlement site and were also consulted about the house designs. When entitled households moved to the resettlement

Table 1.1 Pre-project (1994) income data based on Resettlement Action Plan[10]

	State-resettled households (n=84)		*Cash-compensated households (n=156)*
	Farming families	*Families dealing with trading*	*Families dealing with both trading and farming*
Average annual income per household in 1994 as presented in the report	$366	$2,646	$3,455
Average annual income per household in 1994 (adjusted value for 2011 considering inflation and dropping of six zeros from TL in 2005)	$1,000 ₺1,600	$7,600 ₺12,000	$9,500 ₺15,000
Average annual income per person in 1994 (adjusted value for 2011 considering inflation and dropping of six zeros from TL in 2005)	$250 ₺400	$1,900 ₺3,000	$2,300 ₺3,750

Source: Tahtali Water Supply Project Resettlement Action Plan, State Hydraulic Works, 1994, p. 31.

Note: ₺ represents the new Turkish lira which dropped six zeros in 2005.

Table 1.2 Pre-project conditions with selected indicators

	State-resettled households (n=79)	*Cash-compensated households (n=76)*	*Uncompensated households (n=52)*
Percentage of households who owned lands	10%	38%	10%
Average land size (decares)	1.4	16.1	1.6
Percentage of households who own livestock	51%	72%	62%
Average room/person	0.6	0.9	0.7
Percentage of households paying rent for the house	12%	0%	8%

Source: field surveys conducted in 2011.

village, the houses and infrastructure were ready, but no grazing lands or forests were available. The primary school was operating but a health unit had not been established.

The resettlement site had a water supply, sewage and electricity infrastructure. The houses were composed of two floors with a total of 170 m^2 inner space and a garden of 400 m^2. The upper floor was designed as the living area and the lower floor was intended as an agricultural depot. As the officers did not allow construction of barns in the garden, reportedly many resettlers ended up selling their animals.

Lands were allocated to the resettlers one year after the resettlement. The average size of parcels given to each household was 7 decares. While this was larger than the average land size this group had before (1.4 decares) (Table 1.2), it was much smaller than the average land size, which amounted to 27 decares in the control village (see Table 1.3). The displacees reported that most of the lands were infertile, there was no irrigation water and some of the lands had not been adequately cleared from rocks and bushes.

The resettlers were required to reside at the resettlement site for ten years in order to obtain the title deeds. They were not allowed to sell or rent out the houses or lands during this period. This not only constrained their mobility to look for employment but also halted their access to bank credits as they did not legally own any assets to show as guarantee.

Reportedly, the resettlers had difficulty in finding jobs for about one year until when farmers from other villages came to collect agricultural workers. The new resettlement village was administered by the Torbali municipality, whereas most industrial jobs were at Pancar municipality which was actually closer to the site. Yet, as Pancar municipality followed a policy to employ its own residents, it took them a few more years to have access to these industrial jobs.

The irrigation wells were opened in the fifth year. However, due to the high costs of electricity and disagreements among the members, the established irrigation cooperation soon lost its functions and only a few villagers, who had greenhouses, continued irrigating.

A specific credit was provided only once to promote vineyards. Some had faked establishing a vineyard and obtained the money for other purposes. Others tried their best to do it properly but grape prices fell drastically at the harvest. Eventually, they all faced difficulties in paying back the debts and some ended up selling the lands even though this was not legal.

After a few years the plots at the village centre were sold through bidding for construction of shops and work places. The owners were required to build the shops according to officially approved architectural plans within two years. Most of the buyers could not manage this in the given time as they did not have the financial means and court cases were filed by the government to claim back the parcels.

At the fifth year of resettlement, the resettlers started to pay back the money for the houses and land. This time, inflation was to the advantage of the displacees as the amounts requested for the resettlement assets had lost their value

Table 1.3 Income and living standards of displacee groups in 2011

	Control group (n=76)	*State-resettled households (n=79)*	*Cash-compensated households (n=76)*	*Uncompensated households (n=52)*
Average number of house changes after displacement (asked for the last ten years for the control group)	0	1	2	4
Average room/person	0.7	1.1	1.0	0.7
Percentage of households presently paying rent	0%	0%	10%	60%
Percentage of households who own cultivable land	78%	75%	28%	11%
Average land size (decares) (for the entire group including those without land)	27	7	5	1
Percentage of households who own livestock	67%	21%	7%	15%
Average number of livestock per household: 1 local livestock unit (LLU) = 1 cattle = 0.2 sheep = 0.16 goat[a]	5.7	0.5	0.4	1.3
Percentage of men (age between 15 and 64 inclusive) who are working	77%	79%	68%	82%
Percentage of women (age between 15 and 64 inclusive) who are working	61%	57%	32%	54%
Average number of years of education for the younger generation (age between 17 and 35 inclusive)	8	8	9	8
Average annual household income as of February 2011[b]	$14,440 ₺22,920	$13,280 ₺21,080	$15,180 ₺24,100	$11,090 ₺17,600
Average annual income per person as of February 2011	$3,360 ₺5,330	$3,510 ₺5,570	$3,810 ₺6,040	$2,820 ₺4,480
Average value of assets (except for cultivable lands)	$25,000 ₺40,000	$52,000 ₺83,000	$109,000 ₺173,000	$23,000 ₺36,000
Average value of assets (including cultivable lands)[c]	$134,000 ₺212,000	$81,000 ₺128,000	$128,000 ₺203,000	$28,000 ₺45,000

Source: field surveys conducted in 2011.

[a] Local livestock unit is taken according to the Pasture Regulation, published in official gazette no. 23419, date 31/07/1998.

[b] ₺1 = US$0.63 (according to the currency rate of Central Bank of Turkey on 1 February 2011).

[c] It was not possible to obtain a value for each parcel. As the values of parcels ranged between ₺5,000 and ₺8,000, the average 1 decare of land is assumed to be ₺6,500.

significantly. Over the years the payments decreased to a negligible amount (US$190/year as of 2011) and could be easily paid.

According to the statements of the state resettled households, it took them around 3–5 years to restore their finances and secure some sort of employment. It is understood that many of the households also obtained some cash compensation from family assets and this had helped greatly during this period.[11] As most of the lands were infertile, many ended up planting olive trees provided free by the government. Only a small part of the families continued farming as the main income source, whereas many found informal labour jobs in agriculture or other sectors (Table 1.4). Some also found industrial labour opportunities. They were often satisfied with these types of jobs which provided consistent cash flow in contrast to the unreliable agricultural income that depended on several factors and was received only once a year.

They were also generally pleased with the houses. At the time of the research, the provisional ten years had been filled up and many had rented the lower floors or rebuilt them for their sons. According to the survey results, 52 per cent of the resettlers claimed that they were as well or better off than before which was slightly higher than the control group. The data suggests that the average income level of this group was 5 per cent higher than the control group (Table 1.5).

Table 1.4 The primary occupation of the economically active population who are working (age between 15 and 64 inclusive)

	Control group (n=76)	*State-resettled households (n=79)*	*Cash-compensated households (n=76)*	*Uncompensated households (n=52)*
Total number of persons in this age group covered by the survey	171	152	91	99
Farmers	66%	20%	17%	11%
Agricultural labour	9%	26%	8%	21%
Daily labour	6%	11%	15%	18%
Industrial labour	7%	14%	14%	14%
Forest labour	0%	3%	0%	10%
Small trading and artisanship	8%	10%	4%	9%
Public transportation	2%	12%	32%	12%
Other	2%	4%	10%	5%
Total	100%	100%	100%	100%

Source: field surveys conducted in 2011.

Table 1.5 Self-claimed change in income level and the perceived reason for this change

	Reason stated for the change in income	*Control group (n=76) (%)*	*State-resettled households (n=79) (%)*	*Cash-compensated households (n=76) (%)*	*Uncompensated households (n=52) (%)*
Households who claimed to be better off	Personal reasons (e.g. children grown up)	4	8	8	6
	Land gain	0	6	0	0
	Increase in job opportunities	7	14	15	14
	Obtaining a house	0	1	0	0
	Not specified	7	5	5	5
	Sub-total of households who claimed to be better-off	**18**	**34**	**28**	**25**
Sub-total of households who claimed to have equal level of income		**30**	**18**	**16**	**24**
Households who claimed to be worse off	Personal reasons (e.g. getting older, death of spouse)	7	7	5	8
	Land/animal loss	2	17	28	17
	Decrease in job opportunities	4	15	7	10
	Incurring new costs (e.g. fuelwood, water)	2	1	9	4
	Accommodating in rental houses	0	0	0	4
	Dis-articulation of families and social networks	0	0	0	4
	Increase in costs of inputs, decrease in price of products	30	1	0	0
	Not specified	7	7	7	4
	Sub-total of households who claimed to be worse off	**52**	**48**	**56**	**51**
Total		**100**	**100**	**100**	**100**

Source: field surveys conducted in 2011.

Cash-compensated households

Almost all the households who were cash-compensated moved to the nearby urban centres. Some had started to invest much earlier and had slowly built their houses before the displacement. Most households constructed 2–4 floors as separate apartments where each sibling could have a flat.

A majority of this group ended up in court for the compensation amounts and it is understood that in almost all cases the amount was increased. However, the cash was paid to the lawyers by the court, who then conveyed the money to the displacees. As the displacees did not have direct access to the court decisions and information, they never knew whether they received the right amount. Due to high payments required by the lawyers (generally 20 per cent) and lack of a control mechanism to check fraud, it is understood that large sums of money may have been lost to the lawyers.

Despite efforts it was literally impossible to gain reliable data regarding the amount of cash compensations. Due to high inflation, the dropping of zeros from Turkish lira in 2005 and payments having been received in instalments with court cases, almost no one could quantify the amount of cash compensation. Some thought it was high enough to buy even better lands and some thought it was very little.

All those who had legally owned a property that would be submerged had received their compensation. However, in controversial situations (e.g. multiple ownership claims over the same parcel) or customary ownership claims, the court cases could last several years, thereby delaying the payments.

According to the claims of the key informants, around 20 night clubs offering gambling and adultery services were opened in the closest town at the time compensation payments were made. As the money had melted away, those clubs had also slowly disappeared. The survey results suggest that this group had moved house twice on average and 14 years after the displacement 90 per cent resided in their own houses (Table 1.3). Land and house investments in urban areas proved to be very profitable and their assets had gained significant value. Some of the families also invested in tradable public transportation licences (such as taxis and public minibuses) (Table 1.4), which not only gained momentous value but also provided a very good income source over the years. According to the surveys, this group earns higher and educated their youngsters better than the other groups. The percentage of working women is lower as agricultural type jobs are non-existent in urban centres, but also because there is less need for the women to work as the households have sufficient income (Table 1.3). Despite their comparatively improved position, however, those who thought that they were at least as well off as before were less in number than the other groups (Table 1.5). According to the quantitative data, on the other hand, the income level of this group was 13 per cent higher than the control group (Table 1.3).

Uncompensated households

Not surprisingly, those who did not receive proper compensation suffered most. Many landed at the resettlement site first and rented the lower floors. The officers kept on chasing these families out and dismaying the house owners with cancelling their entitlement had they rented out the lower floors. Some managed to establish their lives in the nearby urban centres whereas others returned to the resettlement site after a while to benefit from their social networks and agricultural labouring jobs.

To those who were entitled but not resettled, the officers kept on promising that the construction of the houses would start 'next year'. Having experienced the earlier 'second assessment', those entitled remained hesitant about entering into jobs with securities for several years. They received rental aid (approximately US$60/month in 2011) from the government; however, this was not enough to rent an adeqaute house. Reportedly, they were threatened by the officers with being 'resettled' elsewhere than Izmir in case they filed court cases against the government. After 12 years of waiting, only two households had braved filing a case against the government to claim their right to resettlement.

Not surprisingly, the uncompensated group had changed houses four times on average, ending up with the poorest housing conditions, lowest earnings and asset values. At the time of research 60 per cent of these households were still residing in rental houses. One would expect a significant amount of impoverishment to be reported by this group. Surprisingly, the percentage of households who reported that they were worse off was not much different than the other groups (Table 1.5). Notwithstanding, the quantitative data suggested that this group earned 20 per cent less than the control group (Table 1.3).

Control group (Cileme village)

The control group (Cileme village) was a nearby village of similar size to the resettlement site. While there were a few households who lost part of their lands that was in the project area, the village in general had not been affected by the land acquisition.

The main income source of the village was agriculture and animal husbandry, and the average land size amounted to 27 decares. The youngsters wanted to work at the industries close by but this was not easy as there were no transportation facilities. It was surprising to hear about the land tenure issues in the village. Generally, the ownership for agricultural land was clear, but there were several disagreements for the house plots in the village centre. This was because the historical transactions had not been registered at the title deed office and over the generations the lands had kept on being officially divided among the legal inheritors while the same lands were in practice used and inherited by the occupants. Presently, there are tens of official inheritors for each parcel and there is no longer anyone who remembers the transactions. Hence the court cases have been going on for several years. This is why the average value of their assets (other than cultivable lands) is less than other groups (Table 1.3).

One would expect (at least most of) the control group to claim that their income and living standards were equal to ten years before. But around half of this group reported that their situation was actually worse and many associated this with the general agricultural policies of the country that resulted in high input costs and low product prices (Table 1.5). Reportedly, the agricultural income had been decreasing every year.

Discussion of the findings

The Tahtali case, while chosen with an expectation to qualify as a successful resettlement, demonstrated a series of failures against few achievements. The achievements of the project can be counted as provision of 344 houses for the displaced households, 90 per cent of whom were composed of landless families, and delivery of cash compensation to the rest of the displacees for all submerged properties, although timeliness and adequacy of the payments remain uncertain.

The case study confirmed various implementation defects identified in the literature. The obvious ones include lack of population census, impact assessment and proper planning, underestimation of number of people to be displaced, lack of institutional commitment and consultation with affected people, undervaluation of assets and cuts in compensation payments, lack of sufficient and adequate lands, lack of compensation for lost common resources and lack of livelihood restoration measures. The planning and implementation deficits had effectively created an 'uncompensated' group whose sufferings can neither be excused nor justified with any development initiative.

Despite the different experiences the groups had gone through, it was surprising that the percentage of people who felt worse off was almost the same (around half) for all the groups (Table 1.5). When people were asked 'why' they felt better or worse off, the answers were diverse, including gain or loss of lands and animals, lack or availability of job opportunities, and personal- and family-related factors such as becoming older or an increase or decrease in number of household members (Table 1.5).

On the other hand, the quantitative results provided a different perspective. When the average income levels per person were compared with the control group it was observed that the state-resettled earned 5 per cent and cash-compensated earned 13 per cent higher, whereas the uncompensated remained 20 per cent lower than the control group (Table 1.3). Although the representativeness and reliability of the income data presented in the Resettlement Action Plan remains questionable due to lack of sufficient information on the methodology and conversion rates used,[12] in 2011 the cash-compensated appeared to earn 65 per cent and the state-resettled appeared to earn at least 84 per cent more than the income levels reported in 1994.

The average land size increased for the state-resettled households, whereas it had decreased for both the cash-compensated and uncompensated (Tables 1.2 and 1.3). Regarding average values of family assets (including lands), the cash-compensated and the control group almost owned the same amount of assets. Not surprisingly, the majority of the uncompensated group still resided in rented houses and lagged far behind the others in terms of value of owned assets.

Regarding the income level of households, there was a noticeable difference between the quantitative and qualitative findings. It is interesting that while half of the households claimed to be impoverished across all groups, quantitative data suggested that only the uncompensated group was impoverished. It is not easy to explain this difference. Is it about the subjectivity of the question 'being better or worse off' that may not only pertain to income in people's perceptions? Did the emotions or disappointments about the process affect the answers? Was this about personality or how displaced people wanted to present themselves to a researcher? If we had aimed to assess the success of Tahtali Dam, which finding should we rely on?

As the samples were randomized for the control and state-resettled groups it is perhaps possible to argue that '14 years after the displacement, the average income level of the state resettled households was 5 per cent higher than the control group'. Unfortunately, such generalization is not possible for the increased income level of the cash-compensated or the decreased income level of the uncompensated groups as snowball sampling does not provide statistical reliability. Regardless, the results are likely to be indicative.

Conclusion

The resettlement implementations vary drastically throughout the world. On the one hand, there are projects in which displaced people receive nothing at all; on the other hand, there are well-planned projects that might have brought a better quality of life to the oustees. Perhaps a large majority falls into neither but somewhere in-between.

In my view, more than anything, this study showed how complicated it can be to assess the outcomes of displacement. Clearly displacement may result in many different impacts and impact groups and isolating and looking into just one group may seriously bias the overall assessment. Lack of pre-project records and statistics, large populations, need for longitudinal data and difficulties in accessing the displaced people who naturally become mobile after displacement lead to the typical limitations in DIDR research and make it a challenge to conduct broad evaluations.

Using a combined methodology of quantitative and qualitative tools proved very beneficial for the study. Qualitative tools were very valuable in gaining insights about the problems and injustices throughout the compensation and resettlement processes. Without this information it would not be possible to either identify or define the chain-like misapplications that marginalized and impoverished the uncompensated group. On the other hand, the quantitative data was also indispensable as it provided an opportunity to calculate and compare the income levels and other socio-economic indicators across the displaced groups. While the qualitative and quantitative findings were generally complementary, it was thought provoking that the outcomes were different regarding the change in income levels. Was this due to a methodological problem in assessing incomes? Was it due to the subjectivities in being 'better-off'? Or was it a political response by the people?

The quantitative data suggested that the socio-economic conditions of the households who were not compensated had significantly deteriorated after displacement. On the other hand, the data recorded an increase in the average income levels of the state-resettled and cash-compensated groups. Yet, an important question that needs further research and verification is what we should attribute this income increase to. Was it about general economic progress in the region? Was it due to a fortunate site selection? Were there other factors that impacted on the outcomes? Or can there really be hidden opportunities in DIDR, such as increased freedom and mobility, if backed up with a land option and adequate cash compensation, as argued by Sarvimäki *et al.* (2009)?

DIDR research is immune to neither methodological nor political bias. Given the political interests in certain outcomes, complexity of the phenomenon, research limitations and evolving nature of the consequences over time, how can we conceptualize 'success' in DIDR? How can we assess the projects fairly and constructively? How can we facilitate holistic and accountable evaluations? There is much to be asked and researched in DIDR.

Notes

1 The last assessment of the Arenal Hydroelectric Project that displaced around 500 households was conducted six years after the displacement through a household survey that covered 100 per cent of the resettled households (W. Partridge, personal email communication, 8 September 2014). In the Shuikou Hydroelectric Power Plant diplacement that affected around 84,000 people (Zhu *et al.*, 2000, pp. 2–3) a total of 524 resettled households from a sample of 35 villages were interviewed for a period of five years that started around two years before and continued until three years after the physical relocation (Zhu *et al.*, 2000, p. 39). The report (Zhu *et al.*, 2000) does not disclose the sampling methodology or standard error for the findings. The evaluation of the Dalian Water Supply Project that displaced 259 households was made 1–2 years after the resettlement through 31 household surveys and focus group meetings, although not much information (i.e. how many meetings with which groups) is provided for the latter (ADB, 2000, pp. 66, 68). The report mentions that the surveyed households were 'randomly' selected (ADB, 2000, p. 5) whereas it does not specify the randomization method or standard error for the findings. For the Arenal and Shuikou Projects, the change in income levels is assessed in quantitative terms whereas in the Dalian Project the affected people are asked a closed-ended question regarding whether and how their income levels had changed (the choices included definitely better off, slightly better, the same, poorer).

2 The amendment was made with Law No. 1306 that was accepted on 16/06/1970 and published in the official gazette on 29/6/1970.

3 The total population of state-resettled households was 307 and the sample size was 79; the total population of the control group was 345 and the sample size was 76. At a confidence interval of 95 per cent, this has limited the maximum error to less than 10 per cent at household level and 5 per cent at individual level for both groups.

4 The relevant governmental offices include the General Management and Izmir District Management of State Hydraulic works, which was responsible for the construction and expropriation works of the dam, Izmir District Management of Ministry

of Public Works and Housing, which has taken over the resettlement responsibilities of General Management of Village Affairs after its dissolution in 2005, and Izmir Water and Sewage Administration (IZSU), which was responsible for the operation of the dam and expropriation of the protection zone.

5 Tahtali Dam is referred to as Izmir Water Supply Project in this report (World Bank, 1994).

6 This Resettlement Law (No. 2510) was replaced with the New Resettlement Law (No. 5543) in 2006.

7 According to the claims of the displaced households, around 10–15 families who were not residing in the area managed to construct small huts in Keler and receive state resettlement through negotiations with the village headman. At the time of research two of these families still resided at the resettlement site whereas the others had sold their assets and moved back to their village.

8 This study identified only five persons who were widows at the time of displacement. All interviewed widows were cash-compensated and living in the urban city. One stated that she was at the same income level as before, whereas the other four claimed that they were worse off.

9 Because the valuation of the expropriated assets would be held ten years earlier (in 1988) than the valuation of the resettlement land and houses. In the meantime the assigned expropriation value of their assets would lose all its worth due to inflation.

10 It should be noted that the research methodology, characteristics of the respondents and survey forms were not presented in the Resettlement Action Plan. The state resettled households were grouped as trading and farming families but the number of surveys conducted with each of these groups was not provided. The data originally presented in the Plan (SHW, 1994) covers only the 1994 annual income as US$/household/year. Yet, the currency rate is not provided. In 1994, the currency for US$1 had increased from 17,000 TL in January to 38,000 TL in December in Turkey (Central Bank of the Republic of Turkey, 2014). When converting the 1994 income from US dollars to Turkish lira, this chapter took a conservative approach and used the December value. The values were adjusted to inflation by using the inflation calculator of the State Statistics Institute (1994). The average family size is given as four in the report. Hence, in order to estimate the yearly income rate per person, the household income is divided by four. As the research methodology is not well-explained and necessary conversion rates and other assumptions are not clarified, the reliability and representativeness of the presented data remains questionable.

11 The state-resettled households were asked to donate all their cash compensation to opt for state resettlement. However, when the compensation amounts were increased upon application to the court, they were not asked to deposit this 'increased part' and were able to keep it for themselves. Most of the interviewed households did not remember the amounts they received and some were also hesitant about speaking on compensation matters. Therefore, it was not possible to find out about how many of the respondents had received compensation and how much, or assess its importance in the overall resettlement outcome for this group.

12 See endnote 10.

References

Alvares, C., and Billorey, R. (1988). *Damming the Narmada*. Penang: Third World Network.

Amornsakchai, S., Annez, P., Vongvisessomjai, S., Choowaew, S., Thailand Development Research Institute, Kunurat, P., Nippanon, J., Schouten, R., Sripapatrprasite, P., Vaddhanaphuti, C., Vidthayanon, C., Wirojanagud, W. and Watana, E. (2000). *Pak*

Mun Dam Mekong River Basin Thailand. Available online at www.centre-cired.fr/IMG/pdf/F8_PakMunDam.pdf (last accessed 5 September 2014). World Commission on Dams.

Asian Development Bank (ADB) (2000). *Special Evaluation Study on the Policy Impact of Invluntary Resettlement*. ADB.

Asian Development Bank (ADB) (2006). *Involuntary Resettlement Safeguards: ADB Evaluation Study*. Available online at www.adb.org/documents/involuntary-resettlement-safeguards (last accessed 5 September 2014): ADB.

Babus, F. (2006). *Osmanli'dan Gunumuze Etnik – Sosyal Politikalar Cercevesinde Goc ve Iskan Siyaseti ve Uygulamalari*. Istanbul: Ozan Yayincilik.

Central Bank of the Republic of Turkey (2014). *Foreign Currency Rates*. Available online at http://evds.tcmb.gov.tr/cgi-bin/famecgi?cgi=$ozetweb&DIL=TR&ARAVERIGRUP=bie_dkdovizgn.db (last accessed 5 September 2014). Ankara: Central Bank of the Republic of Turkey.

Cernea, M. (1996). Sociological practice and action research (Part I). *Journal of Applied Sociology*, 13, 79–99.

Cernea, M. (1997). Sociological practice and action research (Part II). *Journal of Applied Sociology*, 14, 105–123.

Cernea, M. (1998). Impoverishment or social justice? A model for planning resettlement. In H. M. Mathur, and D. Marsden (eds), *Development Projects and Impoverishment Risks: Resettling Project-Affected People in India* (pp. 42–66). Delhi: Oxford University Press.

Cernea, M. (2003). For a new economics of resettlement: A sociological critique of the compensation principle. *International Social Science Journal*, 55, 37–45.

Cernea, M. M. (2004). Impoverishment risks, risk management, and reconstruction: A model of population displacement and resettlement. *UN Symposium on Hydropower and Sustainable Development*. Bejing: United Nations.

Cernea, M. M. (2008a). Compensation and investmet in resettlement: Theory, practice, pitfalls, and needed policy reform. In M. M. Cernea, and H. M. Mathur (eds), *Can Compensation Prevent Impoverishment? Reforming Resettlement Through Investments and Benefit-Sharing* (pp. 15–82). Oxford: Oxford University Press.

Cernea, M. M. (2008b). Reforming the foundations of involuntary resettlement: Introduction. In M. M. Cernea, and H. M. Mathur (eds), *Can Compensation Prevent Impoverishment? Reforming Resettlement Through Investments and Benefit-Sharing* (pp. 3–10). New Delhi: Oxford University Press.

Cook, C. C., and Mukendi, A. (1994). Involuntary resettlement in bank-financed projects: Lessons from experience in sub-Saharan Africa. In C. C. Cook (ed.), *Involuntary Resettlement in Africa* (pp. 32–42). Washngton, DC: World Bank.

Eriksen, J. H. (1999). Comparing the economic planning for voluntary and involuntary resettlement projects. In M. M. Cernea (ed.), *The Economics of Involuntary Resettlement: Questions and Challenges* (pp. 83–146). Washington, DC: World Bank.

Horowitz, M., Koenig, D., Grimm, C., and Konate, Y. (1993). Resettlement at Manantali, Mali: Short-term success, long-term problems. In M. M. Cernea (ed.), *Anthropological Responses to Resettlement: Policy, Practice, and Theory* (pp. 228–250). Boulder, CO: Westview Press.

International Finance Institution (IFC) (2002). *Handbook for Preparing Resettlement Plan*. IFC.

Joseph, J. (1995). *Resettlement and Rehabilitation of Displaced Tribal Families of Sardar Sarovar Project in Maharashtra*. Unpublished paper presented to the International Conference on Development Induced Displacement and Impoverishment. Oxford: Refugee Studies Programme of Oxford University.

Karimi, S., Nakayama, M., Fujikura, R., Katsurai, T., Iwata, M., Mori, T. and Mizutani, K. (2005). Post-project review on a resettlement programme of the Kotapanjang Dam Project in Indonesia. *International Journal of Water Resources Development*, 21(2), 371–384.

Koenig, D. (2006). Enhancing local development in development-induced displacement and resettlement projects. In C. de Wet (ed.), *Development-Induced Displacement: Problems, Policies and People* (pp. 105–140). New York: Berghahn.

Lassailly-Jacob, V. (1996). Land-based strategies in dam-related resettlement programmes in Africa. In C. McDowell (ed.), *Understanding Impoverishment: The Consequences of Development-Induced Displacement* (pp. 187–199). Providence, RI; Oxford: Berghahn.

Mathur, H. M. (2006). Resettling people displaced by development projects: Some critical management issues. *Social Change*, 36(1), 36–86.

Mburugu, E. K. (1994). Dislocation of settled communities in the development process. In C. C. Cook (ed.), *Involuntary Resettlement in Africa: The Case of Kiambere Hydroelectric Project* (pp. 42–49). Washington, DC: World Bank.

Mejia, M. (1999). Economic dimensions of urban resettlement: Experiences from Latin America. In M. M. Cernea (ed.), *The Economics of Involuntary Resettlement: Questions and Challenges* (pp. 147–188). Washington, DC: World Bank.

Ministry of Environment and Urbanization (2014). Baraj Iskani Calismalari Suruyor – Guncel haberler 01.09.2019. Available online at www.csb.gov.tr/turkce/index.php?Sayfa=faaliyetdetay&Id=1032 (last accessed 5 September 2014).

Morse, B., and Berger, T. (1992). *Sardar Sarovar Report of the Independent Review*. Ottawa: Resource Futures International.

Nayak, R. (2000). Risks associated with landlessness: An exploration towards socially friendly displacement and resettlement. In M. M. Cernea, and C. McDowell (eds), *Risks and Reconstruction: Experiences of Resettlers and Refugees* (pp. 79–107). Washington, DC: World Bank.

Partridge, W. L. (1993). Successful involuntary resettlement: Lessons from the Costa Rican Arenal Hydroelectric Project. In M. M. Cernea, and S. E. Guggenheim (eds), *Anthropological Approaches to Resettlement: Policy, Practice, and Theory* (pp. 351–374). Boulder, CO: Westview Press.

Roy, A. (1999). *The Cost of Living*. London: Flamingo.

Sarvimäki, M., Uusitalo, R., and Jäntti, M. (2009). *Long-Term Effects of Forced Migration (IZA Discussion Paper No. 4003)*. Bonn: Institute for the Study of Labor.

Scudder, T. (1984). *The Development Potential of New Lands Settlement in the Tropics and Subtropics: A Global State-of-the-Art Evaluation with Specific Emphasis on Policy Implications*. New York: U.S. Agency for International Development (AID).

Scudder, T. (1991). A sociological framework for the analysis of new land settlements. In M. Cernea (ed.), *Putting People First: Sociological Variables in Rural Development* (pp. 148–187). New York: Oxford University Press.

Scudder, T. (2005). *The Future of Large Dams: Dealing with Social, Environmental, Institutional and Political Costs*. London: Earthscan.

State Hydraulic Works (SHW) (1994). *Izmir Water Supply Project*. Ankara: State Hydraulic Works.

State Statistics Institute (1994). *Inflation Calculator*. Available online at www3.tcmb.gov.tr/inflationcalc/enflasyonyeni.php (last accessed 5 September 2014). Ankara: State Statistics Institute.

Syagga, P. M., and Olima, W. H. (1996). The impact of compulsory land acquisition on displaced households: The case of the Third Nairobi Water Supply Project, Kenya. *Habitat International*, 20(1), 61–75.

Tamandong, S. (2008). Can improved resettlement reduce poverty? In M. M. Cernea, and H. M. Mathur (eds), *Can Compensation Prevent Impoverishment? Reforming Resettlement Through Investments and Benefit-Sharing* (pp. 394–422). New Delhi: Oxford University Press.

Tata Institute of Social Sciences (1997). Experiences with resettlement and rehabilitation in Maharashtra. In J. Dreze, M. Samson, and S. Singh (eds), *The Dam and the Nation* (pp. 184–214). Oxford: Oxford University Press.

Wescoat, J. (1999). *Ex-Post Evaluation of Dams and Related Water Projects – Contributing Paper Prepared for Thematic Review IV.5: Operation, Monitoring and Decommissioning of Dams*. Cape Town: World Comission on Dams.

World Bank (1994). *Resettlement and Development: The Bankwide Review of Projects Involving Involuntary Resettlement 1986–1993*. Washington, DC: World Bank Environment Department.

World Bank (1998). *Recent Experience with Involuntary Resettlement: Thailand Pak Mun*. Available online at http://documents.worldbank.org/curated/en/1998/06/693488/recent-experience-involuntary-resettlement-thailand-pak-mun (last accessed 5 September 2014). Washington, DC: World Bank Operations Evaluation Department.

Zhu, Y., Ter Woort, M., and Trembath, B. (2000). *Successful Reservoir Resettlement in China: Shuikou Hydroelectric Project*. Washington, DC: World Bank EASES Discussion Series.

2 Reinvigorating a critical discussion on 'development' in development-induced displacement and resettlement

A study of non-displacement impacts

Narae Choi

Introduction

Nearly a decade ago, when I first proposed a research project on development-induced displacement and resettlement (DIDR), a common response in development studies was that it is a valuable endeavour but a decades-old problem. However, as a neophyte to the field, I found deeply troubling the way in which displacement and resettlement were carried out in the case of a railway upgrading project in Metro Manila, the Philippines. Moreover, it was still a striking, destabilising experience for those who were forced to leave their homes and communities, however many times that cases of DIDR might have been repeated in the long history of development. The more I become engaged with the topic, the more problematic I find the view of DIDR in the broader development studies. Vandergeest *et al.* (2007) capture the status of DIDR accurately by pointing out that the development literature rarely situates the 'obviousness' of displacement, while the DIDR literature is 'oblivious' to the wider debates on development.

Is DIDR really the same old problem or perhaps DIDR is too conveniently agreed as a foregone conclusion? Cases of displacement have persisted, if not increased, as a silent companion of land-based development and have been noted as 'a global problem', taking place almost everywhere in rich and poor countries alike and in urban as well as rural areas (UN-HABITAT 2011: 1). Considering that involuntary resettlement policies have not yet proven to be sufficiently effective in mitigating the negative impacts of displacement (Oliver-Smith 2010), DIDR does remain as a widespread and unresolved problem. Nonetheless, DIDR's standing in the wider development arena appears to have weakened and I attribute this to the possibility that discussions in the field of DIDR have been out of touch with critical questions about development itself. Such questions include whether displacement is inevitable in the first place (which is a different question from whether displacement harms are inevitable) or, conversely, whether development predicated on displacement is necessary; or, more boldly, whether development without displacement is possible. In this chapter, I investigate why these challenging questions may have been 'displaced' from DIDR research and explore the ways to resuscitate more critical discussion on development with displacement.

First, I propose that the focus on resettlement issues tends to limit the possibility of questioning the necessity of displacement in the first place and the model of development that requires population displacement. This is further explained by the 'placebo' effect of resettlement policy whereby its presence, regardless of the actual performance, appears to be sufficient to justify development with displacement, thereby reinforcing the strong myth that development can eventually generate positive outcomes. Second, in order to broaden the discussion on DIDR, I make a conceptual departure from the current focus on those physically displaced by deliberately looking for the effects that do not involve forced migration. 'Displacement' in the DIDR literature is by now broadly interpreted to mean being deprived of territory on which people had relied on for livelihood and had formed social relationships (Penz *et al.* 2011). That is, displacement connotes not only forced migration but moreover broader social, economic and environmental dislocations. While acknowledging this, I use displacement in a narrow term of forced migration and call those who have stayed in the same area as non-displaced (or non-migrants) and the impacts they experienced as non-displacement or non-migration impacts. Using the aforementioned case of the railway upgrading project, which required the clearance of informal settlements along the railway tracks and thus ended up removing over 35,000 families from their homes, I examine the experiences of people remaining in the project area. The presence of non-displaced but affected people expands the conceptual boundary of 'development' impacts beyond 'displacement' impacts and challenges the underlying assumptions of the current operation that resettlement policy can mitigate the adverse impacts of development.

Displacement of 'development' in DIDR discussions

Development-induced displacement (DID)[1] has been controversial mainly because the necessity of displacement is still debatable, unlike other types of displacement such as conflict-induced displacement (CID) or natural disaster-induced displacement (NID). For CID, displacement takes place within a complicated political situation where it is difficult to foresee (let alone prevent) the coming of displacement or to pinpoint parties accountable for preventing such incidents. For NID as well as for CID, the urgency of coping with the calamity overrides the quest for its causes.

For DID, that population movement is considered and chosen as part of a planned change raises a series of poignant ethical and political questions (see de Wet and Drydyk in this volume), which often comes down to the core question of how we distribute the costs and benefits of development among relevant stakeholders (McDowell 1996; Serra 1993). The distribution question makes DID more complicated than other types of displacement from an interventionist point of view. People displaced by conflicts or natural disasters are less ambiguous victims of a situation beyond their control that triggers immediate action than those displaced by development projects who would have not been victims if a choice against displacement had been made, or if any harmful risks of migration and resettlement had been effectively addressed. Furthermore, their sacrifice is often justified for a greater cause or in exchange for other benefits. I will explore these different positions in reverse order, starting from a view that development albeit at the cost of DID generates benefits.

Unlike conflicts or disasters with inherently negative connotations, development is generally associated with positive values that tend to overshadow a range of conflicting interests and rights surrounding the situation of DID. Notably, the perception of public good has been the main discourse through which complex impacts of 'development', including potential displacement harms, are summarised (Mehta 2008; Vandergeest *et al.* 2007). The cost–benefit analysis (CBA) is an operational tool that conveys a strong emphasis on positive effects by endorsing a project when its benefits exceed costs. The underlying assumption of the CBA is that if the adverse effects of development are left to the law of large numbers, over a large number of projects, the distributional effects would cancel out if the gains and losses are distributed at random among the population (Kanbur 2007).

However, when the actual distribution of benefits and costs is not discussed within the scope of the project, social costs such as displacement, which are not easily quantifiable or measured in monetary terms, are often externalised and borne disproportionately by displaced people (Cernea 2003, 2007).[2] Utilitarian aggregation in the CBA is also criticised in terms of sharing benefits, for being only concerned with the increase in utilities in sum and being indifferent to inequalities in individual utilities (Sen and Foster 1997). Drydyk in this volume outlines a set of values that have emerged in policy debate about development since the 1950s: well-being, equity, empowerment, environmental sustainability, human rights, cultural freedom and integrity against corruption. They form the development ethics values framework, with which we can distinguish worthwhile development from maldevelopment as well as evaluating the process and outcome of development. The framework allows us to demonstrate that even worthwhile development can be put under scrutiny by values such as equity and empowerment – central values to distributional and procedural justice – thereby indicating that the 'balance sheet' approach of the CBA is a crude tool for evaluating the 'merits of a project'.

In response to the need of factoring the costs together with the benefits in the distribution of development effects, involuntary resettlement was introduced as a measure targeted at compensating cost-bearers. Whether or not resettlement policy has extenuated the adverse impacts of displacement is an empirical question. Doubtless, it is important to have a legal framework protecting the rights of displaced people and compensating them for the harm inflicted on them (see Price and Morel in this volume). Nonetheless, the evaluation of policy implementation is inconclusive, while indicating that having a safeguard policy is not in itself sufficient for delivering its said goals. The gap repeatedly emerging between policy and implementation has led DIDR research to focus on exploring 'why policy guidelines designed to prevent impoverishment are not achieving stated objectives' (Rew *et al.* 2000: 5).

While it is a legitimate concern and a valuable contribution, I argue that a recent discussion in the DIDR field has become rather bogged down in 'getting involuntary resettlement right'. The existence of resettlement policy as a mitigation measure seems to have reduced the space of critically reflecting on development itself, by way of promising that the high risks faced by displaced people of undergoing hardship can be prevented. It is problematic if resettlement policy, regardless of its actual performance, is 'believed to' address potential harms. Price in this volume demonstrates that resettlement outcomes are not rigorously assessed as part of project evaluation. In this regard, I question whether resettlement policy, albeit differing from the CBA in caring for adverse impacts of development, has an effect similar to the CBA of reinforcing a strong bias towards the benefits of development. Furthermore, it represents a managerial ideal that promises potential harms can be prevented through effective management.

The positive promises of development projected into the future have long been under scrutiny from a range of perspectives, challenging everything from their ineffective delivery to the narrowness of prevailing conceptions of development itself (Rapley 2007; Rist 2008). The most fundamental critique comes from post-development thinking that rejects a social-engineering view that suggests socio-economic structures can be transformed through planned 'intervention' (Sumner and Tribe 2008). In particular, the modernist ideal of increasing the production of commodities, although originating from the specific tradition of Western history, has gained the character of a myth by drawing its legitimacy from a number of widely shared and seemingly indisputable truths such as economic theories and models (Rist 2008). 'Development' has then become a series of practices to be applied to different contexts, with a depoliticising effect of silencing the contradictions and conflicts that might arise (Ferguson 1994; Rist 2008).

Displacement is a sharp rebuttal in itself to the belief in manufacturing 'good' development, as it demonstrates clearly that development is not beneficial to all concerned and there are losers in the process of development. The continuous resorting to involuntary resettlement in addressing the skewed balance between the costs and the benefits is another poignant illustration of how strongly the high hopes for intervention have survived its unsuccessful (or at best mixed) track record in reality. It also implies that the priority of decision making is firmly on the benefits that a developmental change is supposed to bring and indicates that displacement has been marginalised by the power to define and implement the idea of 'public interest'. Ongoing struggles by affected people have challenged the decisions to proceed with projects displacing people and the power imbalance in decision making. However, the conventional mode of operation has not yet been transformed to the extent that development *without* displacement becomes a norm rather than an exception (Oliver-Smith 2010). When critical thinking loses its ground in the field of DIDR, the continuation of population displacement is increasingly unquestioned. In part, I attribute the 'displacement' of critical questioning from debates around DIDR to the rather narrow focus on displacement and resettlement. Once we enter the terrain of resettlement policy, the room to question a situation where 'development' is precipitated on displacement is limited, since by definition, resettlement already takes DID as a given. Although involuntary resettlement policy came into existence with the best intention to prevent or minimise displacement harms (Cernea 2000; McDowell 1996), its position that displacement harms can be avoided through effective mitigation is nevertheless fundamentally different from the position that displacement itself can be avoided. The framework put forward by the World Commission on Dams (2000) offers an alternative way of thinking by mainstreaming risk prevention and rights protection in the decision-making process (see de Wet, Drydyk and Dolores, this volume). This allows the space for questioning and challenging the rationale for a displacement-inducing project itself, where risks are high and rights can be undermined, against a broader set of values and through a more thorough deliberative process of evaluating development.

In view of this, I amplify the need to move the current discussion on displacement beyond the realm of resettlement and elevate it to a level at which the main focus is more on 'development' than on 'displacement'. I attempt to achieve this by making a conceptual detour from the controversy surrounding whether and how the impacts of DID can (ever) be mitigated, which seems to have reached an impasse between markedly different positions (Penz *et al.* 2011; Rew 1996). The managerial view that development harms can be mitigated has prevailed in practice. Noting that the presence of involuntary resettlement policy might have served the function of depoliticising the discussion on DID, I focus deliberately on what is being missed by the current intervention and investigate the possibility that other people may have been affected in the process of DID *without* experiencing physical displacement. They are identified in this research as 'non-displaced' people. In the DIDR literature, there has been a concern for the population other than physically displaced people (Mahapatra 1998; Scudder 1996) but little has been investigated on the actual experience of non-displaced people. Likewise, some of the involuntary resettlement policies express explicit concerns for impacts other than forced migration, by defining displacement in broad terms to include displacement from income sources, from social networks and from cultural sites of significance. However, the extent to which they are operationalised remains unclear. Hence, the focal point of the empirical investigation of my study will be on identifying and understanding these non-displacement impacts.

Empirical case study of non-displacement impacts

The study of non-displacement impacts is premised on the view that development is a fundamentally transformative process, whether being negative or positive, and its impacts can be much wider in scope and more diverse in kind than the most visible ones such as forced migration. Using an empirical case study of a railway upgrading project in Metro Manila, I examine how settlers remaining in the urban locality are affected by the consequence of land clearance and population displacement. Given the predominantly negative experiences of displaced people, I started my research by hypothesising that non-displaced people may similarly qualify as 'losers' adversely affected by the changes wrought by DID. Furthermore, they may be 'hidden' losers whose loss was not even recognised and redressed by an intervention such as a resettlement programme.[3]

Background and methodology

The first phase of the North Rail–South Rail Linkage project was part of priority infrastructure projects of the Arroyo administration (2001–2010), covering the section under the management of the Philippine National Railway (PNR) that passes through Metro Manila. Its main aim was to alleviate traffic congestion in Metro Manila by rehabilitating the rail tracks and upgrading train services. From the outset, clearing the right of way for the project was the main concern, because a large informal settlement had existed alongside the railway for decades in some cases. The social implications of their displacement were anticipated and duly acknowledged in a bilateral loan agreement that was signed in 2005 between the Republic of the Philippines and the Republic of Korea, as the release of the loan was contingent on the provision of adequate resettlement for displaced people. Accordingly, under the leadership of the National Housing Authority (NHA), a relocation programme was implemented in 11 different sites within and outside Metro Manila over a period that stretched from as early as 2003 to 2010. As a result, around 35,000 families were relocated. The railway project itself started in 2007 and completed in 2010, with the new trains running on the rehabilitated tracks and carrying a large volume of passengers.

A previous study was conducted in 2007 when the process of land clearance and relocation was still taking place in tandem with the railway project, both of which were conducted in phases (Choi 2008). Despite the provision of a relocation programme, the railway project turned out to be a stereotypical DIDR case in which the high risk of impoverishment and disempowerment was not effectively mitigated. Myriad limitations arose from the remote and isolated location of resettlement sites and their incompleteness in terms of infrastructure and services. Beyond this unfortunate outcome of DIDR, I noted the possibility that the project might have had additional impacts on the residents remaining in the project. In order to examine whether, and how, the remaining population was affected, I revisited the project area along the railway in 2010 after land clearance and population displacement was completed.

Once the 'messiness' of DIDR was settled, a degree of physical transformation in the local landscape was striking, which is vividly captured by a set of two photos taken at the same location along the railway tracks, one in 2007 and the other in 2010 (Figures 2.1, 2.2). They not only provide a real 'feel' for the change but also suggest that there remain more settlements and urban residents in the locality, for whom the underlying socio-economic significance can go far beyond the visible changes.

Figure 2.1 The railway area in 2007

Photographer: Beomchan Choi.

Figure 2.2 The railway area in 2010

Photographer: Beomchan Choi.

Semi-structured interviews were conducted with the people remaining in the section between the España station and the Caloocan station, selected on the basis of accessibility (e.g. houses with open doors or windows or with people sitting outside). A total of 67 interviews were conducted, including 16 displaced people who had stayed on or returned from the relocation sites, either temporarily or permanently. The accounts of displaced people were considered in the analysis for the purpose of understanding life along the railway prior to the clearance as they were very much a legitimate part of the locality before they lost their home. A range of experiences of the local change following land clearance and displacement were analysed across three domains of housing, livelihoods and social relationships, which turned out to be the main concerns of urban residents living within and around the informal settlements.[4]

Housing impacts

To secure an operational area for improved train services, a line was drawn on a very compact urban settlement formed along the railway tracks, dividing the residents to be removed from those to stay. First of all, only the informal houses built on the land owned by the PNR were targeted for demolition. Houses on private land or other public land were excluded from demolition, even if they were informally constructed, and the clearance stopped at the border between the PNR property and the land of other ownership. On the other hand, some of the informal houses still remain on the PNR land as the PNR property was not completely reclaimed through this project. The size of the cleared land also varied in different sections, the measurement for which ranged from 5 metres away from the centre of the rail tracks to 25 metres. In a given section, however, the land was cleared in such a way that houses standing on the border line were demolished only up to the point where they fell within the demolition zone. That is, not all the remaining houses survived the clearance intact as some of the remaining houses were literally 'chopped off', as local people described it (Figure 2.3).

Partially demolished houses introduce a grey zone that does not allow the post-clearance railway area to be simply categorised as demolished and non-demolished areas. Accordingly, the housing impact of the clearance is also classified into three types – no housing loss, a partial housing loss and a complete housing loss – with the first two types constituting the cases of 'non-displaced' people in this research. It should be noted that the categorisation of housing impact is only for residential houses, while investments in non-residential houses were also lost by the clearance, with ensuing livelihood implications. Although housing impact types are simple, more distinctive features emerge between the groups when examined against their tenure status.

Whereas displaced people were all informal settlers and thus lost their house completely, the tenure status of non-displaced people is much more diverse and includes both formal and informal settlers. Nearly half of non-displaced people (25 out of 51 cases) still remain informal settlers and could avoid displacement simply because they live on land that does not belong to the PNR. A significant difference between those without a housing loss at all and those with a partial housing loss is that the former includes a far higher proportion of formal settlers (62.9 per cent) compared to the latter (25 per cent). This is visually depicted in Figure 2.4.

Formal settlers in both groups are either legal land owners or house owners including a group of former informal settlers (six out of 51 non-displaced people) who are undergoing the process of tenure formalisation by pursuing a deal of direct purchase with the owner of the land that they have occupied for a long time. Those in the process of tenure formalisation were previously informal settlers themselves but have obtained a more secure position than the remaining informal settlers, who are now experiencing an intensified fear of forced eviction after seeing their family members and neighbours displaced through the railway

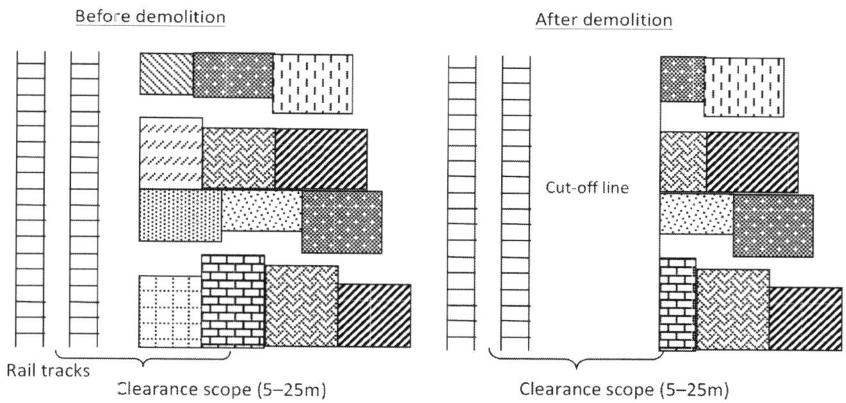

Figure 2.3 Partial demolition

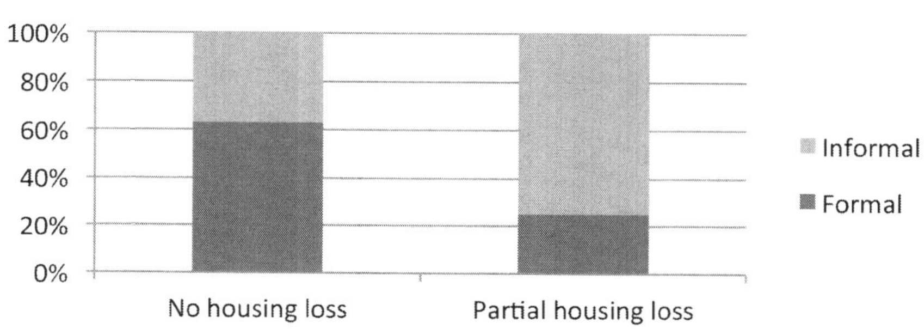

Figure 2.4 Proportion of informal and formal settlers

project. Some of them are indeed faced with other eviction threats by private and public land owners. The presence of remaining informal settlers and the ongoing threat of eviction underline how informal land use is pervasive in urban areas and how tenure insecurity undermines urban residents' daily lives.

Livelihood impacts

It is not only informal tenure that became vulnerable at the time of formal urban change following large-scale land clearance and displacement. Informality is found to be a common mode of arranging and investing in resources among the residents living in and around informal settlements, regardless of whether or not they are informal settlers themselves. The livelihoods of the remaining residents were affected when they arranged for physical capital to be used for livelihoods in the informal settlements or when they were part of the local livelihood network and made their living in the local economy. Some were affected by a combination of both.

Even though non-displaced people did not lose their residential house completely, some of them experienced tangible impacts on their physical asset by having part of their house demolished or by losing a rental house or a shop that they owned in the informal settlement. This had a secondary impact on livelihoods when the lost space had been used for income-earning activities such as a home-based small business or as a source of income such as an eatery, a shop or a rental house, resulting in a double loss whereby the investment in a physical asset was foregone and the income generated from it was also lost.

Accompanying such physical transformations are less visible and more subtle changes stemming from the displacement of informal settlers, which reconfigured the socio-economic relationships in the local economy. As for the physical capital stock, it turned out that non-displaced people were extensively engaged in the local livelihood networks consisting of customers, goods and service providers, middlemen, personnel for delivery and sales people. As long as they were part of these local economic networks, their home- or neighbourhood-based livelihoods were affected by the rupture following the loss of a large population. Consequently, business owners or street traders operating in the local economy experienced a decline in their business and household income to the extent that subsistence businesses making marginal profits were put on the verge of extinction.

Adversely affected livelihoods underline the important role that locally embedded social capital played in providing a pool of people who enabled and offered multiple, small income-earning opportunities. In this regard, locality as a function of location and the scale of the economy are critical for those who sustain themselves by selling a number of relatively cheap products or by providing services at a low price. This is one of the prime reasons why the displaced people who have stayed on or returned from resettlement sites strive to stay in urban centres like the densely populated settlements along the railway (location) where they find abundant livelihood opportunities (the scale of the economy) even though the overall purchasing power in the area may not be so high.

Social impacts

Differentiations also emerged among urban residents living in this compact area with regard to the ways in which their social milieu was affected by local changes. Whereas quite a few non-displaced people had personally close relationships with displaced people and thus experienced changes in their social lives, many others remained socially indifferent as they did not interact very much with displaced people or with people in the locality in general. Such distant or limited relationships are rather strikingly confirmed in the positive evaluations of societal changes by those who tended to attribute the problems in the locality to displaced informal settlers and consequently welcomed their removal as an improvement in the local living environment.

The multifaceted nature of the change was qualitatively illustrated by the evaluations of urban residents who acknowledge both positive and negative aspects. For instance, one research participant stated that even though the livelihoods in the locality were considerably undermined, the railway project is expected to bring better transportation. This elicits mixed responses such as the one shown by another respondent who feels 'sad' about losing his displaced neighbours and 'pity' for them because of the hardships in the relocation sites but simultaneously feels 'happy' that the area has become a better environment.

Discussion

Urban residents were affected by local changes to the extent that they organised their resources, livelihoods and social relationships within by now demolished informal settlements. Such engagement and subsequent impacts were widely observed among people with varying degrees of tenure and livelihood security. For instance, formal settlers managed income-generating activities within the local informal economy and, conversely, many formal contractual workers were also found to be living in informal settlements. That urban residents engage with informality selectively across different life domains leads to two important impact outcomes: (a) a household was affected differently across life domains, with some experiencing multiple adverse impacts; and (b) a substantial proportion of the researched households remained unaffected in any of the domains.

Table 2.1 summarises how each household was affected in the domain of housing and livelihoods. When considered together, there are 42 affected households (out of 67), with 11 households experiencing only a housing impact, 13 households only a livelihood impact and 18 households impacts in both domains.

Households being affected only in one domain indicate that people can move in and out of formal and informal sectors across life domains. That is, being informal in one domain does not necessarily mean that their status in other domains is also informal. On the other hand, the 18 households that were affected in both housing and livelihood terms demonstrate the permeability of informality across life domains. Non-displaced people whose lives were very much embedded in the local environment might have experienced an increased sense of insecurity

Table 2.1 Combined impact patterns across housing and livelihoods

Housing impact only	11 households
Livelihood impact only	13 households
Housing and livelihood impacts	18 households
No impacts	25 households

after part of their residential house or their shop in the informal settlement was demolished and their livelihoods as well as support networks were undermined. In this regard, displaced people who lost their houses completely are likely to have experienced multiple impacts and in fact make up half of the doubly affected group (nine out of 18 households) as the demolition of their whole settlement often meant the dissolution of their socio-economic environment as well. Lastly, it is noteworthy that a substantial number of households (25 out of 67) remained unaffected despite living close to the demolished informal settlements, thereby reinforcing the first point that urban residents engage with informality selectively. Selective engagement with informality and consequently differential impacts across life domains complicates the existing discussion on the distribution of development impacts as it is difficult to explain how individual households were affected as a whole (or to rate them as losers or gainers) and also to compare the aggregate impacts of different households.

Conclusion

Within the DIDR field, the central concern has been with physically displaced people who bear the most obvious social costs of development in the form of forced migration. However, empirical findings from my research demonstrated that urban residents who did not move from their locality also experienced diverse changes across life domains, although the collective picture of impacts is not so straightforward. The complexity arises from the fact that remaining residents were differentially affected, including those *not* affected, and also had different capacities to recover, which does not make them outright 'losers' as a group. In comparison, displaced people have at least one clear commonality despite intra-group heterogeneity: they lost their residential space, and thereby are unambiguous losers in this regard. For non-displaced people, however, the significance of adverse impacts is balanced out by those who have remained indifferent and unaffected.

By demonstrating that the composition of affected people is diverse and the patterns of impacts are complex, my study challenges the conventional method of conceptualising development impacts epitomised by the CBA, which reduces such diversity and complexity to aggregate numbers that account only for tangible effects. In addition, the existence of people who were adversely affected in the process of DIDR while staying put in the project area also gives more weight to the costs even in the limited equation of the CBA, making it harder to strike a balance between benefits and costs. Resettlement as a measure to compensate the costs has proven to be ineffective in addressing the most visible risks of losing a shelter and livelihoods experienced by those who are forcefully moved. It then appears to have a limited capacity to accommodate other affected people. That is, once we consider a range of impacts, including those without forced migration, the anticipation is that it would be harder to reach an easy conclusion that a project is a worthwhile development as it is accompanied with physical displacement *and* other impacts.

This brings us back to the point where we have to consider all the risks, rights, benefits and losses involved in a complex process such as a developmental change in order to understand comprehensively who is a loser and who is a winner, and by what criteria. In between the 'good' (an emphasis on positive promises of development) and the 'bad' (a notion that DIDR leads to negative outcomes), the 'ugly' or rather difficult truth is that DIDR is a complex situation and thus calls for a sophisticated approach. While the study of non-displaced people underlines the importance of a disaggregated and comprehensive approach to unpacking the complexity surrounding a developmental change, it is questionable to what extent the multi-scale and multidimensional implications of a developmental change can be addressed by current interventions. Other social and environmental losses that arise from beyond land-taking and forced migration are duly recognised in some of the most advanced involuntary resettlement policies (e.g. Operational Policy (OP) 4.12 of the World Bank); but it appears that there is little operational room for addressing such an extensive set of potential risks/harms, particularly against time and other resource pressures that are often geared towards generating positive impacts (de Wet 2006; and Chapter 5). It tells something about the way in which the mainstream development is practised at the moment, whereby resettlement policy implementation becomes a compliance issue and thus remains as an ideal rather than an outcome. To move beyond the limit of a given intervention and also not to fall into the trap of fatalism that DIDR is a by-product of development, I emphasise that development continues to require critical imagination and creative ways of realising them.

Notes

1 I distinguish DID from DIDR, as displacement of people is not naturally followed by their resettlement unless a resettlement programme is provided. Given this, DID is used for describing a broader situation where displacement takes place but resettlement is not necessarily assumed.

2 There has been an attempt to give a weighting to a specific group such as the poor so as to make the outcome of distribution more egalitarian but the distributional weighting has rarely been conducted in reality (Kanbur 2007; Pearce and Swanson 2007).

3 Indirect impacts are difficult to identify and arguably the existing involuntary resettlement policies have a limited capacity to consider and address them. For instance, the World Bank Involuntary Resettlement Policy (OP/BP 4.12) accommodates the loss of

access to, and sources of, livelihoods even in the absence of physical displacement, but does not consider other indirect effects of a project.

4 In this chapter, I understand that formal land ownership is proven by possession of a formally registered title (under the New Civil Code of 1950) and that land invasion without paying rent to, or obtaining approval from, the formal land owner makes land users informal.

References

Cernea, Michael M. (2000), 'Risks, safeguards, and reconstruction: a model for population displacement and resettlement', in Michael M. Cernea and Chris McDowell (eds), *Risks and reconstruction: Experiences of resettlers and refugees* (Washington, DC: World Bank), xv, 487.

—— (2003), 'For a new economics of resettlement: a sociological critique of the compensation principle', *International Social Science Journal*, 55 (175), 37–45.

—— (2007), 'Compensation and investment in resettlement: theory, practice, pitfalls, and needed policy reform', in Michael M. Cernea and Hari Mohan Mathur (eds), *Can compensation prevent impoverishment? Reforming resettlement through investments and benefit-sharing* (Delhi; Oxford: Oxford University Press), xxviii, 441.

Choi, Narae (2008), 'Putting "relationships" into the Impoverishment Risks and Reconstruction (IRR) model: a case study of the Metro Manila railway project in the Philippines', Master of Philosophy (MPhil) thesis submitted to the University of Oxford.

de Wet, Chris (ed.) (2006), *Development-induced displacement: Problems, policies and people* (Studies in Forced Migration, vol. 18, New York; Oxford: Berghahn), ix, 218.

Ferguson, James (1994), *The anti-politics machine: 'Development', depoliticization, and bureaucratic power in Lesotho* (Minneapolis; London: University of Minnesota Press) xvi, 320.

Kanbur, Ravi (2007), 'Development economics and the compensation principle', in Michael M. Cernea and Hari Mohan Mathur (eds.), *Can compensation prevent impoverishment? Reforming resettlement through investments and benefit-sharing* (Delhi; Oxford: Oxford University Press), xxviii, 441.

McDowell, Chris (1996), *Understanding impoverishment: The consequences of development-induced displacement* (Refugee and Forced Migration Studies, vol. 2; Providence, RI; Oxford: Berghahn).

Mahapatra, L. K. (1998), 'Risks for the tribal oustees', in Hari Mohan Mathur and David Marsden (eds), *Development projects and impoverishment risks: Resettling project-affected people in India* (Delhi: Oxford University Press), xvi, 296.

Mehta, Lyla (2008), 'Why are human rights violated with impunity? Forced displacement in India's Narmada Valley', in Katarzyna Grabska and Lyla Mehta (eds), *Forced displacement: Why rights matter* (Basingstoke; New York: Palgrave Macmillan), xvi, 261.

Oliver-Smith, Anthony (2010), *Defying displacement: Grassroots resistance and the critique of development* (Austin, TX: University of Texas Press), xi, 289.

Pearce, David W. and Swanson, Timothy (2007), 'The economic evaluation of projects involving forced population displacements', in Michael M. Cernea and Hari Mohan Mathur (eds), *Can compensation prevent impoverishment? Reforming resettlement through investments and benefit-sharing* (Delhi; Oxford: Oxford University Press), xxviii, 441.

Penz, Peter, Drydyk, Jay, and Bose, Pablo S. (2011), *Displacement by development: Ethics, rights and responsibilities* (Cambridge; New York: Cambridge University Press), xiii, 344.

Rapley, John (2007), *Understanding development: Theory and practice in the Third World*, 3rd edn (Boulder, CO: Lynne Rienner Publishers), v, 265.

Rew, Alan (1996), 'Policy implications of the involuntary ownership of resettlement', in Chris McDowell (ed.), *Understanding impoverishment: The consequences of development-induced displacement* (Refugee and Forced Migration Studies, vol. 2; Providence, RI; Oxford: Berghahn), ix, 257.

——, Fisher, Eleanor, and Pandey, Balaji (2000), 'Addressing policy constraints and improving outcomes in development-induced displacement and resettlement projects', (Oxford: Refugee Studies Centre and the Department for International Development).

Rist, Gilbert (2008), *The history of development : From Western origins to global faith*, 3rd edn (London: Zed), xiii, 288.

Scudder, Thayer (1996), 'Development-induced impoverishment, resistance and river-basin development', in Chris McDowell (ed.), *Understanding impoverishment: The consequences of development-induced displacement* (Providence, RI; Oxford: Berghahn), ix, 257.

Sen, Amartya Kumar and Foster, James E. (1997), *On economic inequality* (Oxford: Clarendon Press), xii, 260.

Serra, Maria Teresa Fernandes (1993), 'Resettlement planning in the Brazilian power sector: Recent changes in approach', in Michael M. Cernea and Scott E. Guggenheim (eds), *Anthropological approaches to resettlement: Policy, practice, and theory* (Boulder, CO; Oxford: Westview), vi, 406.

Sumner, Andrew and Tribe, Michael A. (2008), *International development studies: Theories and methods in research and practice* (Los Angeles, CA; London: SAGE), xiii, 176.

UN-HABITAT (2011), *Losing your home: Assessing the impact of eviction* (Nairobi: United Nations Human Settlements Programme (UN-HABITAT)).

Vandergeest, Peter, Bose, Pablo, and Idahosa, Pablo (2007), 'Introduction', in Peter Vandergeest, Pablo Bose, and Pablo Idahosa (eds), *Development's displacements: Ecologies, economies, and cultures at risk* (Vancouver: UBC Press), viii, 281.

World Commission on Dams (2000), *Dams and development: A new framework for decision-making* (London: Earthscan), xxxvii, 404.

3 Risk information sharing

An empirical study on risk perception and depressive symptoms among those displaced by the Three Gorges Project

Juan Xi, Sean-Shong Hwang and Yue Cao

Introduction

In the past few decades, there has been a rapid increase in both the number and scale of developmental projects such as dams, highways, and seaports in the developing world. While aiming to improve the infrastructure in the region, they often necessitate the relocation of a large number of people on or near the site of the projects. More often than not, development-induced displacement and resettlement (DIDR) causes temporary or even long-term economic impoverishment of the relocatees and tears apart their social networks (Cernea, 2009; Scudder, 2009). Efforts around the world to minimize such negative effects have emphasized adequate pre-relocation risk evaluation since the awareness of risks is the first step to prevent their realization in a planned process such as DIDR (Cernea, 2000). Inadequate risk perception of planners has been identified as the key reason for past failure in most relocation projects (Cernea, 1996).

DIDR literature largely focuses on planners' evaluation and prevention of risks, mainly, but not exclusively, based on Cernea's Impoverishment Risks and Reconstruction (IRR) model. To date, however, not much attention has been paid to the risk perception of individual relocatees. While risk evaluation on the part of planners shapes relocation policies, risk perception of relocatees affects their actual experiences of the relocation and resettlement process. Theory suggests that adequate risk perception would prepare individuals better for the coming life changes and facilitate adjustment (Slovic, 1987). Failing to fully recognize the risks on the other side would leave individuals unguarded from the hidden dangers (Slovic and Peters, 2006); regardless relocation officials around the world seldom convey risk information to the relocatees or engage them in the policy-making process (Cernea, 1996).

Using the case of the population resettlement induced by the Three Gorges Project (TGP) in China, this study aims to examine how individual relocatees' risk perception affects their relocation outcome, and particularly its impacts on their mental health. This study speaks to a critical tension in DIDR that although planners are equipped with tools for risk evaluation, affected people have been constantly excluded from this information and thus have been poorly aware of the potential risks. The study would also contribute to the relocation literature by empirically testing the prediction of the risk perception theory that states relocatees' pre-relocation risk perception is beneficial to their relocation outcome.

Background

In 1994, China began the construction of the TGP, the world's largest hydroelectric project located in the mid-section of China's Yangtze River. When completed in 2009, the TGP generated a reservoir of about 1,045 km^2 in a mountainous area. As a result, between 1992 and 2008, 1.27 million people, who lived less than 175 meters above sea level, were relocated (SCGPCCEO, 2009).

Past relocation efforts in China and around the world have led to startling negative outcomes (Billig et al., 2006). In the 1990s, recognizing the catastrophic relocation outcomes as a global pattern across developmental projects, the World Bank commissioned a study from which an IRR model emerged as a guideline for resettlement planners to diagnose, predict, and prevent relocation risks (Cernea, 1997). The basic idea of the IRR model is that catastrophic relocation results are avoidable if potential relocation risks are carefully evaluated ahead of time and counteractive measures are employed to prevent them. Based on global evidence, the IRR model identifies eight commonly found, interrelated relocation risks: landlessness, joblessness, homelessness, marginalization, morbidity, food insecurity, loss of access to common property, and social disarticulation (Cernea, 1997).

Although the IRR model was not explicitly referenced, the TGP planners followed a similar logic to avoid many risks evident in China's past relocation experiences (Heggelund, 2004). The Chinese government adopted a new development-oriented relocation policy (State Council, 1991), which mandated the state to build infrastructure and create conditions for the re-establishment and development of relocatees' livelihood in the post-relocation phase (Duan and Steil, 2003). For example, the State Council has earmarked 40 billion Yuan (US$4.8 billion) investment for the resettlement of the TGP-affected people, which accounts for about 45 percent of the total cost for the whole project (Wang, 2002). Resettlement areas were allowed to "share benefits" of the dam project by receiving a portion of the profits earned from power generation as development funds (State Council, 2001; Cernea, 2009). Farmers were promised to receive new land comparable to that of their former land or otherwise a non-farm job would be arranged for them. The TGP resettlement policy was praised by the World Bank as a model for other developing countries (Bartolome et al., 2000) and planners of the TGP confidently asserted that the resettlement was a development opportunity for the relocated (Wang, 2002).

However, the planned risk-mitigating policies generally assume ideal circumstances whereas they often do not operate as expected in the complex real world (Clarke, 2008; de Wet, 2009). This was true for the TGP relocation in that many mitigating efforts turned out to be ineffective and there were risks that had not even been identified. The submerging of mostly fertile farmland down in the basins forced farmers to move uphill and farm on steep infertile slopes, which led to serious soil run-off and deterioration within the environment. The rising water level caused unexpected landslides, making many places uninhabitable (BBC Chinese Web, 2010). Since 1979, China's economic system had undergone a profound transformation from a planned economy to a market-driven one. Consequently, the government failed to estimate the number of non-farm jobs needed in the region for farmers who have been ousted from their lands and many displaced individuals became landless and jobless, and were forced to survive on meager government allowances (BBC Chinese Web, 2010). In addition, there were many other documented problems such as delays in delivering compensation, improper usage or outright embezzlement of relocation funds, and poor coordination among many layers of local bureaucracies (Tanner, 2005). Such problems effectively hindered the government's efforts to mitigate impoverishment risks.

It has been argued that when institutions have formally evaluated risks and adopted mitigating measures in their planning process, these measures can form a sense of security that may actually be false (Clarke, 2008). The TGP relocation planners developed such sense of security, which was then conveyed to relocatees through intensive propaganda (Heggelund, 2004). Risks and uncertainties were not well discussed and warning messages were not conveyed to the affected population (Wei, 1999; Li et al., 2001). The overwhelming excitement around development-oriented relocation was consistent with the relocatees' hope for a better life. As a result, TGP relocatees were found repeatedly in previous pre-relocation studies to hold a very positive attitude toward the project and relocation (Li, 1996; Ding, 1998). Many relocatees did not pre-perceive any risks and held high expectations of post-relocation life (Li et al., 2001).

Risk perception and the TGP relocation

Risk perception, or the subjective perception of potential risks, is considered fundamental to the survival of human beings as risks can be averted only when they are perceived in advance (Slovic, 1987). Empirical studies in the fields of health behavior, traffic accidents, financial investments, and environmental hazards have demonstrated that increased risk perception prompts both decreased risk-taking behavior and increased risk-reduction efforts and risk-mitigation measures (Slovic et al., 1981; Brewer et al., 2007; Vidrine et al., 2007; McGee et al., 2009). With respect to DIDR, it is believed that an adequate risk perception facilitates an anticipatory socialization and prepares relocatees for the upcoming life changes (Scudder and Colson, 1982). Moreover, when properly mobilized, relocatees can contribute to a successful resettlement not only by taking energetic actions in reconstructing their own livelihood (Cernea, 1997), but also by exploring and negotiating alternatives in relocation arrangement when the original one does not work out (de Wet, 2006). In this way, the relocation process becomes more flexible and adapts to the changing social, economic, and ecological environment (de Wet, 2006).

However, in reality, planners seldom provide adequate information on potential risks to relocatees (Goodland, 2004). Populations to be relocated are usually considered as obstacles to developmental projects rather than participants who can make great contribution to the success of these projects (Li et al., 2001) and should actually benefit from the project as much as others. To gain their cooperation in moving out of the affected area, government officials tend to exaggerate the potential benefits while only briefly mentioning potential risks (Xi and Hwang, 2011). Officials usually withhold risk information, arguing that exposing relocatees to risk information would only increase their resistance to the relocation plan. Past studies usually focus on planners' evaluation of relocation risks, leaving individual relocatees' perception of relocation risks and its effects on their relocation outcomes largely unstudied.

Research question and hypotheses

Recognizing the gap, this study aims to empirically examine the relationship between relocatees' risk perception and relocation outcome, with a particular focus on mental health. As mental distress is associated with wide ranging social consequences, including impaired performance in many different social roles, it has been considered as an important indicator of relocation outcome (Porter and Haslam, 2005).

With its emphasis on policy making, the relocation literature has not yet developed substantive discussions on the mechanisms in which individual relocatees exercise their agency to improve their relocation and resettlement outcome. The stress process model, which has been frequently used by sociologists and social psychologists to study mental health issues, provides great insights into understanding how individual relocatees manage their circumstances and mitigate relocation-related risks upon perception. Substantiated by numerous empirical evidences, the stress process model proposes that social and psychological resources such as social support, sense of control, and self-esteem are protective resources that individuals often draw upon to battle life challenges (Thoits, 2006). These resources would cushion individuals from harsh situations. They would also intervene in the causal link between a stressor and mental distress (Lin and Ensel, 1989).

A key insight from the stress process model is that resources and coping could be mobilized only when the situation is perceived as challenging (Lazarus and Folkman, 1984). Thus, a lack of risk perception among relocatees may lead to fewer intervention efforts and when faced with unprepared challenges, frustrated relocatees are more likely to respond with depression. On the contrary, adequate risk perception at a pre-relocation stage may lead affected people to mobilize resources and evoke coping efforts that eventually reduce the stressfulness of the actual relocation. Guided by risk perception theories and the stress process model, we hypothesize that the TGP relocatees who perceive little or no risks would suffer more from relocation-induced distress. Risk perception is postulated to affect relocatees' mental health both directly and indirectly. A process is anticipated whereby high risk perception triggers relocatees to make mitigating efforts to combat the risks by mobilizing social and personal resources and therefore preempts or reduces resettlement-related stress.

Research methods: data collection and analysis

Data

Data used in this study come from a prospective panel study involving both pre-relocation and post-relocation interviews conducted three years apart. The original study consists of 975 designated relocatees and 555 non-movers recruited from five communities (clusters) randomly selected from Wanxian Relocation and Development Region (WRDR) which was formerly a part of the Sichuan Province where 80 percent of designated migrants resided (Weng, 1999). First, we randomly selected three rural and two urban communities from two strata of communities in the region. Second, we selected households from the selected communities by conducting censuses in three small communities and utilizing systematic sampling in the two larger ones. Face-to-face interviews were conducted with a household member aged 16 years or older in late 2002 and early 2003 by 29 sociology graduate students from two Chinese universities. A follow-up survey was conducted in early 2006, in which we successfully traced and interviewed 1,056 subjects—a success rate of about 70 percent. Among those who were successfully traced, 420 had been relocated, 286 had not yet moved, and 350 were non-movers whose houses were above the future water line.

This study did not use the whole sample of the original study, but rather focused on the 420 relocated respondents to whom relocation outcome and coping measures were relevant. Among them, 50 percent were female. Thirty-nine percent of the respondents were urban residents and 61 percent were rural residents. A typical sample respondent was 46 years old with a little more than six years of education. Finally, the relocatees have been relocated for an average time of 22 months (cf. range from 1 to 36 months).

To address possible biases that might result from the attrition, we conducted a sensitivity analysis and found that urban residents were more likely to be missed in the follow-up survey. To correct the possible implications of the attrition, we computed the hazard rate of attrition, which was equal to the predicted probability of exclusion, minus one (Beck, 1983), and included the hazard rate as *an attrition correction factor* in our main analysis.

Measurement

Depressive symptom was measured by the 20-item CES-D scale (Radloff, 1977). The scale asked respondents whether they had experienced any depressive symptoms from a list of 20 items during the past week. The same scale was used in both pre-migration (the reliability coefficient $\alpha = .87$, indicating high internal consistency among the items) and post-migration surveys ($\alpha = .89$). We focused on changes in depressive symptoms from time one to time two as our dependent variable in regression analysis. Subtracting the pre-relocation CES-D scores from the post-relocation CES-D scores, each respondent served as his/her own control and thus automatically ruled out the pre-existing differences in CES-D among respondents. It thus captured the amount of depressive symptoms elevated by the forced relocation.

To rule out the possibility that the observed over-time changes in depressive symptoms might actually be caused by some other macro-level conditions or historical events in China during the three-year study period, we conducted a sensitivity analysis comparing over-time changes in depressive symptoms among relocatees, non-movers, and designated movers who were yet to be moved. Only relocatees reported a significant elevation of depressive symptoms during the study period (4.31; $p<.0001$), while non-movers (1.02; $p=0.18$) and those who were yet to be moved (0.56; $p=0.52$) did not report increased depressive symptoms. The difference between the movers and others was statistically significant. The sensitivity analysis lent support to interpreting changes in depressive symptoms from time one to time two as induced by relocation.

Risk perception was measured during the *pre-relocation* survey by asking respondents whether or not they had perceived the following relocation-related risks: (1) property loss; (2) income loss; (3) forced to convert to a new livelihood; (4) worsening of housing conditions; (5) severing ties with relatives; (6) inability to get along with new neighbors; and (7) other risks. Responses were coded 1 for yes, and 0 for no and the sum of the seven items yielded a count measure.

Social support was measured by asking respondents whether or not they had talked to or contacted any of the following individuals with whom they do not share a residence: (1) parents; (2) adult children; (3) siblings; (4) other relatives; (5) good friends; (6) neighbors; (7) colleagues; (8) local cadres; and (9) other significant others during the past 30 days. The sum of the nine items yielded a count measure. In this study, we focused on changes of social connection from time one to time two to measure social support mobilized by perceived risks.

Sense of control was measured by Pearlin's (1989) mastery scale. The first- and second-wave reliability coefficients for the mastery scale were 0.74 and 0.78, respectively. *Self-esteem* was measured by the well-known scale developed by Rosenberg (1965). The first- and second-wave reliability coefficients for this scale were 0.77 and 0.78, respectively. As in the case of social support, we focused on changes in these psychological resources from time one to time two.

Finally, we used a positive comparison scale (Pearlin, 1989) to capture the effects of *positive coping*. Respondents were asked: "Compared to those whom you know, would you say that you are (a) much worse, (b) somewhat worse, (c) about the same, (d) somewhat better, or (e) much better in terms of (1) income; (2) occupation; (3) social prestige; and (4) social connections (*guanxi*)?" Responses to the four questions were summed to form a scale with scores ranging from 4 to 20. The scale had a reliability coefficient of 0.79 and 0.81 respectively for the first and second waves, respectively. The difference between the time one and time two measures was used in the analysis.

Analytic strategy

The panel data were analyzed in this study by a difference regression model in which change scores were used whenever available. Using difference scores, the model focuses on the within-individual variations over time and automatically controls for pre-existing, cross-individual differences in measured variables and unmeasured time-invariant variables (Allison, 2005). This feature enables researchers to specify models more economically while greatly reducing specification errors. For example, many stable personality traits such as optimism and pessimism might be associated with both the levels of risk perception and depressive symptoms (David et al., 2006). They were differenced out of the model and thus controlled for automatically. Therefore, the change score estimator is nearly always preferable in non-experimental studies (Allison, 2005).

Results

Table 3.1 reports descriptive statistics of key variables measured from pre- and post-relocation surveys. Based on observations among Western populations, the mental health literature has identified a CES-D score of 16 as the cut-off point for a clinically significant level of depressive symptoms (Radloff, 1977). If this holds for the Chinese population, our sample on average had a very high level of depressive symptoms even before the relocation took place. The stress associated with the anticipation of an impending relocation might explain the high pre-relocation CES-D score (Hwang et al., 2007). Moreover, at the time of our pre-relocation survey, the Three Gorges area has already undergone great changes. This includes the construction of the dam, the preparation work for the reservoir, and the fact that many residents whose houses were at the lower grounds were moving or had already moved out. The changes in respondents' living environment along with the anticipation of their own relocation would both contribute to the high levels of depressive symptoms reported at the pre-relocation survey. While the anticipation of an impending relocation could be stressful, the relocation itself further elevated the average CES-D score significantly. There was a 4.3 increase in mean CES-D score from the pre- to post-relocation survey. On the other hand, the respondents, on average, reported less than 1 risk, which was surprisingly low. While there was no significant change in social support from the pre- to post-relocation survey, the changes in psychological resources were significant and negative. It seemed that the relocation took tolls on respondents' sense of control, self-esteem, and their capability to use positive coping to balance their emotion.

Breaking down the whole sample into two risk perception groups, there were 200 respondents (47 percent) who perceived one or more relocation-related risks and 220 respondents (53 percent) who failed to perceive any relocation-related risk before the relocation. Table 3.2 compares descriptive statistics between two risk perception groups regarding the changes in the dependent and independent variables from time one to time two. Although both groups demonstrated an increase in their symptoms of depression from time one to time two, the average amount of increase for the no risk perception group (6.21) was much larger than the corresponding measure for the group that perceived some risks (2.34). The difference between the two change scores was highly significant.

Table 3.1 Means and proportions at pre- and post-relocation survey for key variables (n=420)

	Pre-relocation		*Post-relocation*			
	Mean/proportion	*SD*	*Mean/proportion*	*SD*	*Changes*	
Depressive symptom	21.94	(10.25)	26.25	(10.21)	4.31	***
Risk perception	0.90	(1.11)				
Social support	3.55	(1.43)	3.69	(1.58)	0.14	
Sense of control	21.40	(4.78)	19.98	(4.60)	–1.42	***
Self-esteem	35.45	(5.27)	34.78	(4.51)	–0.67	*
Positive coping	10.64	(2.90)	10.28	(2.37)	–0.36	*
Time since relocation			22.14	(11.77)		

Note: *** p<.001; * p<.05.

Table 3.2 Comparing changes in key indicators before and after relocation

Changes in key indicators before and after relocation	*Respondents who have initially perceived some risks (n=200)*		*Respondents who have not perceived any risks (n=220)*			
	Mean	*SD*	*Mean*	*SD*	*Differences*	
Changes in depressive symptoms	2.34	(11.47)	6.21	(11.83)	–3.87	***
Changes in social support	0.19	(2.02)	0.09	(1.96)	0.10	
Changes in sense of control	–0.73	(6.23)	–2.06	(5.91)	1.33	*
Changes in self-esteem	–0.35	(5.73)	–0.99	(6.16)	0.64	
Changes in positive coping	0.03	(3.19)	–0.70	(3.08)	0.73	*

Note: *** p<.001; * p<.05.

As predicted by the risk perception theory and the stress process model, Table 3.2 indicates that risk perception did result in respondents mobilizing resources and coping. The two risk perception groups had different change scores on resources and coping measures. Although the forced relocation process damaged relocatees' sense of control and self-esteem in general, vigilant relocatees were affected to a much lesser degree. This is consistent with the stress process literature, which claims that individuals can restore their sense of control when facing a life stressor by actively managing their situation and initiating mitigation efforts (Thoits, 1994). Finally, the no risk perception group experienced a decrease in positive coping while those who did anticipate risks reported an increase, which indicated that vigilant relocatees were more active in managing their emotions. These results supported our hypothesis that the lack of risk perception is associated with higher levels of relocation-related depressive symptoms while risk perception enables relocatees to activate or restore more protective resources and evoke more coping.

Table 3.3 presents the results of a regression analysis using the difference model. Model 1 focuses on differences in change scores of depressive symptoms across levels of risk perception. The regression coefficient indicates that for each additional risk perceived before the relocation takes place, there was a 1.79 point decrease in the elevation of depressive symptoms during the study period. Although we included an attrition bias correction factor in the analysis (Beck, 1983), it was not significant. In other words, there was no evidence to suggest that the attrition of respondents caused bias in the model.

Table 3.3 OLS regression analysis of TGP relocation-related depressive symptoms using difference model (n=420)

	Model 1			*Model 2*		
	Coef.		*Beta*	*Coef.*		*Beta*
Risk perception	–1.79	***	–0.17	–1.16	*	–0.11
Changes in social support				–0.66	*	–0.11
Changes in sense of control				–0.82	***	–0.43
Changes in self-esteem				–0.20	*	–0.10
Changes in positive coping				–0.54	***	–0.14
Time since relocation				–0.08		–0.08
Constant	10.22	**		7.78	**	
Attrition correction factor	–7.64			–3.68		
Adjust R^2	0.03			0.33		

Note: *** p<.001; ** p<.01; * p<.05.

To test the mediation hypothesis, we added change scores in resources and coping into the model. The mediation hypothesis would be supported if the coefficients associated with risk perception observed earlier were reduced when changes in resources and coping were controlled (Baron and Kenny, 1986). Model 2 shows that although the effect of risk perception was still significant, the controlling reduced its magnitude from −1.79 to −1.16 (a 35 percent reduction). This indicates that about 35 percent of the protective effect of risk perception on depressive symptoms functioned through its effect on resources and coping (Baron and Kenny, 1986). Consistent with previous studies, social support, sense of control, self-esteem, and positive comparison were effective factors that protect relocatees from suffering relocation-related depressive symptoms (Pearlin, 1989). Although simple, Model 2 was efficient because it automatically controlled for all measured or unmeasured time-invariant variables such as gender, age, education, and many stable personality traits that were associated with both risk perception and depressive symptoms. In sensitivity analysis, we also controlled for changes in household income and changes in negative life events experienced within 12 months prior to each survey. Controlling for these variables did not bring noticeable changes to the results reported above.

Relocatees whose pre-relocation depression was at maximal/minimal level could only experience a decrease/increase in post-relocation measure even without the effect of risk perception. The ceiling effect might bias the results because perceived risk might elevate the anticipatory stress observed at the pre-relocation survey. To account for the ceiling/flooring effects, we conducted two sensitivity analyses. In the first sensitivity analysis, we controlled for pre-relocation depressive symptoms. In the second one, we deleted respondents whose pre-relocation depressive symptoms levels were among the top or the bottom 5 percent. Both analyses confirmed the reported beneficial effects of risk perception.

Conclusions and discussions

Using data from a prospective panel study on a sample of the TGP-induced relocatees, this paper was devoted to understanding the role of pre-relocation risk perception in relocatees' mental health experiences. We found that risk perception at the pre-relocation stage helped to reduce depressive symptoms of relocatees by enticing them to mobilize protective recourses and coping mechanisms.

Several limitations curb the conclusions that can be drawn from this paper. For example, we did not have a wide variety of coping/mitigation measures. In supplemental analyses, while we did include other variables tapping into the mitigation efforts, such as seeking for relocation-related information and bargaining for more compensation, none of them had a significant effect on depressive symptoms. Despite these limitations, the findings of the paper are generally consistent with theoretical expectations and suggest that failure to perceive potential risks before relocation has damaging consequences on relocation outcome. Although the TGP planners strived to improve relocation outcomes, our study indicates that risk evaluation and mitigation by planners and government alone could not guarantee a successful psychological adjustment after the relocation. This shows that risk perception is not only a procedural step that should remain in the realm of planners but is indeed a vital tool for the relocatees to cope with project uncertainties.

Excluding individual relocatees from risk information undermines their mitigation efforts and exposes them to unexpected difficulties without adequate preparation. The latter, in turn, may lead to worsening relocation outcomes. Based on our findings, we argue that the transparency of risk information is an indispensable component of a successful relocation program. Relocatees should have access to risk information and be able to participate in the planning and re-planning process so that they can fully exercise their agency to mitigate possible risks. This bottom-up planning, however, requires a strong political will from the top echelons of the government agency and intensive work in the field to establish mechanisms through which risk information can be shared by all social actors involved and for joint decision making.

References

Allison, P. D., 2005. *Fixed Effects Regression Methods for Longitudinal Data Using SAS*. Cary, NC: SAS Institute.

Baron, R. M. and Kenny, D. A., 1986. The Moderator–Mediator Variable Distinction in Social Psychological Research: Conceptual, Strategic, and Statistical Considerations. *Journal of Personality and Social Psychology*, 61(6), pp. 1173–1182.

Bartolome, L. J., de Wet, C., Mander, H. and Nagraj, V. K., 2000. *Displacement, Resettlement, Rehabilitation, Reparation and Development. Thematic Review 1.3 prepared as input into the World Commission on Dams*. Available at: www.dams.org [Accessed July 12, 2010].

BBC Chinese Web, 2010. Three Gorges Project Re-settlers 'Increases 30,000'. Available at: www.bbc.co.uk/zhongwen/trad/lg/china/2010/01/100121_dam_relocation.shtml?s [Accessed July 12, 2010].

Beck, R. A., 1983. An Introduction to Sample Selection Bias in Sociological Data. *American Sociological Review*, 48, pp. 386–398.

Billig, M., Kohn, R. and Levav, I., 2006. Anticipatory Stress in the Population Facing Forced Removal from the Gaza Strip. *Journal of Nervous and Mental Disease*, 194, pp. 195–200.

Brewer, Noel T., Chapman, G. B., Gibbons, F., Gerrard, M. and McCaul, K. D., 2007. Meta-Analysis of the Relationship between Risk Perception and Health Behavior: The Example of Vaccination. *Health Psychology*, 26, pp. 136–145.

Cernea, M. M., 1996. Understanding and Preventing Impoverishment from Displacement: Reflections on the State of Knowledge. In: C. McDowell, ed. *Understanding Impoverishment*, Providence, RI: Berghahn, pp. 13–32.

Cernea, M. M., 1997. The Risks and Reconstruction Model for Resettling Displaced Populations. *World Development*, 25, pp. 1569–1587.

Cernea, M. M., 2000. Risks, Safeguards, and Reconstruction: A Model for Population Displacement and Resettlement. In: M. M. Cernea and C. McDowell, eds. *Risks and Reconstruction: Experiences of Resettlers and Refugees*. Washington, DC: World Bank, pp. 1–50.

Cernea, M. M., 2009. Financing for Development: Benefit-Sharing Mechanisms in Population Resettlement. In: A. Oliver-Smith, ed. *Development & Dispossession*, Santa Fe, NM: School for Advanced Research Press, pp. 49–76.

Clarke, L., 2008. Thinking about Worst-Case Thinking. *Sociological Inquiry*, 78, pp. 154–161.

David, D., Montgomery, G. H., and Bovbjerg, D. H., 2006. Relations Between Coping Responses and Optimism-Pessimism in Predicting Anticipatory Psychological Distress in Surgical Breast Cancer Patients. *Personality & Individual Differences*, 40, pp. 203–213.

de Wet, C., 2006. Risk, Complexity, and Local Initiative in Forced Resettlement Outcomes. In: C. de Wet, ed. *Development-Induced Displacement: Problems, Policies, and People*. Oxford and New York: Berghahn, pp. 180–202.

de Wet, C., 2009. Does Development Displace Ethic? The Challenge of Forced Resettlement. In: A. Oliver-Smith, ed. *Development & Dispossession*, Santa Fe, NM: School for Advanced Research Press, pp. 77–96.

Ding, Q., 1998. What are the Three Gorges Resettlers Thinking? In: Q. Dai, ed. *The River Dragon Has Come!* Armonk, NY: M. E. Sharpe, pp. 70–89.

Duan, Y. and Steil, S., 2003. China Three Gorges Project Resettlement: Policy, Planning and Implementation. *Journal of Refugee Studies*, 16, pp. 422–443.

Goodland, R., 2004. Free, Prior and Informed Consent and the World Bank Group. *Sustainable Development Law and Policy*, Summer issue, pp. 66–75.

Heggelund, G., 2004. *Environment and Resettlement Politics in China*. Burlington, VT: Ashgate Publishing Company.

Hwang, S., Xi, J., Cao, Y., Feng, X., and Qiao, X., 2007. Anticipation of Migration and Psychological Stress and the Three Gorges Dam Project, China. *Social Science and Medicine*, 65, pp. 1012–1024.

Lazarus, R. S. and Folkman, S., 1984. *Stress, Appraisal, and Coping*. New York: Springer.

Li, H., Waley, P. and Rees, P., 2001. Reservoir Resettlement in China: Past Experience and the Three Gorges Dam. *The Geographic Journal*, 167, pp. 195–212.

Li, J., 1996. Survey and Policy Study on Attitude of Three Gorges Rural Migrants. *Social Science Research*, 96(2). Available at: www.chinariver.org/big5/articles/leekk.html [Accessed June 30, 2010].

Lin, N., Ye, X. and Ensel, W. M., 1999. Social Support and Depressed Mood: A Structural Analysis. *Journal of Health and Social Behavior*, 40, pp. 344–359.

McGee, T. K., McFarlane, B. and Varghese, J., 2009. An Example of the Influence of Hazard Experience on Wildfire Risk Perceptions and Adoption of Mitigation Measures. *Society and Natural Resources*, 22, pp. 308–323.

Pearlin, L. I., 1989. The Sociological Study of Stress. *Journal of Health and Social Behavior*, 30, pp. 241–256.

Porter, M. and Haslam, N., 2005. Predisplacement and Postdisplacement Factors Associated with Mental Health of Refugees and Internally Displaced Persons: A Meta-Analysis. *Journal of American Medical Association*, 294, pp. 602–612.

Radloff, L. S., 1977. The CES-D Scale: A Self-Report Depression Scale for Research in the General Population. *Applied Psychological Measurement*, 1, pp. 385–401.

Rosenberg, M., 1965. *Society and the Adolescent Self-Image*. Princeton, NJ: Princeton University Press.

Scudder, T., 2009. Resettlement Theory and the Kariba Case: An Anthropology of Resettlement. In: A. Oliver-Smith, ed. *Development & Dispossession*. Santa Fe, NM: School for Advanced Research Press, pp. 25–48.

Scudder, T. and Colson, E., 1982. From Welfare to Development: A Conceptual Framework for the Analysis of Dislocated People. In: A. Hansen and A. Oliver-Smith, eds. *Involuntary Migration and Resettlement*. Boulder, CO: Westview Press, pp. 267–287.

Slovic, P., 1987. Perception of Risk. *Science, New Series*, 4799, pp. 280–285.

Slovic, P., Fischhoff, B., Lichtenstein, S., and Roe, F. T. C., 1981. Perceived Risk: Psychological Factors and Social Implications. *Proceedings of the Royal Society of London. Series A, Mathematical and Physical Sciences*, 376, pp. 17–34.

Slovic, P. and Peters, E., 2006. Risk Perception and Affect. *Current Directions in Psychological Science*, 15, pp. 322–325.

State Council (No. 74:3), 1991. *Regulations on the Compensation for Land Acquisition and Resettlement of the Construction of Large and Medium-Sized Water Conservancy and Hydroelectric Projects*. Decree of the State Council of PRC.

State Council (No. 299:1), 2001. *The Regulation on Changjiang Three Gorges Project Resettlement*. Decree of the State Council of PRC.

State Council Gorges Project Construction Committee Executive Office (SCGPCCEO), 2009. *The Three Gorges Projects has Relocated 1.27 million people, Resettlement Task is Basically Completed*. In Chinese. Available at: www.3g.gov.cn/xxxq.ycs?GUID=3114 [Accessed June 8, 2010].

Tanner, L., 2005. *Broken Promises and Loss of Trust: The Corruption Stemming from the Use of the Development Resettlement Policy at the Three Gorges Dam Site*. Contemporary Topics in Forced Migration, Working Paper 3. San Diego: Forced Migration Laboratory, Center for Comparative Immigration Studies, University of California.

Thoits, P. A., 1994. Stressors and Problem-Solving: The Individual as Psychological Activist. *Journal of Health and Social Behavior*, 35, pp. 143–160.

Thoits, P. A., 2006. Personal Agency in the Stress Process. *Journal of Health and Social Behavior*, 35, pp. 143–160.

Vidrine, F. I., Simmons, V. N. and Brandon, T. H., 2007. Construction of Smoking-Relevant Risk Perceptions Among College Students: The Influence of Need for Cognition and Message Content. *Journal of Applied Social Psychology*, 37, pp. 91–114.

Wang, J., 2002. Three Gorges Project: The Largest Water Conservancy Project in the World. *Public Administration and Development*, 22, pp. 369–375.

Wei, Y., 1999. Major Problems and Hidden Troubles in the Relocation of the Three-Gorges Project: Yunyang County, Chongqing City (in Chinese). *Strategy and Management*, 16, pp. 11–12.

Weng, L., 1999. *Environmental Monitoring and its Management of the Three Gorges Project*. Paper present at the Third Annual Seminar on Environmental Issues in China, Wuhan.

Xi, J. and Hwang, S., 2011. Relocation Stress, Coping, and Sense of Control among Resettlers Resulting from China's Three Gorges Dam Project. *Social Indicators Research*, 104, pp. 507–522.

4 'They are not family, they just live with us!'

Exploring the practical, social and ethical implications of defining the household

Pierre Gouws

Households: so familiar yet so diverse!

Resettlement planning often uses the household as a unit of entitlement for resettlement. Guidelines to international policies on resettlement, such as the World Bank Guidebook to Involuntary Resettlement (World Bank, 2004) and Guidance Note 5 of the International Finance Corporation (International Finance Corporation, 2012) include numerous references to the 'household' as part of (*inter alia*) surveys, planning and negotiations. Specifically, the World Bank Guidebook to Involuntary Resettlement states that, as a general rule, those losing assets should be compensated for their losses, and the unit of loss typically determines the unit of entitlement (World Bank, 2004, p. 47):

> The 'unit of entitlement' is the individual, the family or household, or the community that is eligible to receive compensation or rehabilitation benefits. Determining the appropriate unit of entitlement, especially if the resettlement process disrupts current household relationships, is necessary to ensure that entitlements target those adversely affected and to clarify the responsibilities of agencies managing compensation and rehabilitation ... If more than one person owns or customarily uses expropriated resources, then they are entitled to share in compensation. For example, if a household of eight loses a house and 2 hectares of land held in the name of one person, the members of the household are collectively entitled to at least a house and 2 hectares of land of comparable value or to another form of compensation or rehabilitation acceptable to them.

In rural areas of Africa (which is the primary focus of this chapter), customary ownership of assets is fairly often encountered in resettlement projects, where structures, land and crops are typically shared by multiple members living within a household. As such, the household often is used as the unit of entitlement (especially on large-scale resettlement projects).

The terminology in the resettlement discipline includes the 'household' as a potential unit of entitlement, and as such the 'household' fulfils an important function to assist resettlement planning to categorise and manage not only compensation, but also other resettlement aspects such as livelihood restoration and social welfare.

However, hands-on experience in resettlement planning has demonstrated that defining the household is a challenging aspect in itself. In fact, the literature is rife with studies from statistics, economics, demographics, anthropology and other disciplines that face the same challenge. The construct of a 'household' is influenced by semantic, cultural, social, psychological, anthropological, economic and ethical aspects. Certainly, attempts have been made to widen and narrow the definition of a household, and although it has been characterised as abstract and artificial, limited in scope, ethnocentric (bound to time and culture) and static, these criticisms have not led to the abandonment of the household concept (Burch, 2001).

Privately owned mining companies across Africa regularly face the complexities of resettlement planning when developing new operations or expanding their current operations. Professional experience of the author as a resettlement specialist shows that some mining operations in countries such as Ghana, Tanzania and Zambia have attempted to develop resettlement plans 'in-house', and when implementation of the resettlement plan commenced there were typically grievances and disputes around compensation and unfair treatment on a household level. These typically included cases where polygamous husbands' wives felt they were being treated unfairly, cases where there were tenants present and there were social and economic interdependencies between the displaced household and tenants, and cases where there were adult children and/or migrant household workers who were absent at the time of census and were therefore not considered eligible for resettlement due to a mismatch between the census household definition and cultural definitions of a household and its members.

Once these disputes arose, it was often the first time that these developers became aware of the potential issues and implications of developing (or failing to develop) a consistent and applicable household definition. Coast *et al.* (2010) state that while research designers and data collectors (and by implication, experienced social practitioners and/or resettlement practitioners) may have clear ideas of why the construct of a 'household' is necessary and develop a clear understanding of household definition, other analysts or developers who are not familiar with data collection and planning processes may approach this aspect very differently. These developers might look at a household definition and assume that this also corresponds to the unit of production, consumption and socialisation central to the developmental process, or might not even look at the definition at all because they assume they know what a household is (Coast *et al.*, 2010).

Coast *et al.* (2010) indicate that the household is a device used to engage (or enumerate) individuals: the household is the sampling unit while the individual is the observational unit (i.e. in order to collect information on individuals, the sample is determined by using households). The goal of a census is to ensure that all persons are surveyed and that no one is double counted (each person should only belong to one household) (Coast *et al.*, 2010). These authors indicate that there is usually recognition that it is a reduced social unit and that compromises (usually regarding level of detail) are made in using this definition, but it provides a set of rules for enumerators to follow and allows a level of comparability over time.

So what *is* a household? Something so seemingly simple has a range of possible definitions, from definitions used in formal national population censuses to the definitions adopted by dictionaries. Some examples of different definitions of a household include:

- 'A person or a group of persons, related or unrelated, who live together in the same house or compound, share the same housekeeping arrangements, and eat together as a unit' (Ghana Statistical Service *et al.*, 2009, p. 11).
- 'A person, or a group of persons, who occupy a common dwelling (or part of it) for at least four days a week and who provide themselves jointly with food and other essentials for living … Visitors, both foreign and South African, as well as boarders who stayed with a household on census night … [are] part of that household. People who were absent on census night, but were not counted elsewhere (either because they were working, travelling, at a church vigil, at an entertainment centre, and so on), and returned to the household [the following day], were counted as part of the household. Live-in domestic workers and live-in employees were regarded as separate households' (Statistics South Africa, 2003, p. vi).
- 'A group of persons who normally live and eat together, whether or not they are related by blood or marriage, and who are answerable to the same household head' (Kenya Census 1999, as cited in Coast *et al.*, 2009, p. 7).
- 'A group of persons living together and sharing living expenses' (Tanzania Census 1988, as cited in Coast *et al.*, 2009, p. 7).
- 'Respondents who live in the same housing unit or in connected premises and have common cooking arrangements (eat their food together)' (Ethiopia Census 1994, as cited in Coast *et al.*, 2009, p. 7).
- [A common set of] 'arrangements made by persons, individually or in groups, for providing themselves with food and other essentials for living … The persons in the group may pool their resources and have a common budget; they may be related or unrelated persons or constitute a combination of persons both related and unrelated' (United Nations, 2008).
- 'A group of persons who share the same living accommodation, who pool some, or all, of their income and wealth, and who consume certain types of goods and services collectively, mainly housing and food. In general each member of a household should have some claim on the collective resources of the household. At least some decisions affecting consumption or other economic activities must be taken for the household as a whole' (European Commission, 2009).

As demonstrated in the above definitions, a 'household' commonly refers to an individual or a group of persons living together in a dwelling, who eat together, share common housekeeping arrangements, may share a common budget and (in some cases) are answerable to a head (Beaman and Dillon, 2012; Coast *et al.*, 2009). None of these factors can be taken separately to infer a household; they are intrinsically linked and interdependent. As with many theoretical constructs, it is the application thereof that poses the challenge.

Variations on household definitions can lead to significant changes on aspects such as household size and poverty and livelihood analyses. Beaman and Dillon (2012) determined that household welfare and production measures are significantly influenced by changes to the definition of the household, and also found that the addition of more criteria (e.g. living together, eating together, sharing common housekeeping arrangements) to the definition of a household tends to increase the average size of the household rather than decrease it. Conversely, Leone *et al.* (2009) report that there is a distinct difference in the professional culture of demographers, statisticians and survey designers' understanding of the construct of a household and that of a Tanzanian cultural grouping's understanding (the Masaai, in this case). These authors found that while a Masaai household declared 37 people as part of the household, a Tanzanian census definition would categorise these people into six separate households. This inconsistent understanding is widespread throughout Africa, and is similarly reported in countries such as Nigeria (Udry, 1990), Senegal and the Gambia (Van de Walle and Gaye, 2005) and Kenya (Muga and Onyango-Ouma, 2009).

Such cultural and linguistic differences in understanding a household can have substantial implications for resettlement projects as resettlement practitioners cannot simply assume that there is mutual understanding of who is part of a household. If the definition of a household implicitly or explicitly changes between resettlement planning, implementation and subsequent monitoring, the information obtained on key monitoring criteria such as household size, livelihood restoration monitoring and poverty analyses may be different. Notably, institutions such as the International Finance Corporation and the World Bank do not define a 'household' – the World Bank (2004, p. 48) states that the Bank accepts the borrower's census definition of 'household'. It is therefore the responsibility of the developer/borrower to define the 'household', and this definition therefore forms a critical piece to set the stage for the remainder of resettlement planning.

In addition to the challenges of defining the household, normally for planning and statistical analysis purposes a 'household head' is also defined. Resettlement planning is no exception to this. For example, typical census surveys enumerate household members in relation to the household head (e.g. 'wife of the household head' and 'son/daughter'), and typically compensation is paid into a bank account held by the household head. The World Bank (2004, p. 48) states that '[i]n practice, title to replacement land, structures, and any other household assets is generally vested in the head of the household'. Practically, the household head is also assumed to be the person in the household who takes the lead on making decisions regarding resettlement.

According to Hedman *et al.* (1996, p. 64), there are complexities with the definition and use of the term 'household head':

> The term head of household is used to cover a number of different concepts referring to the chief economic provider, the chief decision maker, the person designated by other members as the head, etc. … Generally, the definition of head of household reflects the stereotype of the man in the household as the person in authority and the bread winner. And even where the definition is adequate, criteria used by interviewers are often vague and leave room for subjective interpretation.

Budlender (2003) put forward that the enumerators for the South African census defined 'head of household' as 'male or female, and is the person who assumes responsibility for the household', however did not specify the *type* of responsibility. She suggested that this concept becomes even more unclear and open to interpretation when considering different sociological, cultural and other groupings and how they understand the 'head of household' concept. In many African cultures, the household head is the oldest male. In a multi-generational household, the oldest male is not the main income-earner, or may not even control the household resources. Ideologically, states Budlender, the oldest male is the 'head', but not the economic head.

In order to mitigate complexity of who the household head is and/or what the role entails, the term 'householder' has been coined, referring to the person who rents or owns the dwelling, and has been used in several developed countries (Budlender, 2003). However, this also poses problems in several cases (Budlender, 2003):

- Polygamy, where one man is a householder in several households.
- Migrant labour, where the male householder is not a member of the household because he is absent most of the time.
- Situations such as:
  - homeless persons or nomads where there is no dwelling;
  - students living in a dwelling that is owned by the father of one of them;
  - dwellings that belong to one person who is not living in the dwelling but allows the household to use it based on kinship or other ties;
  - a farmworker household which has access to housing on the farm because they work there, but where the householder is the farmer employer (unless a contract is signed);
  - wealthier households where the house is registered in the wife's name to protect the household against bankruptcy of the husband's business, rather than because the wife has greater control over resources; and
  - joint, or even communal, ownership.

These definitions offer glimpses into the complexity of accurately defining a household head. Often resettlement surveys allow households to nominate their own household head without questioning the criteria underlying this nomination. Interviews are held with the household head to gather data on household members, the livelihoods of the household and the various assets within the household. This approach, although faster and more cost effective, may result in an incomplete picture of the actual household situation. A study by Fisher *et al.* (2010) in rural Malawi demonstrates that income data reported by male household heads is significantly under-represented in comparison to reports by their wives. The authors state that this is more likely in households where the household head is away at least part of the time (such as migrant workers), when household livelihoods are more complex, for instance, by involving more earners, and the household is more sophisticated as it has educated female members or is located in a bigger town. In mining developments that cause displacement in rural Africa, migrant workers and complex livelihoods are often aspects to consider in resettlement projects.

Clearly, not only is the definition of a household caught in complexity, but identifying a household head aggravates the potential of misunderstanding and misrepresentation. Furthermore, in many rural African settings, one or more households may reside in jointly shared areas of land (homesteads) – usually established through some form of social relation or economic interdependency. This adds another layer of complexity to resettlement, when households that are grouped together need to be re-established in a similar configuration to maintain the social or economic relationship. Should this important linkage not be recorded when, for example, surveys are conducted only on households, the planning process will result in social disarticulation once households are relocated individually to host areas.

Given these challenges surrounding constructing and applying the definitions, the question remains whether it is necessary or practical to maintain the 'household' as a construct in resettlement planning. The household serves as a possible means around which social relations can be understood, and as a construct it allows some form of categorisation and simplification to these social relations to create a workable social unit.

The following case studies present two brief examples of where the interface between terminology and practical application of household and household headship becomes complex.

So, is your house or your household your home?

A number of resettlement programmes initiated by private mining companies in the rural Western Region of Ghana have adopted the use of 'compounds' (similar to homesteads) as the unit of entitlement. These compounds contain a number of structures within demarcated physical boundaries, and often house multiple related or non-related families who cohabit and share living arrangements. Compounds feature shared structures and facilities such as kitchens, bathrooms and toilets, as well as cocoa drying platforms in the centre of the compound (see Figures 4.1, 4.2, 4.3) – all of which are occasionally shared between compounds. Each dwelling has multiple rooms, which are considered individually owned. Compounds may house individuals, related and non-related families and tenants, each with differing claims to ownership of the rooms in the overall dwelling. The compound is typically 'owned' by an individual, who may reside (possibly as a tenant) on another compound. The dwelling supports the social dynamics between inhabitants on a compound – the close proximity provides a stronger support network and ample opportunity for socialisation. When additional rooms are required to accommodate an expanding household (or tenants), these can simply be added onto the current dwelling.

Resettlement planning needs to appreciate that the 'compound' has a specific social and economic interdependent arrangement between the inhabitants that ideally needs to be re-established, aiming to at least maintain or (preferably) improve the current conditions. However, from the description above it is evident that such a social arrangement offers a particularly challenging environment to conduct a household census for resettlement planning. For example, double-counting or the omission of individuals becomes a real risk when asset or compound owners reside as tenants in other compounds – and blurs the lines between ownership and social relations (both critical pieces of the resettlement

Figure 4.1 Typical compound structure with multiple rooms

Photographer: Marisa du Toit.

Figure 4.2 Room additions to the main structure

Photographer: Marisa du Toit.

Figure 4.3 Central cocoa drying platform in the foreground

Photographer: Marisa du Toit.

puzzle). An asset or compound owner who resides in compound A, but with the asset located in compound B, may under customary arrangements be reported as part of a household in compound B – even though the owner does not live with, eat with or share a common household arrangement with households in compound B. Conversely, the asset or compound owner living in compound A may be reported as a tenant in the household they are living in at compound A (in cases where the 'owner' rents out their compound for income and resides as a tenant in another compound), without acknowledgement that they own assets in compound B. Equally likely in this case is that the tenant is reported as part of the main household, as the tenant often lives with and eats with the owners – but may not necessarily share common household arrangements.

Failure to clearly communicate the definition of a household to the respondent during the census surveys increases the risk of misunderstandings substantially. Furthermore, cases where certain residents such as adult children and tenants fit some – but not all – of the criteria (living together, eating together, sharing common household arrangements and/or budget, and answerable to a head) complicate consistent and reliable enumeration. Without well-designed surveys based on clear understanding and preparation for these cases, the resettlement planning process risks miscategorising individuals as a result of a household-level census.

In addition, re-establishing the household at a new destination involves consideration of the dynamics between multiple households living in a compound and often in a single structure. In this case, the terminology of householder (a person who owns the dwelling) and household head (who is often a nominated representative of the household) becomes too simplified to successfully implement resettlement. The social relations within the compound also need to be considered in order to ensure that the livelihood strategies within and between households are fully understood. Although individual households would in many resettlement programmes be entitled to their own replacement dwelling, interviews with members of cohabiting households in this project indicated that their preference would be to continue to cohabit in a similar fashion to their current arrangements in order to maintain social and economic interdependencies.

In this setting, the question then becomes: What constitutes a household, and how can resettlement be effectively planned when the social relations within and between households are so complex? Utilising the four standard themes for defining a household (living together, eating together, sharing common household arrangements and/or budget, and answerable to a head), the challenge also lies in *applying* the concept of a household within this setting. When asked about household members during census enumeration, respondents listed the inhabitants but it soon became clear that multiple households reside within a single dwelling (they eat separately and make decisions separately). In a case where enumerators enquired about residents living in the adjoining room as part of the household, interviewees responded: 'They are not family, they just live with us!' While it was explained that the household does not necessarily relate to a family, this conversation demonstrates that the resettlement practitioners' and the resettled communities' languages differed.

Ultimately, the private mining company in this case study adopted an approach of negotiating on a 'compound' level, assuming that the compound is the unit of entitlement. This approach also assumed that compensation would be paid to the compound owner, who would distribute compensation as required.

This approach offered some advantages by simplifying the resettlement planning process, mostly as a result of dealing with a less detailed unit of entitlement that is based on physical boundaries. This approach also clearly identified who would receive the compensation (namely, the compound owner). Furthermore, the current social arrangements of residents within compounds' dwellings theoretically would be maintained, in the event that compound dwelling arrangements are replicated at the host site.

However, a number of suspected disadvantages were also associated with this approach. A compound remains a physical entity, and attempts to group social relations based on a physical boundary run the risk of miscategorising the true social unit and/or not defining vulnerable individuals or households appropriately. The compound owner may also not be the person of choice for compound residents to make decisions around resettlement and entitlements, and there is also an increased risk of the compound owner disproportionately distributing the compensation to the asset owners on the compound. Furthermore, livelihood restoration support provided to compound residents may be less effective as the planning and implementation occurs on a compound level rather than a household level. As indicated in the previous discussion as well, more complex situations such as the presence of tenants who own their own compounds that they rent out increases the risk of double-counting or being excluded from resettlement benefits.

This approach is suspected to have offered more disadvantages than advantages, and further evaluation is required upon completion of these resettlement projects. Clearly, should households be used as the unit of entitlement, resettlement practitioners should be prepared to accommodate complex social arrangements. Despite this challenge, the household as a sampling unit allows resettlement planners to obtain information regarding individuals – whereas compounds as a sampling unit may risk losing detail or miscategorising individuals.

Forbidden dilemma: head or tail?

A second case of complexity in applying the concepts of households and household heads involves polygamous households. Where polygamy is practised, resettlement planning normally considers each wife's household as a separate household. However, what about cases where polygamy is illegal but is nevertheless practised?

In Burundi, although polygamy was officially abolished in 1993, the practice is still known to occur, especially among ethnic groups living on the Imbo and Moso plains (SIGI, 2013). Historically, much of the Burundian legislation has been biased against females. For example, the inheritance laws of Burundi state that, under customary law, rural women cannot inherit land from their fathers or husbands. Widows cannot inherit land from their husbands and often their brothers will not welcome them back into the family home, leaving widows landless and homeless (SIGI, 2013). Although this has been recognised as discriminatory practice by the Burundian government, attempts at equalising the law have reportedly fallen by the wayside (SIGI, 2013).

Polygamy in Burundi offers unique challenges to not only development projects that cause displacement but also repatriation programmes. Palmesi (2014) indicated that development projects were considered in the Gitarani commune of the Muyinga Province that would result in physical and economic displacement. In this area, there are many polygamous cases where the husband abandons his wife and takes a new wife in a new area. The abandoned wife/wives then live alone with their children and visits from, and assistance by, the husband are extremely rare. The women tend to consider themselves the sole or unique wife of a given husband, while the husband considers his wife as the woman he is currently living with. Since polygamy is illegal in the country, many of the 'first wives' who are concerned that their husband has taken new wives consider themselves 'abandoned wives' and, in many cases, the husband's family reclaims the wife's land – leaving the wife landless. The abandoned wives are technically single mothers (due to the illegal nature of polygamy), face much social stigmatisation and are not accepted back into their families.

The 'abandoned first wives' can be considered eligible unique 'households' in resettlement processes, entitled to compensation and assistance of the resettlement programme. However, the most significant risk is that the husband could return to the wife and legally claim the compensation. While the 'single mothers' (abandoned second/third etc. wives) are entitled to constitute an individual female-headed household, some state that they are the 'first wife' in the hope that the husband will share some of the compensation (if he receives any). This approach is not only overly optimistic, but also influences households' eligibility for compensation, effectively leaving them classified as part of 'male-headed' households. Ultimately, this means that these vulnerable single female-headed households will not receive the additional support typically provided to vulnerable households. This leaves these women with a two-sided coin, where there is risk for stigmatisation and ostracising on the one side and risk for losing their compensation on the other.

This not only creates a practical problem in effectively defining the household head, but also poses an ethical and legal problem to resettlement practitioners, and is a striking example of where country policy and resettlement practice fail to meet. With polygamy considered illegal, resettlement practitioners should still attempt to ascertain the true nature of the household social relations. Considering that accepting the reported social relations at 'face value' could lead to significant hardship, understanding this issue in resettlement becomes imperative. However, with the substantial risk associated with these women admitting they may have a polygamous husband, investigating this in a sensitive but also ethical manner will require significant care and effort. Resettlement programmes funded by international funders (e.g. International Finance Corporation, 2002, p. 26) require that gaps between practice and policy such as these need to be identified and measures to close these gaps must be developed. Making these measures practical and culturally appropriate, however, becomes challenging when there are such differences between country legislation and culture and international requirements. Specifically, legislation around the constitution and family law also needs to be investigated to determine whether these may have implications for the resettlement process. Defining household headship accurately in this case is essential as it not only has significant consequences for the resettlement process, but also influences vulnerability and stigmatisation of the affected persons.

A fuzzy solution to a complex conundrum

Questions around household definition and household headship have been posed for decades, and while there are common themes to the various definitions, the application of these themes is not necessarily simple. These definitions relate to critical aspects of the displacement and resettlement field, such as livelihoods and vulnerability criteria. Considering the displacement and resettlement field, a number of critical aspects need to be engaged further.

First, the 'terms' or 'language' that we as resettlement practitioners use should ideally be consistent with that of the displaced population – and underlying assumptions for key terms such as 'household' and 'household head' need to be mutually understood and agreed upon.

Second, social relationships within households need to be investigated sufficiently. An understanding of these relationships and the contribution thereof to the household's social and economic structure needs to be well developed to avoid unintended negative social impacts through resettlement.

Where vulnerable groups are present – especially in cases where the laws of the country and cultural practices maintain vulnerability – it is critical for resettlement projects to not only be cognisant with these socio-legal and socio-cultural influences but also to sensitively engage with these issues to protect vulnerable groups. Other laws (such as the constitution, land laws, inheritance laws, ownership laws and family laws) may have an indirect impact on resettlement and therefore these need to be included when developing the legal framework for resettlement.

Defining the household remains a task of complexity, and no single universal definition of the household and household head is practical – rather it remains a 'fuzzy' concept (as argued by Coast *et al.*, 2009) to be informed by local customs and cultures. Importantly, resettlement practitioners should explicitly state their defining criteria for a 'household'.

Resettlement practitioners must keep the overarching goal of defining the household in mind when planning for resettlement. The term 'household' offers a workable social unit around which to plan and implement resettlement, and offers a means to survey individuals in a community. The unique contributions of each person to produce a 'household' need to be understood in order to re-establish these social and economic relationships successfully.

Conducting interviews with only the household head may provide an incomplete picture of the actual tapestry of social and economic relations within the household – interviews with multiple household members is beneficial. Again, resettlement practitioners must keep the goal for identifying a household head in mind. The household head is required to make decisions around *inter alia* distributing compensation and entitlements. While there is a multitude of theoretical definitions, the practice of identifying a household head is an aspect that should primarily be led by the household members, who understand the culture and social relations. Resettlement practitioners need to ensure that household members are fully aware of the roles and responsibilities associated with nominating a household head. In patriarchal societies where the male of the house traditionally is the household head, additional safeguards may need to be built into the entitlement framework to ensure that the interests of women and other vulnerable groups are protected.

Defining alternative units of entitlement (such as homesteads or compounds) offers some advantages but risks losing the detail around livelihood strategies and social relations. Focusing on a purely individual (namely project-affected person) level faces similar risks. Therefore, there is still a use for defining the household as the unit of entitlement as it attempts to strike a balance between the individual and the larger social groupings, and remains the most practical construct to use when customary use is prevalent in resettlement projects. The recommendation of the World Bank (2004) to have the unit of loss determine the unit of entitlement remains solid, practical guidance to gauge the appropriate unit of entitlement.

Resettlement practitioners need to remain aware that resettlement theory should be informed by practice, and that the context should dictate the specific approach. Households operate as a gestalt (where the whole is more than the sum of its parts), and resettlement practitioners should remain sensitive to this fact. The innate wisdom of displaced populations needs to be utilised on resettlement projects, and although terms such as 'household' and 'household head' are understood differently between cultures it remains a useful and practical grouping to use on resettlement projects.

References

Beaman, L. and Dillon, A., 2012. Do household definitions matter in survey design? Results from a randomized survey experiment in Mali. *Journal of Development Economics*, 98, pp. 124–135.

Budlender, D., 2003. The debate about household headship. *Social Dynamics: A Journal of African Studies*, 29, pp. 48–72.

Burch, T.K., 2001. Families and households, behavioral demography of. In: N.J. Smelser and P.B. Baltes, eds, *International Encyclopedia of the Social and Behavioral Sciences*. Elsevier, pp. 5265–5271.

Coast, E., Randall, S. and Leone, T., 2009. The commodity chain of the household: From survey design to policy planning. In: IUSSP, *XXVI IUSSP International Population Conference. Marrakech, Morocco, 27 September–2 October, 2009*. Unpublished.

Coast, E., Randall, S. and Leone, T., 2010. The commodity chain of the household: From survey design to policy and practice. ESRC End of Award Report, RES-175-25-0014. Swindon: ESRC. Available at: http://personal.lse.ac.uk/coast/RES-175-25-0014.pdf [Accessed 16 February 2013].

European Commission, 2009. *System of National Accounts*. New York: United Nations. Available at: http://unstats.un.org/unsd/nationalaccount/docs/SNA2008.pdf [Accessed 12 January 2014].

Fisher, M., Reimer, J.J. and Carr, E.R., 2010. Who should be interviewed in surveys of household income? *World Development*, 38, pp. 966–973.

Ghana Statistical Service (GSS), Ghana Health Service (GHS) and Macro International Inc., 2009. *Ghana Demographic and Health Survey 2008*. Accra, Ghana: Ghana Statistical Service. Available at: http://pdf.usaid.gov/pdf_docs/PNADO176.pdf [Accessed 18 February 2013].

Hedman, B., Perucci, F. and Sundström, P., 1996. *Engendering Statistics: A Tool for Change*. Luleå, Sweden. Available at: http://www.scb.se/statistik/_publikationer/LE0202_1996A01_BR_X93%C3%96P9601.pdf [Accessed 18 December 2014].

International Finance Corporation, 2002. *Handbook for Preparing a Resettlement Action Plan*. Washington, DC: International Finance Corporation.

International Finance Corporation, 2012. *Guidance Note 5 Land Acquisition and Involuntary Resettlement*. Available at: www.ifc.org/wps/wcm/connect/4b976700498008d3a417f6336b93d75f/Updated_GN5-2012.pdf?MOD=AJPERES [Accessed 22 June 2014].

Leone, T., Coast, E. and Randall, S., 2009. Did you sleep here last night? The impact of the household definition in sample surveys: A Tanzanian case study. In: *British Society for Population Studies Annual Conference. Brighton, England, 9–11 September 2009*. Available at: http://personal.lse.ac.uk/coast/Coast_Didyousleep.pdf [Accessed 18 February 2013].

Muga, G.O. and Onyango-Ouma, W., 2009. Changing household composition and food security among the elderly caretakers in rural western Kenya. *Journal of Cross-Cultural Gerontology*, 24, pp. 259–272.

Palmesi, M., 2014. Resettlement in Burundi [e-mail] (personal communication, 22 June 2014).

SIGI (Social Institutions and Gender Index), 2013. *Gender Equality in Burundi*. Available at: http://genderindex.org/country/burundi [Accessed 18 February 2013].

Statistics South Africa, 2003. *Census in brief*. Pretoria: Statistics South Africa. Available at: www.statssa.gov.za/census01/html/CInBrief/CIB2001.pdf [Accessed 15 January 2013].

Udry, C., 1990. Credit markets in northern Nigeria: Credit as insurance in a rural economy. *World Bank Economic Review*. Available at: www-wds.worldbank.org/external/default/WDSContentServer/IW3P/IB/1990/09/01/000009265_3980630181123/Rendered/PDF/multi_page.pdf [Accessed 12 January 2014].

United Nations, 2008. *Principles and Recommendations for Population and Housing Censuses, Revision 2*. New York: United Nations. Available at: http://unstats.un.org/unsd/demographic/sources/census/docs/P&R_%20Rev2.pdf [Accessed 12 January 2014].

Van de Walle, E. and Gaye, A., 2005. Household structure, polygyny, and ethnicity in Senegambia: A comparison of census methodologies. In: E. van de Walle ed., *African Households: Censuses and Surveys*. Armonk, NY: M.E. Sharpe, pp. 3–21.

World Bank, 2004. *Involuntary Resettlement Sourcebook: Planning and Implementation in Development Projects*. Washington, DC: World Bank.

Part II

Ethics of development-induced displacement and resettlement

5 Spatial- and complexity-based perspectives on the ethics of development-induced displacement and resettlement

Chris de Wet

Introduction

Development projects give rise to the involuntary displacement and/or resettlement of some 15 million people worldwide each year (Cernea 2008: 20). Such resettlement has left resettled people better-off in some cases (e.g. the Aswan High Dam on the Egyptian side, Pimburetwa Dam in Sri Lanka and the Arenal Dam in Costa Rica in Scudder 2005: ch. 3). However, the literature suggests that overall such successes are a minority phenomenon, and that the socio-economic consequences for those who have to move to make way for such developments are typically very negative, with relocatees being left worse-off in the long term (Scudder 2005: 61–62), with Cernea's impoverishment risks[1] becoming reality in many situations (Cernea 2000, 2005). Reasons for this are considered below. Conventional approaches to development, while not without value, have effectively not succeeded in improving this dismal track record. It is here argued that this is not only because of limitations in such conventional approaches to development, but, more fundamentally, because of what characterises forced resettlement.

The chapter argues that central to development-induced displacement and resettlement (hereafter DIDR) is that it involves externally initiated spatial and related social changes via a resettlement project that is a complex institutional process, not least because it has to deal with such changes. It asks whether perspectives from complexity theory may help in understanding these issues, difficulties with the resettlement process and how best to deal with such problems.

The fact that, in spite of policy developments and best efforts, resettlement continues to hurt many people, and brings us to the many vexing ethical issues confronting us in DIDR, which, it is here argued, relate substantially to the nature of the spatial dimension of resettlement, rather than to the conflicted nature of development. I analyse these issues, to which, in the nature of ethical dilemmas, there are no clear 'solutions', and I suggest ways of trying to grapple with them through an approach that I call 'resettlement diagnostics'.

Characteristics of development-induced resettlement

Resettlement as externally initiated spatial and related social change

Group resettlement arising out of development projects is effectively imposed, inasmuch as development projects such as dams, irrigation schemes, mines and urban renewal projects are initiated from outside. Such projects, and the group resettlement to which they give rise, involve spatial change, as they incur spatial transformation and reorganise land use patterns such as the introduction of new infrastructure and people having to move from one area to another. This has significant related social consequences.

Human settlement has a strong spatial/place-related aspect. I see people as settled, not only in a specific place, but in place as such: socially and culturally 'emplaced'. 'Emplacement' portrays an association and identification that a person or a group of people has with a socially constituted place/territory that is recognised by others. Emplacement relates to being a member of the group or community associated with that place, with the concomitant rights and obligations of such membership, with regard to involvement in social relationships and the institutional life of the group, access to resources, livelihood, protection and meaning. Emplacement thus involves a socio-spatially constituted local citizenship (de Wet 2008).

At base, DIDR involves people being moved (usually against their will) away from one or several areas where they have been living for a significant period of time, and then either being moved to one or several new areas that have been planned for them, or being provided with compensation to find a new place elsewhere for themselves. This externally initiated move therefore involves imposed spatial and related social change, which includes economic, political and institutional changes.

With DIDR, people are plucked out of their old physical and social settings, environmental and institutional resource bases, and relationship networks that they have used to manage and to meet their everyday economic and socio-political realities. They are dis-emplaced, and have to reconstitute, i.e. re-emplace, themselves socially, politically and economically in a new environment. Resettled people tend to find themselves in larger and socially more heterogeneous and complex settlements than before, with access to less space and land – in particular, less arable land. They are now part of wider bureaucratic and power structures, with less control over their circumstances, both political and economic. Externally initiated development projects, such as those that transform land use and therefore spatial and social patterns, tend to involve increased outsider control of the way that land is subsequently used, and resettlers often lose control of their land, as well as overall power, in the process (de Wet 2006).

The kind and degree of spatial and corresponding social transformation critically influences not only where people find themselves, but also the manner in which, and the extent to which, they are able to re-establish themselves economically and socially, in their new situation. Based on the evidence of many cases worldwide, Scudder argues that involuntary group resettlement, as well as new land settlement, is best understood as a process whereby re/settled people may be seen as moving through four broad stages in behavioural terms[2] (Scudder 1985, 2005: ch. 2). For our purposes, one of the two most important is the second stage, a period of extreme stress, during which people adjust, and behave so as to avoid and reduce stress. They become risk-avoiding, socially and otherwise inward-turning and conservative, and behave as if they were in a closed social system. This accounts for the broad uniformity in responses observed worldwide during Stage Two. Differences in the kinds of stress and risks they face and adjustments and behavioural responses they make will be significantly related to the kinds of spatial and related transformation and adjustment demanded by resettlement in particular situations. The way resettlement is planned and implemented will be of central importance in this regard, as will the circumstances and characteristics of particular resettlers.

In Stage Three, as people find their economic, social and institutional feet again, they settle down and open up, and behave as if they were now in an open system (Scudder and Colson 1982: 41). Open systems may be seen as systems that 'interact with their environment' (Cilliers 1998: 4). Inasmuch as resettlers are reconstituting themselves after the upheaval and dislocation of the move, there is, however, a predictable range in the kinds of economic, institutional and social rejuvenations that need to occur if a social grouping is to achieve the community formation and economic development envisaged in this stage. This element of predictability does not, however, prescribe the specific detail of the way in which these various kinds of rejuvenations and behavioural responses take place. This level of detail is likely to be influenced by the ways in which the setting and situation has been changed/transformed by the actual resettlement, i.e. what socio-spatial options it has closed down and opened up in a particular situation. Socio-spatial transformation thus directly impacts on the way resettlers are able to move out of Scudder's Stage Two into his Stage Three and further, in terms of the resettlement process.

Socio-spatial transformation also influences the ways in which Cernea's range of impoverishment risks become realised, because, in the absence of effective planning, funding, implementation and political will, the above processes of change usually lead to the dissolution, or severe weakening, of people's 'capital contexts', that is, the physical and socio-political-institutional resource contexts in which people were able to access and process various kinds of capital. This leads to 'de-capitalisation' and thus to impoverishment. In conjunction with Scudder's and Cernea's analyses of resettlement, the spatial component thus allows us to account for and to anticipate the widespread and similar kinds of processes and consequences discussed above. Thus, forced resettlement tends to involve people: being moved into larger and denser settlements; being farther away from land, water and jobs; being further from kin and former neighbours; becoming involved in, and vulnerable in the face of, wider administrative and political structures; and becoming caught up in accelerated socio-economic change – all of which follows on from the imposed socio-spatial change which is a fundamental aspect of forced resettlement. Examples of such similarities occur in resettlement projects, whether resulting from dams, such as Akosombo, Aswan or Kariba; the establishment of national level villagisation projects, such as in Ethiopia under the Derg or in South Africa under apartheid; or urban modernisation projects, such as in Ghana or in South Africa (see de Wet 2006: 183–185). Likewise, the kind and extent of the spatial–social changes involved vary across particular cases of DIDR; this will exercise a significant influence upon variations in the way the resettlement process plays itself out, and in its consequences in different situations. Understanding this influence is central to our ability to understand and to anticipate (as distinguished from predict in any causal type fashion) resettlement outcomes.

The resettlement process is not amenable to rational planning and procedures

However, while resettlement projects across the world display significant similarities as well as differences, which we are mostly able to account for with the aid of the above-mentioned resettlement theory, the specific details of the way in which a particular resettlement process plays itself out are not predictable or controllable in any straightforward causal-linear or rational-planning manner. This is for a range of reasons. What actually happens on the ground, i.e. the way official resettlement policy actually plays itself out, is the outcome of a range of factors, such as competing groupings within the policy domain, or the sufficiency or (more usually) shortage of political will, resulting in further shortages of other requirements, such as finances, staff, skills, planning and, critically, time (de Wet 2006). The dynamics of individual resettlement projects, and the way they unfold, vary significantly, and this feeds back into the kinds of socio-spatial changes to which the resettling people have to be assisted to adapt by the resettlement project that is moving them. Resettlement may thus be usefully understood as a complex institutional process that is characterised by ongoing feedback and adaptation as it develops. In the next section, I apply a complexity approach to the analysis of DIDR.

A complexity-related approach to the analysis of DIDR

Much has been written about complexity analysis. Because of limitations of space, I here give a very brief picture of the approach in the words of John Urry, and then discuss some of the implications, as I see them, for the analysis of resettlement.

> Overall, complexity approaches combine system *and* process thinking … [and aspects] … of diverse and non-linear changes in relationships … of the systemic nature of processes … systems that have the ability to adapt and co-evolve as they organize through time … Complexity investigates emergent, dynamic and self-organizing systems that interact in ways that heavily influence the probabilities of later events. Systems are irreducible to elementary laws or simple processes.
>
> (Urry 2005: 3)

Within a complex system, 'changes in the elements and dimensions mutually feedback to each other in a continually dynamic manner' (Ramalingam and Jones 2008: 17).

Complexity analyses thus raise questions as to how we are to best deal with matters such as variable-based analyses, generalisation across cases and policy issues. Anthropological case studies have identified significant similarities across cases of resettlement worldwide. These similarities are discussed in this chapter, and I have attempted to synthesise various theoretical perspectives in order to help us account for broad similarities as well as differences in resettlement instances and trajectories. Can complexity theory/analysis help resettlement analysis in its quest to understand and generalise the similarities and differences across those cases, and to move responsibly towards 'the transferability of best practice' (Ramalingam and Jones 2008: 30), and therefore towards responsible policy more widely, and towards a defensible ethics of resettlement?

I suggest that the concept of path dependence from complexity theory may cast light on the similarities in terms of the ways in which the resettlement process unfolds/is seen to unfold (e.g. Scudder's stages, Cernea's impoverishment risks), as well as on differences that emerge between cases.

> Path dependence explains how the set of decisions [conditions] one faces for any set of circumstances is limited by the decisions that one has made or situations one has faced in the past, even though the past circumstance is no longer relevant.
>
> (Praeger 2007)

The decisions one faces as a resettler in the present are influenced by decisions and actions taken in the past as well as in the present by others, such as resettlement officials and fellow resettlers. While there are obviously differences across cases, substantial evidence shows us that there are significant similarities across the world in terms of the ways in which DIDR is planned, implemented and experienced – not least in the ways in which it closes down options and flexibilities, through a limited range of possible procedures, plans and designs for resettlement areas, and managerial styles on the part of the implementers (de Wet 1995: ch. 2–3; Scott 1998). Such basically similar kinds of socio-spatial transformation (see de Wet 2006: 183–187 for a discussion and examples of such socio-spatial transformation), similarity of initial conditions, i.e. resettlement plans and implementation styles, and the difficulties and stresses of adaptation in Stage Two, place restrictions on the range of options open to future path dependence, and ways in which it can unfold, in spite of feedback and adaptation in the light of local circumstances.

The post-relocation path dependence scenario at the beginning of Stage Three is thus not wide open. How patterns emerge over time is the outcome, not only of non-linearity and contingency, but, also and significantly, of the nature of the on-going resettlement process. It builds on what has gone before, in terms of the socio-spatial transformation, and the decisions and events that have occurred earlier – but critically so, in Stage Two. This allows us to understand the aspects of similarity and generalisability across different instances of resettlement.

Complexity theory is concerned to understand the feedback process in systems – including human systems – as ongoing and as dynamic. There are broad and significant similarities in terms of what might be seen as 'initial conditions', which have been discussed above, that serve as a limitation on the ways in which a resettlement situation can develop, and that therefore allow us to understand aspects of similarity. However, all resettlement situations are not totally similar at the outset, do not experience these initial conditions as constraining in exactly the same ways and do not develop in exactly the same way. We are not in the realm of scientific universalism or causality.

There is often significant variation in the local context in which DIDR takes place and unfolds over time. Some resettlement projects involve far greater socio-spatial transformation than others; some are better planned, funded, implemented, with better and more sustained follow-up support and services, with greater local legitimacy and more effective local leadership than others. Some enjoy greater social and/or economic stability and success than others. All of this makes for variation in the ways in which particular resettlement processes unfold. While initial conditions influence and inform the way that a complex system develops, they do not determine that dynamic, as complex systems are open systems, open to the ongoing influence of events, both within themselves and from outside, which feedback in an ongoing, dynamic and non-linear manner. Local variation and local events are thus central to the way that a particular resettlement dynamic develops – taking into account the ways and extent to which outside intervention has set up less flexible parameters.

Complexity theory can thus help us to clarify both the interaction between powerfully similar initial conditions (in terms of the way resettlement projects are designed and implemented) and the variable local factors, making for differences as specific projects unfold. Take the example of two rural areas both subjected to the same kind of villagisation-based resettlement project in South Africa around the 1960s. Within one of the areas, the way in which the new residential arrangements were laid out became an initial condition that has for the next 45 years fundamentally directed the way in which political, social, agricultural and ritual relationships have become reorganised in the settlement. However, the same broad resettlement policy impacted very differently at the time of implementation, because of different land tenure arrangements in the two areas. The longer term impacts of resettlement were also very different because one of the areas was located close to an accessible road, and so its people were better educated, and accordingly better able to obtain higher paying jobs closer to home, than in the other area. They were thus better able to move from Stage Two to Stage Three of the resettlement process in Scudder's terms. The two local systems were thus different in some ways, and their ways of relating to the wider outside economic system were very different. The ways in which they were open systems and the nature of the feedback modifying the initial conditions of resettlement were thus significantly different (de Wet 1995: ch. 4–6). This supports the argument that a system such as a resettlement process is an 'emergent, dynamic and self-organizing system that interact[s] in ways that heavily influence the probabilities of later events' (Urry 2005: 3), and in which 'changes in the elements and dimensions mutually feedback to each other in a continually dynamic manner' (Ramalingam and Jones 2008: 17).

Where does this take us in relation to policy? I suggest that, from their empirically and theoretically derived understanding and knowledge of previous resettlement situations, trained and experienced resettlement anthropologists, in ongoing partnership with the affected parties in a particular resettlement situation, are in a position to discern, to diagnose, to anticipate – although not to predict in any straightforward manner – what is common or different with other situations, what processes are unfolding, in that particular resettlement situation. This would call for resettlement anthropologists functioning, not as outside expert consultants, but as what one might term 'participatory resettlement diagnosticians'. In concert with the affected people, they would seek to identify emerging patterns and possibilities, how resettlement scenarios are likely to unfold, in terms of their sound knowledge of past cases, the dynamics of the resettlement process, and the inputs and actions of the affected people. This relates to seeing resettlement as a complex process, with its aspects of feedback and open-endedness. This is a work of something more like diagnosis, of 'what is going on here?' of 'what is likely to happen?', rather than of classification or prediction in any straightforward scientific sense.

Some key ethical issues in DIDR

DIDR, as a complex institutional process involving externally initiated socio-spatial change, has ethical implications. The affected people are moved, whereas other people are not – even if this is 'only for the sake of development that is shown in fair public deliberation to be ethically responsible' (Penz *et al.* 2011: 194). Such a collective move is often traumatic and economically disruptive (Cernea 2000; Scudder 2005: ch. 1–2). Even in the best of circumstances, physically separating the displaced spatially out from other project beneficiaries significantly increases the chances of their being sidelined, overlooked, disempowered and impoverished in so many ways. By being moved against their will, they have also been politically peripheralised, although the particular impact of that dis-emplacement varies by factors such as age, gender, education, income and social position.

It is with these considerations in mind that DIDR emphasises what the movementists refer to as 'the ugly face of development ... the evidence of development's uneven and unfair distribution of costs and benefits' (Penz *et al.* 2001: 18), or as Cernea (2000: 12) puts it, that 'some people enjoy the gains of development, while others bear its pains'.

There seem to me to be two important kinds of ethical issues that arise in terms of the ways in which DIDR challenges and compromises our ability to treat people equitably and apply our ethical principles in a coherent manner

– and that DIDR therefore presents ethical challenges for us, or in my terms, threatens to 'displace ethics'. I conceptualise ethics as 'a systematic concern with the principles by which we seek to distinguish between right and wrong in our behaviour towards other people and towards nature' (de Wet 2009: 78). These ethical issues will apply in situations where there are genuine attempts to treat all parties equitably, to respect the rights of all parties – and where genuine difficulties arise in the attempt to do so, e.g. where various ethical principles cannot be applied together in a consistent manner, or where no clear, unproblematic course of action is apparent. There will be cases where the rights of people in line to be moved for a development project are simply being ignored and overridden in an exploitative and unconcerned manner. Such behaviour is simply morally wrong – but I would want to say that this does not constitute an ethical dilemma or problem, as we are not confronted by having to pick our way between principles, decide between irreconcilable claims on the good, etc. Such exploitation is simply wrong – and it is completely plausible to argue that a resettlement project should be shut down on those grounds.

First, there are issues of how the displacement in resettlement gives rise to situations where it does not seem possible to find a way to treat all stakeholders in the development project equitably, in significant measure as a consequence of the fact that some people have to move.

Penz, Drydyk and Bose discuss various dilemmas that arise directly out of the fact that the kind of development envisaged requires or is deemed to require the affected people to move. Various kinds of trade-off or worse inevitably arise. First, if they are to be displaced by the larger development project, the 'oustees' stand to suffer significant harm – whereas if they are not moved, the project will then not be able to go ahead as planned, and those who were to benefit from it will suffer the harm of withheld development (Penz *et al.* 2011: 151, 158ff). Second, to exclude potential oustees from decision-making processes relating to development projects that would impact them would be to deny them fundamental rights, while to make their consent a central aspect of the decision-making process might be to give them a potential veto power over the overall project, effectively denying the right to development to other people (Penz *et al.* 2011: 171, 188ff).

While Penz, Drydyk and Bose might see these dilemmas as 'cruel choices' (taken from the title of Goulet's foundational (1971) book on development ethics) between different stakeholders in the development process, my concern is that '[d]evelopment projects ... simultaneously promote and undermine human well-being ... and human rights' (de Wet 2009: 79), leading the moved people to suffer. There are strong arguments, backed up by plenty of evidence, that group resettlement is a traumatic and debilitating experience. There seems no way out of the fact that resettlement hurts, definitely in the short term (Colson 1971: 44; Scudder 2005: 22ff;) and, often, also in the longer term. 'Forced resettlement, seemingly inescapably, involves not being able to treat resettled people as ends in themselves, as full beneficiaries of development' (de Wet 2009: 80). As argued below, while imperative, benefit-sharing is not the magic medicine to cancel or dissolve that suffering.

The intention here is not to go into each of these issues; they are argued in detail in the sources quoted (also in de Wet 2012). It is rather to indicate how the spatial dynamic behind group resettlement sets up a train of ethical implications.

Second, issues of complexity and practicability in what is involved in the resettlement process challenge our capacities to proceed ethically in the sense of treating the moved people equitably and fairly, and delivering on resettlement as development. I have briefly outlined these issues in the section on 'Characteristics of development-induced resettlement'. They are directly related to the changes that group relocation, together with the accompanying spatial and social change and reconstruction, set in motion, as well as to our attempts to deal with them in a constructive manner. I contend that '[w]hether or not one believes that the complexities of the resettlement process can in principle be mastered, is of some ethical significance' (de Wet 2009: 83). This is because it relates directly to whether or not one holds that satisfactory outcomes can be underwritten, if not in principle, then with a reasonable and responsible degree of likelihood (one which might persuade the potentially affected parties to enter into an agreement to move). If not, then there do not appear to be satisfactory grounds on which to justify group resettlement. I am inclined to stand more with the pessimists, especially when it comes to the availability of political will and willingness to approach resettlement in terms of a human rights vision on the part of the authorities, as well as in terms of considerations of capacity and resources. I am concerned that issues of efficiency and capacity, of general willingness and wherewithal – or the lack of them – do seem to impinge directly upon our ability to proceed and to follow through, i.e. to act ethically. Even 'doing the right thing', 'going the extra mile' – as with benefit-sharing – to seek to counteract 'uncertainties concerning future harm' (Penz *et al.* 2011: 154) may not be good enough. This is because, to be effective, benefit-sharing itself requires that very efficiency and capacity, willingness and wherewithal in the first place.

These two kinds of issues feed into each other. If we are to soften the sharpness of the suffering caused by the contradiction involved in genuine public interest DIDR, then it becomes essential to deliver, not only in policy, but also in practice, on a rights-based process with developmental and empowering outcomes on the ground. But, therein lies the rub. Multiple case studies and analyses keep on telling us that it is that very delivery that remains highly problematic – for very compelling reasons (see Scudder's detailed analysis of the very high incidence of development failure in dam-related resettlement across the world; Scudder 2005: ch. 3). People have a right to development, and to be treated equitably, and to be empowered. But without delivery of developmental outcomes, those rights mean very little, if anything, and we are back with the powerless losing to the benefit of the powerful.

I suggest that it is the spatial dimension of resettlement, i.e. imposed collective spatial and related social transformation and what it gives rise to, that lies at the heart both of what one might call the 'fairness' and the 'delivery' set of ethical problems – and crucially, the way that they interact and reinforce each other. It is this interaction and negative reinforcement that leads me to argue that our basic ethical problem with regard to DIDR may well be something like this:

Because of the way that the spatial dimension leads the 'fairness' and the 'delivery' sets of problems to feed into each other, we do not seem able to resolve our fairness issues (and related decisions) through a development ethics approach alone; on the other hand, issues of complexity and practicality render both managerial and participatory approaches deeply problematic in terms of guaranteeing delivery. But we need a realistic prospect of delivery to resolve our fairness impasses. So, what will not seem to go away is that it is ethically justified and, indeed, may be required to proceed with group resettlement that is fairly established as necessary to achieve a development project that is demonstrably in the public good. However, the spatial dimension of what resettlement involves, with its seemingly inevitable differentials of power, pain and poverty, severely undermines our ability to achieve the fair and effective ways of going about such resettlement that are necessary in order to make it ethically acceptable. This is the major ethical conundrum at the heart of DIDR.

Some concluding remarks

Development-initiated resettlement in many cases involves people having to move off their own land. Regardless of whether they are compensated adequately, the logic of the development project is usually that it is not possible for the people on whose land the development project is to be established to continue to live as they used to, and for the development project to go ahead. That is why they have to move and as a result they are excluded from living on their own land. Externally initiated exclusion is at the heart of resettlement and its consequences. As long as we cannot do away with models of development that require significant spatial transformation and its subsequent zero sum consequences, we will continue to be confronted by the ethical problems that come with the fact that, whatever else it involves, group resettlement is, at base, characterised by imposed movement and, therefore, by spatial and social change, and by exclusion.

These problems seemingly cannot be done away with, no matter how good our systems of development ethics, project planning and management, benefit-sharing, or democratic planning and options assessment are. What we can do is to face up to these problems realistically, and to acknowledge what we are up against in the attempt to treat people ethically, as we would want to be treated.

I have sought to provide a framework for elucidating the ethical tensions at the heart of group resettlement arising out of development projects, by locating those tensions in the spatial dimension of resettlement. I have suggested a way of working with those ethical tensions through an understanding of the complexity of the resettlement process that spatial imposition sets in motion, and through the metaphor of participatory diagnostics.

Notes

1 Cernea (2000) sees resettled people as being exposed to a range of interrelated risks that, if not consciously countered, will become realised. These are: landlessness,

homelessness, joblessness, marginalisation, food insecurity, increased morbidity and mortality, loss of access to common property, and social disarticulation. If countered, these risks can be inverted into reconstruction opportunities.

2 Stage One, the Planning and Recruitment Stage, starts when project planning and activity commence, and people become aware that 'something is up'. Stage Two, Adjustment and Coping, involves the move and the years immediately thereafter, and is the time of major stress for those moving. Stage Three, Community Formation and Economic Development, follows once people have basically settled down and re-established themselves economically, socially and institutionally. Stage Four, Handing Over and Incorporation, brings resettlement to a successful end as project areas and populations are integrated into the political economy of a region or nation.

References

Cernea, M.M. (2000) 'Risks, Safeguards and Reconstruction: A Model for Population Displacement and Resettlement'. In M.M. Cernea and C. McDowell (eds) *Risks and Reconstruction: Experiences of Resettlers and Refugees*, pp. 11–55. Washington, DC: World Bank.

Cernea, M.M. (2005) 'Concept and Model: Applying the IRR Model in Africa to Resettlement and Poverty'. In I. Ohta and Y.D. Gebre (eds) *Displacement Risks in Africa: Refugees, Resettlers and Their Host Populations*, pp. 195–258. Kyoto: Kyoto University Press; Melbourne: Trans Pacific Press.

Cernea, M.M. (2008) 'Compensation and Investment in Resettlement: Theory, Practice, Pitfalls, and Needed Policy Reform'. In M.M. Cernea and H.M. Mathur (eds) *Can Compensation Prevent Impoverishment? Reforming Resettlement through Investments and Benefit-Sharing*, pp. 15–98. London and New Delhi: Oxford University Press.

Cilliers, P. (1998) *Complexity and Postmodernism: Understanding Complex Systems*. London and New York: Routledge.

Colson, E. (1971) *The Social Consequences of Resettlement: The Impact of the Kariba Dam upon the Gwembe Tonga*. Manchester: Manchester University Press.

de Wet, C.J. (1995) *Moving Together, Drifting Apart: Betterment Planning and Villagisation in a South African Homeland*. Johannesburg:Witwatersrand University Press.

de Wet, C.J. (2006) 'Risk, Complexity and Local Initiative in Forced Resettlement Outcomes'. In C.J. de Wet (ed.) *Development-Induced Displacement: Problems, Policies and People*, pp. 180–202. Oxford: Berghahn.

de Wet, C.J. (2008) 'Reconsidering Displacement in Southern Africa'. *Anthropology Southern Africa*, 31(3/4): 114–122.

de Wet, C.J. (2009) 'Does Development Displace Ethics? The Challenge of Forced Resettlement'. In A. Oliver-Smith (ed.) *Development and Dispossession*, pp. 77–96. Santa Fe, NM: School of Advanced Research Press.

de Wet, C.J. (2012) 'Towards Ethical Outcomes in Displacement: A Search for Coherence, or a Fine Balance?' Blog Commentary on Chapter 7 (Ethical Outcomes) of *Displacement by Development: Ethics, Rights and Responsibilities*, by Peter Penz, Jay Drydyk and Pablo Bose. Cambridge University Press 2011. http://developmentethicsthematicgroup.wordpress.com. Accessed 11 June 2012.

Goulet, D. (1971) *The Cruel Choice*. New York: Athenaeum.

Penz, P., J. Drydyk and P.S. Bose (2011) *Displacement by Development: Ethics, Rights and Responsibilities*. Cambridge: Cambridge University Press.

Praeger, D. (2007) 'Our Love of Sewers: A Lesson in Path Dependence'. *Daily Kos*, 15 June 2007. www.dailykos/story2. Accessed 1 June 2014.

Ramalingam, B. and H. Jones, with T. Reba and J. Young (2008) *Exploring the Science of Complexity: Ideas and Implications for Development and Humanitarian Efforts*. London: Overseas Development Institute. Working Paper No. 285 (2nd edn).

Scott, S.C. (1998) *Seeing Like a State: Why Certain Schemes to Improve the Human Condition have Failed*. New Haven, CT and London: Yale University Press.

Scudder, T. (1985) 'A Sociological Framework for the Analysis of New Land Settlements'. In M.M. Cernea (ed.) (2nd edn) *Putting People First: Sociological Variables in Rural Development*, pp. 148–187. New York: Oxford University Press. Published for the World Bank.

Scudder, T. (2005) *The Future of Large Dams: Dealing with Social, Environmental, Institutional and Political Costs*. London and Sterling, VA: Earthscan.

Scudder, T. and E. Colson (1982) 'From Welfare to Development: A Conceptual Framework for the Analysis of Dislocated People'. In A. Hansen and A. Oliver-Smith (eds) *Migration and Resettlement: The Problems and Responses of Dislocated People*, pp. 267–287. Boulder, CO: Westview Press.

Urry, J. (2005) 'The Complexity Turn'. *Theory, Culture and Society*, 22(5): 1–14.

6 The centrality of empowerment in development-induced displacement and resettlement

An ethical perspective

Jay Drydyk

The displacement of communities by development projects continues to cause political conflict and policy conundrums, as it has for several decades, from the Narmada dams to the Tata Nano plant – just to mention two major examples in one country.[1] The harms and risks that displacement and resettlement pose for the people who are displaced raise important questions about what people are entitled to when they face displacement by development. Are they entitled merely to compensation, or also to restoration of their livelihoods, or sharing in the benefits of the projects that displace them? What recourse and participation in decision making are they entitled to? Are there circumstances in which people are entitled not to be displaced at all without their consent? In this chapter, those questions will be addressed in three ways. First, I will identify the values in terms of which we can identify what can go wrong, ethically, with development that displaces people. Second, I will specify four categories of entitlements and sketch the kinds of factual and ethical considerations that justify them. Third, I will focus on one of those entitlements: people facing displacement by development are entitled to be sufficiently empowered to achieve just outcomes – e.g. restoration of livelihoods and sharing in benefits. The centrality of empowerment is made evident by the many practices and circumstances that can disempower these people and result in highly inequitable outcomes. After illustrating some of these practices and circumstances with one particular case, the Bangladesh Jamuna Bridge Project of the 1990s, I consider one governance model that has been proposed (by the World Commission on Dams [WCD]) to more adequately empower the 'oustees' and other stakeholders.

The development ethics values framework as an ethical assessment tool

Values have emerged in late-twentieth-century discussions and debates over ways in which development policies, projects and practices have gone wrong. In these debates, the criticism is typically not just that development has failed to achieve its own explicit objectives, but rather that it has brought about *some other harms or wrongs*. For instance, one might criticize a programme aiming at modernization or growth not for failing to modernize or increase gross domestic product, but for failing to increase living standards, for failing to reduce poverty or for expanding social inequalities. These criticisms rely upon values that are expected to be realized in worthwhile development, for instance, that development ought to improve well-being and reduce poverty and social inequality. In these examples, the criticism of actual development assumes broad values of well-being and equity. It is in terms of such values that development worth having is distinguished from development gone wrong, or 'maldevelopment'. Denis Goulet was among the first to stress how important it is to draw such a distinction in ethical terms, based on values, and accordingly he is remembered by many as a founder of contemporary development ethics (Goulet, 1971, p. 14, 2006, pp. 5, 45; Drydyk, 2010a, 2011).

In *Displacement by development: ethics, rights, and responsibilities* (Penz *et al.*, 2011), I identify seven such values that have emerged in policy debate about development since the 1950s: well-being, equity, empowerment, environmental sustainability, human rights, cultural freedom and integrity against corruption. It is important to bear in mind that, along with broad agreement that these values distinguish worthwhile development from maldevelopment, there are also differences of opinion about how, precisely, each value ought to be interpreted. Hence it should be understood that I am presenting them not as a precise set of principles, but only as a broad framework for continued discussion – as I hope will be made clear in the following discussion of the first four of those values.

First, worthwhile development must improve people's well-being. This is the first principle of the human development approach founded by the late Mahbub ul Haq (Haq, 1995). From a well-being perspective, because there can be periods of growth in which living standards remain stagnant or even fall, worthwhile development cannot be identified with simple economic growth. There may be much debate about how we should understand 'well-being', but nevertheless there is widespread agreement that good development must enhance human well-being.

Second, development that is worth having must be equitable, both locally and globally. This may mean giving priority to the worst off; it may mean bringing more people to a threshold of decent living standards; it may mean reducing inequalities of what Amartya Sen has called 'well-being freedom' (Sen, 1992, 1993, 1999); it may mean reducing long-term social inequalities along the lines of sex, race, ethnicity, disability, and so on. Notwithstanding these differences of interpretation, there is widespread agreement that good development contributes to reducing these inequalities, while maldevelopment either reproduces or worsens them.

Third, good development is not something that is done to people; rather, people must be the agents of their own development. At one time this was conceived as participatory development; more recently, 'agency' and 'empowerment' have become the leading concepts (Penz *et al.*, 2011, pp. 134–136). In my view, the principal value here is empowerment. Good development connects people with power in such ways that, through their own agency and decision making, they can improve their lives.

Fourth, development is not worthwhile unless it is environmentally sustainable, although wide agreement on the broad principle is accompanied by wide discussion of what 'sustainability' should mean.

While these four values may have been most often invoked in evaluating how development can go wrong, three others are no less important. The fifth is that worthwhile development does not weaken but strengthens human rights. Sixth, worthwhile development enhances cultural freedom to be who we are and who we want to be. Seventh, worthwhile development is not carried out by corrupt means or for corrupt purposes; rather, it is carried out with integrity. These seven values comprise the development ethics framework that distinguishes worthwhile development from undesirable maldevelopment.

The framework illuminates a number of ways in which development that displaces people can go wrong. Consider the case of the Kariba dam, built across the Zambezi River between 1955 and 1959. Designed primarily for power generation, its main beneficiaries were 'electricity consumers, the copper mines, and other industries, who could enjoy low prices for electricity' (Soils and Chalo, 2000, section 3.4). Some 57,000 Tonga people were forcibly displaced and resettled, mainly in order to clear land for the reservoir. Different compensation schemes were introduced in Southern Rhodesia (now Zimbabwe) and Northern Rhodesia (now Zambia). In the former, the scheme provided compensation for land replacement, food during resettlement and exemption from a tax; in the latter, the scheme provided for land replacement and compensation for foregone earnings and lost crops (Soils and Chalo, 2000, p. xi). What can development ethics tell us about a case such as this?

The first question to ask from a development ethics perspective is how the displacement and resettlement affected the displaced Tongas' well-being. In Southern and Northern Rhodesia alike, replacement land was semi-arid, with high risk of crop failure, whereas the Tonga had previously cultivated crops throughout the year in alluvial valley soil (Magadza, 2006, p. 276). Food production fell so deeply as to cause a famine in the period following resettlement (Magadza, 2006, p. 276), and subsequently the Tonga ceased to be self-sufficient in food (Soils and Chalo 2000, p. 57; Magadza, 2006, p. 276). In this respect, the impact on Tonga well-being was negative.

Meanwhile, copper mines and other industries profited from lower energy costs, and city dwellers benefitted from electrification. In the reservoir, a new fishery was established, from which Tonga artisanal fishers benefitted on the north bank; along the south bank a commercial fishery was developed, dominated by immigrant and expatriate interests (Scudder, 2005, pp. 9–13). Magadza has observed retrospectively:

> The Tonga appreciate how the sacrifice of their land has benefited the sub-region, as exemplified by the bright lights of Kariba and Siyavonga Towns, luxury cruises on the lake, and expensive holiday cottages by the lakeshore. At the same time, however, the Tonga resettlement areas have sparse education, health and other benefits … [which] would have been made available

> to them if the Tonga had been given a share in the Kariba benefits via levying the power producers a development levy for the resettlement area.
>
> (2006, p. 283)

Thus, the project had a negative impact not only on well-being but also on equity.

A development ethics perspective would also inquire about empowerment and participation in decision making. In the South, there was some consultation about resettlement sites, but governance was otherwise as disempowering as it could be:

> The district magistrate assembled head men and elders to inform them that the dam would be built and they should be ready on a given date to move to sites that they might help select. Lorry transport and some building materials would be provided. Taxes would be remitted for two years and grain would be issued free of charge until they were once more able to harvest a crop. They could expect nothing else.
>
> (Colson, 1971, p. 20)

Governance in the North, following principles of indirect rule, was more complex. Consultation was carried out through a Local Authority council, whose members (chiefs and their councillors) were appointed by the colonial government (Colson, 1971, p. 21). Although this council was regarded by the Tonga as a 'pawn of the colonial administration' (Scudder, 2005, p. 32), it did manage to negotiate ten concessions from the territorial government (Colson, 1971, pp. 22–23). Still, resistance was strong in some villages, particularly against plans for resettlement in the region of Lusitu. Scudder describes the outcome:

> Having failed to convince the villagers to move, and aware of the imminent closing of the dam, the PA [Provincial Administration] mandated a September date for commencing removal. Lorries were brought in. By then a number of village men had assembled in one neighbourhood to emphasize their unwillingness to move. The administration called in the mobile police. … Failing to negotiate a solution to the impasse, the governor ordered the people into the lorries. The Gwembe men charged the mobile police who, believing their lives under threat, fired. Eight Gwembe Tonga were reported to have died and at least 32 were wounded.
>
> (Scudder, 2005, p. 39)

Cultural losses and stresses have been reported for all resettlement areas for this project (Colson, 1971, pp. 101–133; Scudder, 2005, pp. 40–45). However, the Lusitu site was especially worrisome to the Tonga because it was occupied by people of different ethnicity and language, the Shona-speaking Goba (Scudder, 2005, p. 38). In this and other resettlement sites some Tonga merged into their host populations and lost their language and culture (Soils and Chalo, 2000, p. xx), so that, on top of everything else, even their cultural freedom was diminished.

What development ethics tells us about the Kariba dam, then, is that this was a case of maldevelopment, five times over.

People facing displacement have moral rights that must be realized

Clearly, development ethics can be a valuable critical tool, showing when, how and why some cases of displacement are ethically deplorable cases of maldevelopment. But can it do more? Beyond identifying goals essential to worthwhile development, has it anything to say about the appropriate means of achieving these goals, especially for development that involves displacement? Some progress can be made in this direction by clarifying the *moral rights* that belong to people facing displacement by development. Four such rights are ethically justifiable:

> 1 *Right of good reason*: Everyone has a right to be free (and hence protected) from forced displacement except in the case of demonstrably responsible development (accepted in fair deliberation as a reasonable effort to realize the values that distinguish worthwhile development from maldevelopment).
> 2 *Right of non-victimization*: Everyone has a right to be free from net losses resulting from displacement for development, including inadequately compensated losses of individual or community assets and losses in living standards.
> 3 *Right of equitable sharing in benefits*: Everyone who is displaced for development has a right to share equitably in the benefits of the development that has displaced them. Equity gives priority (but not exclusive concern) to reducing the worst inequalities and to redressing any past victimization by displacement in the area.
> 4 *Right of equitable empowerment*: Everyone who is displaced for development has a right to become sufficiently empowered to achieve outcomes that are equitable (in terms of rights 2 and 3).
>
> (Penz *et al.*, 2011, p. 211)

The first and fourth are procedural rights; the second and third are rights to just outcomes. The 'right of good reason' answers the vexing question of whether it is ever permissible to *forcibly* displace people for purposes of development. (Cases of forcible displacement stand in contrast to cases of voluntary displacement where people give up use of lands through voluntary agreements.) According to international law, forcible displacement is permissible only for projects that are in the public interest. Yet this seems far too lax. In 2005, the US Supreme court ruled that economic development was a constitutionally legitimate 'public use' and 'public purpose' (*Kelo*, 2005; Calfee, 2006; Merrill, 2006). From a development ethics perspective, given the ethical ambiguity of 'development' and 'public interest', this standard of public interest is unacceptably low, since development ethics has higher standards, comprising the seven values of worthwhile development. With this we can say that the right of good reason should protect people against forcible displacement except in the case of 'demonstrably responsible development' that advances the seven core goals of worthwhile development. This invites the question, 'demonstrable to whom', and to this it is reasonable to answer: demonstrable to the public, in a fair deliberation. Simply put, if governments and developers cannot demonstrate to the public, in a fair deliberation, that theirs are projects of ethically worthwhile development, then people have a right not to be forcibly displaced by those projects.

Now consider the right of non-victimization. In the case of the Kariba dam, the Tonga were not adequately compensated. They were given land for land, along with other benefits, but this compensation was not adequate to maintain their living standards. The land they received was much less productive, so that food production fell to the extent that they could no longer feed themselves.

In effect, they were being required to make a greater sacrifice and contribution to development than their fellow citizens, just because they were 'in the way' of development. This is analogous to arbitrary taxation. Being required to make a greater contribution to development than others violates what Des Gasper has called 'contributive justice' (Gasper, 2004, p. 89). That is the principal argument supporting the conclusion that everyone has a right to be free from net losses resulting from displacement for development, including inadequately compensated losses of individual or community assets and losses in living standards.

The same considerations support the third right, to share in the benefits of the development project. Resettling requires effort, yet not everyone is required to resettle for the sake of a development project. If this effort is not rewarded, then a sacrifice of labour and effort is being extracted from people arbitrarily, just because they are 'in the way' of development. *Equitable* benefit sharing is called for because the more powerful segments of a displaced community may otherwise capture a disproportionate share. Moreover, equity demands not just that benefits are to be shared equally, but that they are used to some extent to reduce some of the existing inequalities within the displaced community. For instance, if additional benefits accrue to a displaced community in India, steps should be taken to ensure that they are not captured disproportionately by upper-caste families, and further steps should be taken so that the additional benefits are used to reduce the extent to which dalit and tribal families are disadvantaged. Of course, the extent to which this can be achieved in a single project will be limited; on the other hand, doing nothing is not a morally defensible option. It is not plausible to say that providing equal treatment to advantaged and severely disadvantaged people is treating them alike, since being severely disadvantaged is a morally relevant difference. Reproducing the inequalities of a displaced community through resettlement violates a basic principle of impartiality, namely that everyone's good is to be given equal consideration.

Finally, displaced people have a right to be sufficiently empowered to achieve these equitable outcomes. This means that communities and their members must be able to freely negotiate the terms of their displacement and resettlement; every aspect and stage of a project that displaces people (including the need for the project) must be subject to public approval; resettlers must be involved in decision making in the planning and management of resettlement; they must have the power to arrest development[2] in case commitments to them have not been honoured; and all of this must be subject to quick and fair dispute resolution.

The content of this right to empowerment derives not so much from ethical argument as it does from careful study of the kinds of acts, omissions and circumstances that can block the stakeholders' realization of their other rights, in this case their rights of good reason, non-victimization and benefit sharing. In other words, we can understand the concrete requirements of empowerment, in a given context, by studying what can *disempower* them, in their particular social and political environments.

Sources of disempowerment

The case of the Jamuna Bridge Project in Bangladesh illustrates several potential sources of disempowerment. People were displaced by this project in a particularly striking way: the land was literally swept from beneath the feet of people living on sandy islands known as *chars* (Sarker *et al.*, 2003). In order to shorten the span of the bridge, the river was channelized, which had the effects of quickening river currents, hastening downstream erosion and making that erosion more volatile (Dulu, 2003, p. 94). Within a matter of days, the river washed away *chars* that had been stable for decades (Schmuck, 2000, p. 14). Some families faced serial displacement when *chars* to which they had moved were washed away later (Sarker *et al.*, 2003, p. 76).

Consider the *char* dwellers' rights: (1) Elements of the *right of good reason* were achievable throughout the region affected. The bridge was to replace an extremely dangerous boat crossing that caused delays of several days to travellers and shipping (Ahmad *et al.*, 2003, p. 177). It was also designed to support a railway line, electrical power and communications lines, and a gas pipeline. Bangladeshis who knew about the project were overwhelmingly favourable (Dulu, 2003, p. 93). So the project is likely to have been received as a case of good development, at least for enhancing people's well-being. However, the *char* dwellers were not included in this discussion (JCDP, 1996b, p. 11). Nor is it evident that the other six development values received any attention in public discussion. A belated survey of stakeholders who might require resettlement or compensation was contracted out by the developer to the Bangladesh Rural Advancement Committee (BRAC), a large and well-established development NGO (JMBA, n.d.). They did not survey or inform the 75,000 *char* dwellers until after another NGO began to organize an appeal on their behalf (Dulu, 2003, p. 98 ff). The full and fair public deliberation called for by the right of good reason did not take place in this case. (2) *Right of non-victimization.* The restricted channel caused flooding for 10–12 miles north of the bridge and devastating erosion for 5–7 miles downstream to the south. The local NGO claimed that 4–5 thousand families were rendered homeless and without any source of income (JCDP, 1996a, p. 16). (3) *Right of equitable sharing in benefits.*

There were no provisions for *char* dwellers to share in the benefits of the project, apart from their being at liberty to cross the bridge and apart from trickle-down benefits of economic growth stimulated by bridge construction and usage. (4) *Right of equitable empowerment.* The victimization of the *char* dwellers can be explained in large part by decisions, circumstances and institutional practices that were disempowering. These can be described under six headings.

- *(i)* *Failure to identify the* char *dwellers in advance as stakeholders.* The *char* dwellers were not identified as people who could be affected by the project until the impacts actually took place – long after site selection and in the midst of construction. Even then, project managers declined to recognize them, arguing that it would not be possible to identify this risk before, that erosion is a natural phenomenon and that it would be impossible to assess the degree to which future erosion was caused by the impacts of the bridge (Dulu, 2003, p. 96).
- *(ii)* *Poor dissemination of information about the project.* According to the local NGO, the Jamuna Char Integrated Development Project (JCDP),

  > a sweeping 73 per cent of respondents said that there had been no official attempt to inform them of the plan undertaken by the authority having direct impact on their lives and livelihood. They came to know about the issues only through hearsay.
  >
  > (JCDP, 1996a, p. 11)

- *(iii)* *Absence of negotiation/arbitration.* No formal consultations or negotiations were held between representatives of the *char* dwellers and the developer or government at any time, even after recognition of their 'affected people (or stakeholder)' status. The compensation and resettlement programme that was eventually offered to them was provided unilaterally by the Government of Bangladesh and the developer, the Jamuna Multi-purpose Bridge Authority (JMBA), under pressure from the World Bank (Dulu, 2003, pp. 102–105).
- *(iv)* *Lack of facilitation.* Later, when the *char* dwellers were recognized as stakeholders entitled to compensation, they were still poorly informed about claims procedures, and officials would not assist them in the process (Schmuck, 2000, p. 28).
- *(v)* *Diminished role in management of resettlement.* This does not apply to most *char* dwelling families, who resettled according their own plans. Planned resettlement on the two banks of the river was managed by the JMBA Resettlement Unit, with facilitation by two local NGOs (Rahman, 2001, p. 305). Representatives of the resettlers participated in consultations; however, decision makers were not ultimately accountable to them (Asian Development Bank, 2000, p. 43).
- *(vi)* *Lack of good governance.* The established leadership and representation mechanism did not function well. Local leaders on the *chars* were widely alleged to be corrupt (Schmuck, 2000, p. 26; Rahman, 2001, p. 278), and thus they were not always effective or reliable advocates for the *char* dwellers. Informal groups of *char* dwellers organized themselves to act on various grievances, ranging from compensation procedures to bribery and harassment. These

groups had limited success, at best, and in some cases, 'due to the vested interest of the leaders of the groups ['local important persons'], performance was bad' (Rahman, 2001, p. 299).

A more serious governance gap lay in the absence of compliance protection within the project and outside avenues of recourse to ensure that commitments made to resettlers were honoured. No legal recourse was available in Bangladesh, because the eventual compensation rates offered for land lost to erosion and flooding exceeded the very low rates set in land acquisition legislation. The compensation plans put in place resulted from pressure by the World Bank, due to an application made by JCDP to the Bank's Inspection Panel, which investigates noncompliance of Bank-funded projects to Bank policies. However, in the later stages of the process, when JCDP notified the Panel that various compensations had not actually been paid, they were informed, 'the Panel is no longer involved in the process' as the Bank's lending period for the project had come to an end (Dulu, 2003, pp. 106–108).

The WCD decision-making framework

Empowerment is central to cases like this in two ways. Since empowerment is one of the values of ethical development, the kinds of disempowerment demonstrated by the Jamuna Bridge Project mark these as cases of maldevelopment, even if in other respects the project might have been worthwhile. But not only is empowerment in this way intrinsically valuable for development, it is also crucially important instrumentally, as a means of protecting the moral rights of people facing displacement by development. The many and various ways of disempowering these people can make it all but impossible to realize their rights to equitable outcomes – sharing in benefits and not being victimized. In light of this, we must ask whether the means of disempowerment will be too numerous, too various and too prevalent to overcome. If they are, then we may have to conclude that displacement by development is almost always maldevelopment and should for that reason be avoided in almost all cases. On the other hand, this pessimistic conclusion might be avoided if there are ways to structure development management and governance so as to overcome or avoid these sources of disempowerment. In the remainder of this chapter, I will confine myself for the most part to assessing the management and governance proposals made by the WCD, which made significant progress in its time (in the early 2000s) towards realizing the rights of people facing development. In particular, the WCD proposed a unique decision-making mechanism designed to prevent the disempowering practices that I have just enumerated. Still, the WCD framework for decision making has gaps that need to be filled and, with this in mind, I want to examine how well the WCD recommendations measure up to the demands of development ethics.

While development bank guidelines must be regarded as significant political and moral achievements by those who advocated for them, they have been revealed over time as being toothless and hence useless to many of the people who are disadvantaged by displacement for development. I base this on the observation that the only specific recourse that oustees have to uphold from these guidelines is the Inspection Panel process of the World Bank, and on initial evidence the Inspection Panel process seems to ignore more oustees than it helps (Fox and Treakle, 2003, p. 284). Typically, the problem is that development continues while legitimate oustee claims remain unresolved (Clark, 2009). The WCD proposed a brilliantly simple solution (particularly aimed at dams but in fact applicable to other projects that displace people): that decision making be organized in such a way that development cannot proceed unless stakeholder rights are realized. Five stages of decision making were distinguished, and progress from any one to the next would be barred unless all stakeholder rights had been *realized and verified* in the previous stage.

The first stage is needs assessment – evidence-based analysis of whether the project's outputs or results are needed, and, if so, whether this project (compared with alternatives) offers the best means of producing them. The WCD called for the establishment of a consultative forum including not only potential beneficiaries of the project but also those who could be displaced from territory on which their livelihood depended – either for habitation, production or consumption. This is an important first step in realizing the right of good reason, to ensure that the impacts of proposed development on well-being and equity are at least understood. The WCD also recommended assessments at this stage of (a) possible legal and institutional roadblocks to future participation of stakeholders and (b) environmental and social baseline studies.

The second stage might conventionally be called 'site selection', though the WCD broadened this to allow for consideration of possible project alternatives. By the end of this phase, crucial decisions would be required for (a) evaluation of alternatives, by all stakeholders, on the basis of needs and objectives established in the previous phase; (b) stakeholder agreement on dispute resolution mechanisms; (c) free informed consent by indigenous groups affected; and (d) outline agreements on compensation, mitigation, resettlement, development, monitoring measures and benefit-sharing mechanisms. If free negotiation does not succeed, the previously agreed dispute resolution mechanisms are engaged. Unless an independent review panel confirms that these results have been attained, development would not progress to the next stage.

In the third stage, the outline agreements with oustees and other stakeholders are to be made into legally binding agreements before contracts are tendered for construction. This, again, is subject to verification by a review panel. The fourth stage is commissioning of the project, which is to be contingent on verification that all prior commitments have been met. Further conditions can be written into licensing documents to regulate the fifth stage, operation of the enterprise or facilities.

No doubt, any measure to establish gateways like these would make considerable progress towards empowering people facing displacement by development to achieve equitable outcomes. Yet, there are important ethical gaps in the WCD recommendations. In particular, they do not insist that empowerment be designed to achieve equitable outcomes. Some segments of a displaced community will be more powerful and advantaged. While everyone should be sufficiently empowered to achieve equitable outcomes (including compensation for large-holding and small-holding landowners alike), empowerment schemes should not enable anyone to seize disproportionate benefits. Rather they should be designed to serve the goal of equity. In my formulation (above) of the right of empowerment for people facing displacement, there is a clear connection between the value of empowerment and the value of equity. I understand the right of empowerment as a right to *equitable* empowerment: everyone who is displaced for development has a right to become sufficiently empowered to achieve equitable outcomes. By 'equitable outcomes' I refer specifically to fulfilment of the moral rights of non-victimization and equitable benefit sharing. For reasons that I have already given, equitable benefit sharing must address some of the worst inequalities of disadvantage in the displaced community. (As noted above, reducing every such inequality may not be feasible, but neither is it morally defensible to do nothing.) This may require greater or at least different measures and forms of empowerment for worse-off and less-powerful segments of the community.

This connection was lacking in the WCD framework. The reason was conceptual: the WCD argued for inclusion of all stakeholders in decision making, and 'stakeholders' were conceived generically as all those who had anything to lose or gain if the development in question proceeded. All potential losses figure as risks, in this way of thinking. But from an ethical perspective, not all risks are equal. For some people (for instance, the Tonga displaced by the Kariba dam), displacement is a threat to livelihood and basic human security (for instance, food security). There can also be a risk, again endured by the Tonga, of cultural losses. But suppose there were others who risked losing opportunities for modestly improving their livelihoods as a benefit of a project that displaces others, and still others who might amplify their already considerable wealth through such projects. For both of the latter two groups, barriers to projects that displace others are potentially disadvantageous risks. And yet all are stakeholders. To advocate equal participation rights for all of these stakeholders is in practice incompatible with the value of equity in development, because it may allow more powerful stakeholders to steer decisions unfairly to their own advantage and to the disadvantage of others. This criticism was acknowledged by one Commissioner (Medha Patkar, prominent leader of the opposition to the Narmada dams) who observed:

> [O]nly creating a level playing field for options cannot suffice. We should instead give priority to more equitable, sustainable, and effective options to satisfy basic human needs and livelihoods for all before supporting the additional luxuries of the few, unjustified in the face of many who remain deprived.
>
> (WCD, 2000, p. 322)

That is, the right of empowerment should be realized in ways that give priority to reducing poverty and social inequalities, and that is not an outcome guaranteed by the decision-making framework advocated by the WCD.

Conclusions: from moral rights to empowerment research

I began by identifying seven values that can distinguish development that is worthwhile from 'maldevelopment' that is undesirable. Broadly construed, these values can be widely endorsed by people who have knowledge or experience of development; yet they also leave room for disagreement about details – for instance, about the meaning and measurement of 'well-being' or 'equity'. For that reason, I proposed that these values should be understood not as making up a theory, but rather as forming a framework within which further discussion should take place.

In my treatment of displacement by development, I have made what may be a distinctive use of the concept of rights – distinctive, at any rate, in the context of development thinking. The 'rights-based development' approach typically encourages stakeholders to assert their civil and political rights so as to bring about social change serving development goals. In other words, general rights are used in particular ways as means that are meant to be instrumental to development goals. In contrast, I focused on rights that are specific to one development context: the rights of 'oustees', that is, protections that are deserved, for simple ethical reasons, by people facing displacement by development. Once we take these rights as ends, we can examine various means of empowerment as instrumental to realizing them.

Surprisingly, this ethically oriented starting point opens the way for understanding empowerment in a way that is more empirical. Sources of disempowerment that threaten the full realization of oustees' rights can be found by observation. Procedures and mechanisms for empowering the oustees can be tested against this observational base. Best practices and win–win solutions can be identified (Kabra, 2013). Indeed, similar testing can also be applied to more theoretical and ethical accounts of the meaning of 'empowerment', and I make no exception for my own (Drydyk, 2008; 2010b; 2013). This, I think, should be a productive and mutually informative interaction between development social science and development ethics, with a view to counterposing, against the many and various means of disempowering people displaced by development, a more numerous, various and effective set of measures for empowering them.

Notes

1 Due to conflict between needs for irrigation and electrical power, on one hand, and harms caused by displacement, on the other, the Sardar Sarovar dam was the most controversial of 30 large dam and reservoir projects planned for the Narmada River in the Indian states of Gujurat, Madhya Pradesh and Maharashtra. See Drèze *et al.* (1997) and, for an ethical assessment, Penz *et al.* (2011, pp. 263–267). In 2008 Tata Motors

abandoned plans to construct a new plant for manufacturing its low-cost Nano automobile in the Indian state of West Bengal, in the face of protests against land acquisition and population displacement. See Chandra (2008) and Jha (2013).

2 To 'arrest development' means to stop a project from proceeding to the next stage if prior obligations have not been fulfilled. For example, if stakeholders have not been identified and consulted in needs assessment and site selection, independent monitors should be able to prevent the project from proceeding to the planning stage. For further discussion of such a mechanism, as proposed by the WCD, see the penultimate section of this chapter, 'The WCD decision-making framework'.

References

Ahmad, I., Azhar, S. and Ahmed, S. M., 2003. Construction of a bridge in a developing country: a Bangladesh case study. *Leadership and Management in Engineering* 3(4), pp. 177–182.

Asian Development Bank, 2000. *Special evaluation study on the policy impact of involuntary resettlement*. Manila: Asian Development Bank.

Calfee, C., 2006. *Kelo v. City of New London*: the more things change, the more they stay the same. *Ecology Law Quarterly* 33(3), pp. 545–581.

Chandra, N. K., 2008. Tata Motors in Singur: a step towards industrialisation or pauperisation? *Economic and Political Weekly* 43(50), pp. 36–51.

Clark, D., 2009. Power to the people: moving towards a rights-respecting resettlement framework. In A. Oliver-Smith ed. *Development and dispossession: the crisis of forced displacement and resettlement*. Santa Fe, NM: School for Advanced Research Press, pp. 181–199.

Colson, E., 1971. *The social consequences of resettlement: the impact of the Kariba resettlement upon the Gwembe Tonga*. Manchester: Manchester University Press.

Drèze, J., Samson, M. and Singh, S., eds, 1997. *The dam and the nation: displacement and resettlement in the Narmada valley*. Oxford: Oxford University Press.

Drydyk, J., 2008. Durable empowerment. *Journal of Global Ethics* 4(3), pp. 231–245.

Drydyk, J., 2010a. Book review of Denis Goulet, development ethics at work: explorations – 1960–2002. *Journal of Human Development and Capabilities* 10(2), pp. 299–300.

Drydyk, J., 2010b. Participation, empowerment, and democracy: three fickle friends. In A. Dutt and C. Wilber eds, *New directions in development ethics: essays in honor of Denis Goulet*. Notre Dame, IN: University of Notre Dame Press, pp. 333–356.

Drydyk, J., 2011. Development ethics. In D. Chatterjee ed., *Encyclopedia of global justice*. New York: Springer, pp. 252–254.

Drydyk, J., 2013. Empowerment, Agency, and Power. *Journal of Global Ethics* 9(3), pp. 249–262.

Dulu, M. H., 2003. The experience of Jamuna bridge: issues and perspectives. In D. Clark, J. Fox and K. Treakle, eds, *Demanding accountability: civil-society claims and the World Bank Inspection Panel*. Lanham, MD: Rowman & Littlefield, pp. 93–113.

Fox, J. and Treakle, K., 2003. Concluding propositions. In D. Clark, J. Fox and K. Treakle eds, *Demanding accountability: civil-society claims and the World Bank Inspection Panel*. Lanham, MD: Rowman & Littlefield, pp. 275–286.

Gasper, D., 2004. *The ethics of development*. Edinburgh: Edinburgh University Press.

Goulet, D., 1971. *The cruel choice: a new concept in the theory of development*. New York: Atheneum.

Goulet, D., 2006. *Development ethics at work: explorations – 1960–2002*. London and New York: Routledge.

Haq, M., 1995. *Reflections on human development*. Oxford: Oxford University Press.

Jamuna Char Integrated Development Project (JCDP), 1996a. *Submission to Inspection Panel: a request for inspection on the effect of Jamuna Multi-Purpose Bridge on the Jamuna char inhabitants*. Dhaka: JCDP.

Jamuna Char Integrated Development Project (JCDP), 1996b. *The people's view*. Dhaka: JCDP.

Jamuna Multi-Purpose Bridge Authority (JMBA), n.d. JMBA completed works. Available at: www.jmba.gov.bd/completed.html [Accessed 23 August 2005].

Jha, S., 2013. Analyzing political risks in developing countries: a practical framework for project managers. *Business and Politics* 15(1), pp. 117–136.

Kabra, A., 2013. Conservation-induced displacement: anatomy of a win–win solution. *Social Change* 43(4), pp. 533–550.

Kelo v. City of New London. 125 S. Ct. 2655 (2005).

Magadza, C. H. D., 2006. Kariba reservoir: experience and lessons learned. *Lakes and Reservoirs: Research and Management* 11(4), pp. 271–286.

Merrill, T., 2006. Six myths about Kelo. *Probate and Property* 20(1), pp. 19–23.

Penz, P., Drydyk, J. and Bose, P., 2011. *Displacement by development: ethics, rights, and responsibilities*. Cambridge: Cambridge University Press.

Rahman, H., 2001. *Resettlement in JMBP: assessing process and outcomes. Qualitative evaluation of RRAP (revised resettlement action plan) and project on EFAP (erosion and flood affected persons)*. Dhaka: Power and Participation Research Centre.

Sarker, M. H., Huque, I. and Alam, M., 2003. Rivers, *chars* and *char* dwellers of Bangladesh. *International Journal of River Basin Management* 1(1), pp. 61–80.

Schmuck, H., 2000. *The char-people and the Jamuna bridge in Bangladesh: an independent study on the project for compensating erosion and flood affected persons (EFAP)*. Dhaka: JCDP.

Scudder, T., 2005. *The Kariba case study*. Social science working paper 1227. Pasadena, CA: California Institute of Technology.

Sen, A., 1992. *Inequality reexamined*. Cambridge, MA: Harvard University Press.

Sen, A., 1993. Capability and well-being. In M. Nussbaum and A. Sen eds, *The quality of life*. Oxford: Clarendon Press, pp. 30–51.

Sen, A., 1999. *Development as freedom*. New York: Knopf.

Soils Incorporated (Pty) Ltd. and Chalo Environmental and Sustainable Development Consultants, 2000. *Kariba dam case study: prepared as an input to the World Commission on Dams*. Cape Town: World Commission on Dams.

World Commission on Dams (WCD), 2000. *Dams and development: a new framework for decision-making. The report of the World Commission on Dams*. London and Sterling, VA: Earthscan.

7 Resettlement projects as spaces of exception

Margarita Serje

The experience of resettlement

Recalling her experience of coming to live to Caracol, a resettlement project in Bogotá, Amanda[1] compared it to the first time she arrived as a child at a missionary boarding school. Like many children in rural Colombia, due to long distances, she had to stay at school during the week, subjected to the strict discipline imposed by the nuns.

When she arrived in Caracol, school was a thing of the past. Amanda had come to live in Bogotá when she was a teenager. Her parents had decided to try their luck in the capital in search of better opportunities and, above all, to avoid the intense violence that has haunted the Colombian countryside for many decades. They arrived in the big city with empty hands, and with enormous difficulty they gradually built a house and a life in a *barrio pirata* (informal development) located on the slopes that border the city. It was evocatively called *Nueva Esperanza*: 'new hope'. Each home was designed and built by its inhabitants, following the curves of the mountainside and responding to their particular needs. Although it was located in an area that was difficult to access and had no public utilities, they could 'keep an animal or two and even a small vegetable garden', which also provided herbal plants for home remedies. They had neighbours they knew well and some relatives on whom they could always rely lived close by.

As a consequence of the increasing inflow of occupants and the deforestation of the slope, the area where the neighbourhood was built was declared a high-risk zone for landslides. A few years ago, the city decided to turn it into a metropolitan park and an urban renewal project. They moved the people who had lived there for about 30 years away, resettling them in different 'projects'. This is how, bearing the new identity of 'resettled population', a large group of them came to live in Caracol. Their first impression of the new neighbourhood was that it was 'too ordered and everything was straight'. They had been looking forward to becoming, at last, legal homeowners and to living in modern houses, built with new, industrial materials. But life in the new neighbourhood soon proved to be, as Amanda recalled, similar to the experience of living in the missionary boarding school of her childhood.

The fact that this woman compared her new neighbourhood and her experience of resettlement with the confinement and strict discipline of a rural missionary boarding school was enlightening to me. It drew my attention to the effects that the practices of resettlement projects – considered normal and even desirable – actually have on people's lives. It also confronted me with the larger social function of these projects, that is, with the politics of resettlement. I will explore here this problem, illustrating my argument with examples drawn from the ethnographic work on several cases of resettlement in Colombia. It is not my intention in this chapter to describe the case studies or the findings (see Serje and Anzellini 2012), but rather to reflect on this experience, punctuating my observations with the direct words of the people with whom we worked.[2]

In order to show what actual resettlement programmes look like when put into practice, regardless of the discourse supporting them and the objectives they purport to have, I will focus first on a description of the practices through which they are implemented in a country such as Colombia, where they are seen as an opportunity to bring the advantages and the infrastructure of modern life to the poor and marginalized. I will attempt then to illustrate how these practices function, in fact, as vehicles for processes of normalization. I suggest that resettlement projects effectively create a situation in which there is a *de facto* suspension of what might be considered the customary rights of the inhabitants – that is, their right to their own ways of life. The suspension of these rights constitutes a state of exception, paradoxically produced by the rigid enforcement of an all-encompassing norm. In this way, very specific regulations created and supposedly put in place to avoid the negative effects of resettlement deploy forms of both symbolic and physical violence.

Practices

The standard practices in any resettlement plan, as prescribed by most guides and manuals,[3] include classifying the – usually marginalized – groups to be resettled, objectifying and quantifying their assets and entitlements, determining the technical specifications of their new homes, habitats and livelihoods, and placing many of their life decisions on hold by bureaucratic procedures. It is possible to group these practices into three main categories: those involved in the process of making a 'social diagnosis'; those that constitute the bureaucratic procedures necessary for the identification, evaluation and compensation of assets, and entitlements and the reconstruction of livelihoods; and those regarding the physical design of the new settlement.

The 'social diagnosis'

The first set of practices is concerned with the 'social diagnosis' – a term drawn from the medical sciences that, when used in planning, implicitly pathologizes social situations. Diagnoses are usually accomplished through rapid social assessments due to the short periods of time allowed by the haste of the executing agencies. Their descriptions and analyses are centred on aspects that render themselves to objectification and quantification, which in turn reduces the multiple dimensions of social life to a limited number of quantifiable and instrumentalizable variables (Ferme 1998, Scott 1998, Ferguson 2006). A complex social process such as kinship, for example, is reduced to the number of members by age and gender in the household. The multifaceted reality of a home is reduced to its area, building materials, number of rooms, and so forth.

If the explicit purpose of the 'diagnosis phase' is to characterize the population and their way of life, it ultimately constitutes an enumeration of traits to sort the population involved into categories that are instrumental in the implementation of the predetermined solutions envisaged by the project. A good example may be found in the new generation of initiatives designed to restore the livelihood of displaced persons in Colombia. Since this has proven to be one of the most complex problems resettlement projects have to face, a very simplistic solution has been adopted recently in the form of subsidy programmes, as an alternative to the complexity presented by 'productive projects'.[4] Because censuses and social diagnoses are crucial for defining and regulating who may be the potential beneficiaries of these programmes and their access to compensations and subsidies, their quantification procedures are often contested and subverted and have thus become an important issue in the public debate. A good example of the differences that can be observed in approaches to quantification was the discussion of the concept of 'equitable distribution' that took place at a consultation for an oil project: for the corporation in question it meant distributing equal shares per household, whereas for the community it meant distribution according to household size.[5]

The actual application of the classificatory devices deployed during the diagnosing stage, however, is not to serve as a basis for the design of tailored solutions, since the crucial aspects of the project are determined beforehand. Its function is rather one of inventory and appraisal, as much as of monitoring and supervision, constituting, as James Ferguson has noted, 'a machine for reinforcing and expanding the exercise of bureaucratic state power' (2006: 273), which in this case takes resettlement as its point of entry. This is particularly important, since the groups that are to be resettled are usually poor and marginalized, with no access to resources of power. They include in most cases people who lead their lives in what executing agencies categorize as 'informality': they provide employment and income for themselves and their families based on personal relations (ILO 2013), have no access to institutionalized public services and in many cases lack legal property titles. 'Informality' refers thus to the solutions that the most vulnerable groups devise and provide for themselves. It is a category that denies them participation as peers in social life, as Fraser (2000) has suggested, and invalidates their solutions. Resettlement constitutes in practice a means of suppressing these 'informal' resources to impose formalization.

Procedures

The process of formalization (or 'legalization' as it is usually referred to) takes pace through a second set of practices embodied in seemingly endless bureaucratic procedures, which begin when an array of entities decide to implement a resettlement programme and extend well beyond the moment the actual resettlement has taken place. They include inventories, budgets, contracts, loans and credits, cessions, titles, etc. This sequence of procedures in which the population to be relocated is trapped constitutes an experience similar to a rite of passage: the people involved acquire a new status and a new identity as they undergo a series of events. Through the painful and cumbersome bureaucratic procedures of resettlement, a transition from informal to formal, and from 'traditional' to modern, is performed. But unlike most rites of passage, this one does not recreate the sense of community or mutuality; its procedures are meant to validate and legalize (or to exclude and minimize) the entitlements and assets on a personal basis, enforcing the modern logic of individualism and private property.

This empty rite of passage is finally consummated when its symbolic meaning is materialized in an act that all those to be resettled must perform: the milestone of the process is the physical demolition of their home and their neighbourhood, of the places they have woven with their own histories. With this act, the foundations of their life as creative inhabitants are torn down: from that moment onwards they become merely occupants of the projects.[6] Their past life is emptied of meaning and especially of value, to become marked by the rhythms, formats and limits established by a programme that – far from aiming at recovering the sense of habitation of any particular group of people – is committed primarily to ensuring a 'technically correct' execution and implementation.

Each step of the process must be endorsed, stamped and registered in public offices, introducing two dimensions that are usually alien to the experience of those to be resettled. The first one is that of a new temporality, since the whole process is subjected to the temporal demands of the institutions and corporations interested in carrying out the resettlement. They impose their own pace on the development of the project, based on the cadence of bureaucracy and/or on the corporate rhythm of the turnover time of capital. The second dimension is the imposition of the written word. This process has been described as a powerful colonial device by Latin American critic Angel Rama (1984), through the notion of the 'lettered city' which refers to the city as an artefact conceived and planned according to rules, aims and means laid out in written form. Resettlement projects are similarly configured as legal and architectural devices subordinated to the rigour of the norms and regulations that grant their categories force of law, thus displacing the fluidity of the customary.

All these procedures are garnished with purported 'participation' of the population to be displaced, usually staged according to the disciplinary logic of the church or the classroom, and consisting mostly of individual speeches delivered in the technical and legal language of planning. 'I don't speak government' (the language of government) one of the beneficiaries responded when I asked her why she had not expressed to the assembly the concerns she raised in an interview.

Apart from the fact that the crucial decisions have already been made by planners (such as that of displacing people to make way for projects considered to be of 'public interest'), those that are actually consulted move within a field of predetermined solutions (Serje 2010). The simile used to describe the situation by a consulted 'beneficiary' of one of the projects summarizes the problem: 'I don't eat meat,' he said, 'and they are asking me to choose between sausage and tripe.'

Housing and neighbourhood design

The new 'formal' way of life is materialized in the physical design of the new settlement, the third set of practices characteristic of resettlement projects. The design of the new settlement aims at minimizing costs and maximizing housing solutions, both understood in quantitative terms. As a result, while the planning and execution of these projects may be considered successful, the living conditions and quality of life they provide are usually extremely poor. In the case of the minimal income housing (Figures 7.1 and 7.2), minimizing costs results in reducing the living space for each house (which barely provides minimal conditions for everyday life), using poor building materials and sacrificing general living conditions, in order to maximize the number of beneficiaries. In this way, even when the project intends to reduce risk factors, the new houses are paradoxically considered unsafe, due to their poor quality. 'These are all cheaply built houses', says one of the beneficiaries. 'Mine flooded the first time it rained; others had loose floorboards and the tiles were falling' (ER: 05-2011: 181).

On the other hand, the architecture of low-income houses usually presumes the existence of the modern Western nuclear family: father, mother, a couple of children: the kind of family the state has tried to impose, ever since colonial occupation, through aggressive policies of normalization. The type of family that prevails in countries such as Colombia remains stubbornly different: they are mostly multigenerational extended families, linked by a diversity of kinship bonds that simply cannot fit in these houses. Besides, housing policies in developing countries usually assume the lifestyle of industrialized countries as the desired goal for its population: projects are thus expected to incarnate modern housing standards. In this way, massive housing solutions, and particularly resettlement projects, end up fitting each dwelling with a doll's-house-sized living room, dining room, kitchen and two bedrooms, compartmentalizing human life into restrictive living spaces.

Nothing is farther from the popular urban or rural house in 'third world' countries, where most homes are spaces for numerous productive activities that are central to what in Colombia is called *rebusque* (rummaging), an expression that refers to the various initiatives necessary to make a living in an economy in which 67 per cent of the jobs are 'informal'. Homes are, therefore, multifunctional spaces, accommodating a considerably large floating population, where various productive activities take place, and with a layout that changes from day to night. To fixate them in the spaces prescribed by 'modern housing' only makes sense for development agencies, which see low-income housing as a 'development policy', that is, as civilizing and disciplining instruments.

These minimal living units are juxtaposed with the desolate public spaces that result from the also minimized investment in urban infrastructure and design.

Figure 7.1 Interior, minimal income housing (Proyecto Caracol, Bogotá)

Photographer: Stefano Anzellini.

Figure 7.2 Exterior, minimal income housing (Proyecto Caracol, Bogotá)

Photographer: Stefano Anzellini.

Most projects are configured as strings of terraced houses that resemble more a roadside motel than an actual organic neighbourhood. The end result is an urban structure that, rather than sustaining social interaction or neighbourly cooperation, imposes grids for cadastral purposes. Cadastral systems primarily involve the consolidation of private property based on discrete areas, which often differs from other forms of property that have been maintained over history in both urban and rural environments, where different forms of usufruct rights over the land have persisted. Moreover, cadastral systems were designed in principle to facilitate taxation. Today they have become the means to commercialize basic services (such as water supply, electricity, gas, waste disposal) that are increasingly becoming less public.

In this way, through the invasive regulation of spatiality and temporality implicit in the process of formalization, the groups involved in the resettlement programme are placed in a situation where not only their right to their home(land) is suspended, they are forced into a new way of life determined by foreign concepts of what a house, a neighbourhood or a community should be like, and by new constraints on their livelihoods. The logic of resettlement projects is thus expressed in the displacement of the historical forms of habitation of the populations to be resettled, denying the people involved the right to their customary way of life by expropriating their commons: their landscapes, temporalities, social networks and knowledge, and by normalizing the ways of life that have made it possible for these groups to survive in 'informality'. In this way, as Miller and Rose (2008: 45) point out for governmental interventions in general, resettlement safeguards appear 'to enhance the autonomy of zones, persons, entities, [while they enwrap] them in new forms of regulation – audits, budgets, standards, risk management, targets, shadow of the law, etc.'.

It is on the basis of the suspension of their rights as inhabitants, by transforming them merely into occupants, that the new spatial and social arrangements for the resettled populations are created. What I would like to emphasize here is how these practices are made possible by the context of crisis and the condition of exceptionality that legitimize displacement and resettlement.

Exceptionality

Hannah Arendt (1982 [1951]) and Walter Benjamin (1968 [1940]), among others, have pointed out how the defining feature of sovereign power lies not so much in its ability to define norms and regulations and to establish order, but, above all, in its power to leave legality aside at its convenience, defining areas of exceptionality where power may be exercised with relative and even with full impunity. Sovereignty resides then in the power to demarcate spaces of exception. Agamben (1997: 113) who saw the concentration camp (the archetypal space of exception) as a 'place which is opened when the status of exception begins to become the rule', proposes that the camp, far from being an anomaly set in the past, is, in fact, the 'hidden matrix of the politics in which we are still living'. And since the essence of the camp resides in the materialization of exception, it constitutes a space 'in which bare life and the rule enter into a threshold of indistinction' and therefore, as is the case of resettlement,

> we find ourselves in the presence of a camp every time such a structure is created, independent of the crimes that are committed there and whatever its denomination and specific topography. In all these cases, an apparently innocuous [place] … actually defines a space in which the normal order is de facto suspended.
>
> (Agamben 1997: 113)

In fact, resettlement, as well as its predecessor 'population transfer', has historically been a weapon of war. In the context of war, it was explicitly forbidden by the Fourth Geneva Convention (article 49, 1949); yet, in the context of development, it is considered a legitimate practice. Its legitimacy resides precisely in its condition of exceptionality, as a response to the crisis implicit in risk, disaster, violence and the 'maelstrom of perpetual disintegration and renewal' of development and modernization (Berman 1982: 15). As Ferme points out, 'the discourse of exception has crept into the rhetoric of crisis' (1998: 557–558). If the suspension of rights becomes routine in states of emergency, it also becomes normal in the management of crisis. I have shown here which rights are suspended in the midst of resettlement crisis and by what means: the condition of exceptionality in resettlement is created by introducing a multiplicity of regulations and procedures that work with the logic of the panopticon, identifying, classifying and regulating every aspect of daily life (Foucault 1975). In this way, 'the practices that we normally associate with the peaceful management of society … in the modern projects of state administration rationalization and governance' (Ferme 1998: 556) acquire here a new dimension: they become a factor of both symbolic and physical violence.

Just as Amanda's life at the missionary boarding school was marked by the violence of its iron-clad discipline, her life in the new settlement has been marked by various forms of structural or symbolic violence – that is to say, violence that takes place 'in domains where disciplinary projects of state administration, government and modernization unfold' (Ferme 1998: 556). This type of violence, usually exercised through neglect and marginalization, is implicit in many aspects of resettlement, starting with the rejection that categories such as 'resettled', 'displaced' or 'victim' (in violence induced displacements) produce. On the one hand, such categories inspire fear and distrust in the old inhabitants of the new environment; on the other, the persons described with those terms feel ashamed and resentful. Old patterns of discrimination, isolation and even open aggression are reinforced and new manifestations emerge (ER 10-2011: 152).

Symbolic violence is also implicit in the passage from an 'informal' environment governed by the rules and codes set by the people themselves, to a 'legal' one governed by pre-established but unknown civil codes. Since they live now in a 'formal' neighbourhood and they have become 'legalized homeowners', the occupants of the projects must also face the violence of having to deal with an autistic bureaucracy that demands public service payments, tax payments, as well as maintenance payments for the communal infrastructure and mortgage payments (since the new homes have to be paid for, at least partially, as in most cases the value of the previous home is not fully recognized). This pressure generates clashes and conflicts among neighbours and between neighbours and the authorities (ER 10-2011: 150). The house as private property defines the way in which resettled persons are forced to reorganize their life and their relationship with the local authorities (ER 10-2011: 49). Becoming a 'legalized homeowner' implies burdensome financial obligations for the beneficiaries: 'now we work only to pay utilities and taxes and we do not have enough to eat, we are always in debt!' (ER 06-2010: 139). Their life as 'informals' is effectively over: their new modern life is one of subordination and dependency. Moreover, as a result of the resettlement procedures that transform people into permanent debtors 'the community is gone, now everybody has to fend for themselves' (ER 06-2010: 139).

This situation is sometimes aggravated by the layout of the new neighbourhoods, which can also be seen as a factor of violence, since people in these projects live in a permanent state of overcrowding stress; as Amanda puts it, 'here everything is tight, you can hear every word your neighbours speak, they all know what you do, you are never on your own' (ER 06-2010: 149). The structural design of the houses and neighbourhoods constitutes a disturbing factor, as multiple conflicts arise that have to do with the layout and construction, such as noise and lack of space, among others.

But above all, resettled populations have to face physical violence. First the (usually minimized) violence of their 'involuntary displacement' – as it is euphemistically referred to by the multilateral partners involved in planning and executing these projects – and of the enforcement of the new (formal) ways of life they must adopt. It must not be forgotten that displaced and resettled groups are part of what Hannah Arendt (1982 [1951]) has called 'superfluous populations': groups that are considered disposable, that can be removed and replaced according to the economic needs and demands of larger groups with more power resources. This is evidenced by the fact that many development projects requiring displacement (such as mega-infrastructure or extractive projects) are militarized by public forces deployed to protect the investments rather than the people or the land.

Apart from the violence inherent to displacement, these groups sometimes also have to face direct aggression and crime, particularly in urban resettlements, which tend to be located in marginal areas and in the city's violent frontiers. After being carted off from their homes to a distant, alien resettlement project, they now fear for their lives, never knowing when they may be caught in the middle of a drug or racketing gang war. This is the case of Caracol, Amanda's new neighbourhood. Here they have faced assaults, robberies and even rapes without the support of their former social networks. One of Amanda's neighbours explains that 'even if the old neighbourhood was unsafe, we all knew and took care of each other'. The new situation is different: 'Here we are surrounded by enemies, it's like being at war with guerrillas, you have to watch out and be on your guard at all times' (ER 11-2010: 183). They believe 'these houses are very insecure, can't leave them alone. People feel they can't move around anymore, they have to stay at home to guard the house' (ER 04-2011: 181). Furthermore, this insecurity is explained by some as a direct result of been resettled, since many of them lost the (informal) sources of their livelihood and young people have resorted to gangs and robbery.

The new neighbourhood inspires a feeling of great helplessness. 'I feel here like an ant', said Amanda, and her neighbour completes the thought: 'one feels trapped here; we used to be able to cope better in the old neighbourhood' (ER 06-2010: 110). The conspicuous use of the image of the prison to describe life in the resettlement project is revealing. It appears in numerous testimonies: 'I live here like a prisoner, I can't take the kids out, I cannot leave the house alone, and I do not trust anyone anymore' (ER 06-2010: 139).

The politics of resettlement

Resettlement – whether caused by the risk of natural disaster, violence, climate change or large projects – is, directly or indirectly, related to development as the means of expansion of the modern world system. Most natural hazards result from the forms of occupation and use of landscapes and resources inherent in modern economic development and its addiction to carbon-based energy. Today's violent internal conflicts in the 'third world' are related to land concentration and to the 'new forms of labour' of neoliberal capitalism. Resettlement is therefore both a prerequisite and an outcome of the modern world system; it is instrumental for development (and for its mega projects), and is at the same time an instrumental effect of development policies and projects. This double bind explains why, despite the regulations and safeguards to which resettlement projects might be subjected (or precisely because of them), they constitute spaces of exception.

If we look at resettlement in a historical perspective, it is possible to approach its social function as a spatial strategy; that is, a set of practices through which a spatial reality is created at the same time that the social conditions of its creation are veiled. The global expansion of capitalism has involved a series of spatial strategies that are inseparable from each other. They are constitutive of the geography of the modern world system, of the spatiality of capital (Deleuze and Guattari 1980; Lefebvre 1994 [1974]; Harvey 2006). Among the most important of these strategies are the establishment of private property, which involved the appropriation, privatization and clearing of the commons first in Europe and then in America, Africa and Asia; the creation of boundaries and territories based on the principles of utopian space (as opposed to historical space); the clustering of activities related to the concentration of capital in urban areas that has led to the hyper-urbanization of the planet; and the geographical organization of labour in centres and peripheries: a false opposition that hides the fractal relationship that facilitates the reproduction of capital.

One of the conditions of possibility of all these strategies is the continuous displacement and resettlement of (each time) unprecedented numbers of people to meet the needs of capital. If displacement and resettlement constitute a spatial practice in itself, they also constitute both the spearhead and the cornerstone of the expansion of the modern world system. Some of the darkest chapters of modern history have involved the forced relocation of people to meet the demands of capital: they include (among many others) the systematic resettlement of indigenous populations in colonial America to deploy the catholic-urban project that was implemented by the Spanish crown from the sixteenth century onwards; or what was euphemistically called the 'Middle Passage', that is the transport of millions of enslaved peoples from Africa through the circuits of the Atlantic trade; or the 'Indian Removal Act' of 1830 in the USA. These chapters in the history of resettlement shed light on what may be considered its 'political unconscious' (Jameson 1981): the logic that transforms it into a disciplinary device and into a space of exception.

In spite of the fact that, in the words of Zygmunt Bauman, the corporate market forces that run the world today are 'ex-territorial', in the sense that they are 'free from territorial constraints, from the constraints of locality' (in Berger 2008: 8), the corporate concentration of land has reached unprecedented dimensions in the past decades. In Latin America, corporations have acquired millions of hectares in the past decade (FAO 2013), through different and not always legal means. A century ago, in the early twentieth century, the prevailing notion was that there was abundant land, which was mostly uninhabited. The continent was like an ownerless mine ready to be appropriated and incorporated to the global market, a process that was accomplished through a sequence of boom and bust cycles based on invasive and intensive resource extraction. The difficulty lay in securing the necessary workforce, which was very scarce at the time. Today, at the beginning of the twenty-first century, the picture is overturned: land has now become a scarce resource and it has become much more valuable than human labour. It constitutes one of the most lucrative investments, since it grants private rights not only over the soil, but also the water, vegetation, minerals and other resources. The geopolitics of territorial appropriation has thus changed, and corporations are advancing aggressive land grab initiatives (Serje 2007). The Andes-Amazon region has experienced, during the past decade, an unprecedented process of corporate land acquisition for mining and agribusiness. Governments are using eminent domain to seize what is considered as 'undeveloped' land (that is, land inhabited by local, 'traditional' groups according to non-modern logics) for private development. Most displacement and resettlement processes (both legal and illegal) in the region are linked to this process of land grab.

Since resettlement and displacement – even in risk and disaster situations, that are usually the consequence of the fact that we have subordinated life to the growth and increasing concentration of capital in our planet – are linked to the expansion of the modern world system, there are two unavoidable questions that must be asked with regard to any 'involuntary resettlement' process. The first one is to whose interests is the displacement subordinated. 'Public interest' or the 'common good' do not constitute acceptable answers, since the meaning of these concepts is defined by specific social groups. So, the question still stands: who determines the need for resettlement and in the interest of whose common good? The second question is about the social cost of displacement and resettlement: who must sacrifice their rights as inhabitants, subordinate to debt and bureaucracy, and be subjected to both symbolic and physical violence, and why?

The answer to these two questions probably explains why the protagonists of many resettlement projects feel cheated, as Amanda does:

> We never asked to be taken out of there, they came and promised us a lot of things. Instead we arrived here as destitute, they treat us like children and decide what it is good for us … And in exchange they kept our land.
> (ER 06-2010: 181)

Notes

1 At her request, I do not use her real name.

2 As part of the project *Reasentamiento forzado en Colombia: Una aproximación interdisciplinaria* (Universidad de los Andes) we studied, between 2010 and 2013, seven resettlement cases with an ethnographic approach. We made several family and life histories in each case. References to the ethnographic reports are indicated by the initials ER, the date (month-year) and page number.

3 World Bank manuals provide a good example: 'Involuntary resettlement resource book', 'IFC handbook for preparing a resettlement action plan', 'Populations at risk of disaster: A resettlement guide', all available at: http://documents.worldbank.org/curated/en/home [Accessed 1 February 2015].

4 In Colombia, cash transfers in the form of subsidy reach 62 per cent of producers, while productive projects reach only 2.6 per cent (Ibañez 2014). Subsidies might have unexpected effects that need to be researched, but they do have two well-documented consequences: they tend to create dependency and they reinforce clientele networks.

5 Resguardo Gavilán-La Pascua, Vichada, 04-14-11. Reunion de Consulta Previa para el Proyecto DCPE, Resguardo Gavilan-La Pascua, Vichada.

6 According to Ingold (2007: 81), the inhabitant is one

> who participates from within in the very process of the world's continual coming into being and who, in laying a trail of life, contributes to its eave and texture … imperial powers have sought to occupy the inhabited world throwing a network of connections across what appears, in their eyes, to be not a tissue of trails, but a blank surface. These connections are lines of occupation.

References

Agamben, G. 1997. The camp as nomos of the modern, in de Vries, H. and Weber, S. eds, *Violence, identity and self-determination*. Stanford University Press, Palo Alto, CA, 106–118.

Arendt, H. 1982 [1951]. *L'Impérialisme: Les origines du totalitarisme*. Fayard, Paris.

Benjamin, W. 1968 [1940]. *Illuminations*. Random House, New York.

Berger, J. 2008. *Meanwhile*. Drawbridge Books, London.

Berman, M. 1982. *All that is solid melts into air: The experience of modernity*. Penguin, New York.

Deleuze, G. and Guattari, F. 1980. *Capitalisme et schizophrénie, mille plateaux*. Editions de Minuit, Paris.

FAO. 2013. Dinámicas del mercado de tierras en América Latina y el Caribe. Available at: www.rlc.fao.org/fileadmin/content/events/semtierras/acaparamiento.pdf [Accessed 25 February 2014].

Ferguson, J. 2006. The antipolitics machine, in Harma, A. and Gupta A. eds, *The anthropology of the state*. Blackwell, London, 270–285.

Ferme, M. 1998. The violence of numbers. *Cahiers d'études africaines* 38 (150–152), 555–580.

Foucault, M 1975. *Surveiller et punir*. Gallimard, Paris.

Fraser, N. 2000. Rethinking recognition. *New Left Review* 3, 107–120.

Harvey, D. 2006. *Spaces of global capitalism*. Verso, London.

Ibáñez, A. M. 2014. Ponencia en el Foro 'La tierra en el desarrollo sostenible de la Orinoquía', Universidad de los Andes, Bogotá, Junio. Available at: http://ceo.uniandes.edu.co/foro-tierras-andes [Accessed 1 February 2015].

ILO. 2013. Measuring informality: A statistical manual on the informal sector and informal employment. Available at: www.uneca.org/sites/default/files/uploaded-documents/ACS/AGEIS2013/ageis2013-ilo-manual-informality_en.pdf [Accessed 25 February 2014].

Ingold, T. 2007. *Lines: A brief history*. Routledge, London.

Jameson, F. 1981. *The political unconscious: Narrative as a socially symbolic act*. Cornell University Press, Ithaca, NY.

Lefebvre, H. 1994 [1974]. *La production de l'espace*. Anthropos, Paris.

Miller, P. and Rose, N. 2008. *Governing the present*. Polity Press, Cambridge.

Rama, A. 1984. *La ciudad letrada*. Ediciones del Norte, Hannover, NH.

Scott, J. C. 1998. *Seeing like a state*. Yale University Press, New Haven, CT.

Serje, M. 2007. Iron maiden landscapes: The geopolitics of Colombia's territorial conquest. *South Central Review* 24 (1), 37–55.

Serje, M. ed. 2010. *Desarrollo y conflicto*. Universidad de los Andes, Bogotá.

Serje, M. and Anzellini, S. eds. 2012. *Los dilemas del reasentamiento*. Universidad de los Andes, Bogotá.

Part III

International and national policies

8 Is there a global safeguard for development displacement?

Susanna Price

Introduction

Many land-based projects displace people, sometimes in huge numbers. Whether projects are publicly or privately financed, no global body is tasked with systematically monitoring the numbers of people displaced or the terms of their displacement in development-induced displacement and resettlement (DIDR). The subsequent outcomes for livelihoods and living standards of the people affected are even more opaque. States rarely disclose the number of their citizens who are developmentally displaced or their fate following displacement, while few corporate voluntary codes of conduct address the risk of displacement.

Certain international financial institutions (IFIs), notably the World Bank Group and the regional Multilateral Development Banks (MDBs)[1] developed resettlement policies that require, for both public and private sector projects, publicly accessible resettlement documents with monitoring against resettlement policy benchmarks. For example, the 'resettlement instrument' (resettlement plan or framework) constitutes a 'strategy for achieving the objectives of the policy and covers all aspects of the proposed resettlement', while the borrower must ensure that, at the end of the project, the policy objectives are met (World Bank 2004, p. 376). The 'outcomes' mean achievement of policy objectives of improved or at least restored livelihoods and living standards for people affected (ibid., p. 155) – such outcomes, therefore, depend upon the quality of the resettlement instrument, its implementation and monitoring (ibid., pp. 257, 396).

Such plans, however, cover directly only a small percentage of the total globally displacing projects. In 1994, for example, World Bank projects accounted for just 3 per cent of dam-instigated displacement worldwide and just 1 per cent of urban development and transportation-related displacement (World Bank 1994) – but this share may have fallen further since then. Official inflows to developing countries' net of debt repayment, while significant in a small group of fragile states, reportedly comprised just 1 per cent of total international capital inflows to developing countries in 2012. In contrast, Foreign Direct Investment (FDI), the dominant private financing modality, accounted for 60 per cent of these inflows (World Bank 2013). Similarly, even though IFIs are increasingly directing lending flows through their private sector arms (IFC 2011) the annual *private sector* financing from all IFIs now constitutes a fraction of total capital investment in developing countries (ibid.). Built initially upon detailed case study research and analysis, these policies were incrementally enhanced over several decades of experiential, knowledge-based work. Safeguard reviews, however, appear to create opportunities for 'streamlining, efficiencies and cost-saving' – championed by some, and decried by others who charge that such approaches derogate key institutional responsibilities for processing, approval, implementation and independent monitoring that are necessary, not only to protect people displaced, but also to inform future policy making (see, for example, Bugalski and Pred 2014).

IFI standards on DIDR, however, have a longer reach than their financing share would imply. The World Bank's original involuntary resettlement policy principles have transformed into a global benchmark utilized in multilateral, bilateral and state formulations (Cernea 2005). Moreover, private sector entities must generally engage with international safeguard policy standards if they are doing business directly or indirectly with an IFI – in this way leveraging extends the IFI's policy coverage to associated project components that they do not directly finance. About 18 per cent of all long-term syndicated loans to developing countries include an IFI as one of the participants (IFC 2011, p. 21) – so their partners engage with IFI social and environmental risk management policies generally, including DIDR.

What does this mean for our understanding of resettlement outcomes? Constrained resources for supervision and monitoring limit the extent to which key IFIs monitor, evaluate and report on DIDR outcomes. Monitoring efforts tend to focus on compliance monitoring rather than outcomes for the lives of people affected; while little is known of outcomes of the International Finance Corporation's (IFC) Performance Standards (World Bank 2010). This leaves uncertainty in DIDR outcomes for many IFI-financed projects – and little systematic public reporting for the remaining vast majority of global project investments without direct IFI support. This means, therefore, that we cannot answer affirmatively an important question. Is there globally an effective resettlement safeguard for people displaced by development projects?

This absence of an affirmation matters. The reasons are compelling. First, as will be shown, the number of people internally displaced through multiple causes globally is rising. Second, research and practice demonstrate that DIDR is complex and carries multiple risks for those affected. Third, global aid and investment architecture is rapidly changing, with the emergence of innovative financing modalities creating new DIDR risks because of the difficulty of attributing responsibilities for displacement. Fourth, non-traditional donors and financiers from emerging economies and organizations are creating new patterns of operation, with consequent ambiguities for DIDR. Fifth, liberalization of land markets and escalating FDI bring more foreign land ownership, partnerships or leasing to the developing world with sometimes devastating effects for communities.

This chapter briefly explores these points through the lens of internationally recognized rights- and risk-based standards for DIDR. Despite some significant differences between rights and risks conceptualizing DIDR policy, both sets of standards operate through state regulatory frameworks for DIDR, supplementing those frameworks where necessary. Both highlight the need for enhanced state regulation. This includes the vital – but often neglected – need to enhance and mobilize DIDR skills, knowledge and practice right down the administrative system to the negotiations with people displaced. DIDR research demonstrates that, despite some innovative new laws, particularly in Asia, generally, state laws lean towards land clearing and acquisition through compensation rather than towards sound principles of rehabilitation, and there is considerable variation in practice in local social spaces in negotiations on implementation (Rew *et al.* 2006; Price 2008).

Similarly, both rights- and risk-based standards promote the concept of corporate responsibility for DIDR through corporate self-regulation and voluntary codes of conduct. The Equator Principles and the Export Credit Guidelines[2] boost corporate self-regulation on DIDR – while several sector associations (mining and hydropower)[3] have signed on to lesser standards. Overall, however, while DIDR practitioners have known for some time that international policy can enhance resettlement outcomes, they also know that supportive state laws and institutional capacity are important for realizing outcomes for both rights- and risk-based DIDR standards (World Bank 1994; Robinson 2003). Both rights- and risk-based DIDR principles face gaps in policy articulation, as well as challenges in implementation in both public and private sector spheres. The chapter concludes by highlighting the urgency for better, evidence-based understanding of resettlement policy outcomes for people to inform further action in policy development and realization. This entails follow-through into implementation, monitoring and evaluation of outcomes, with transparent, credible reporting and disclosure.

Why development displacement outcomes matter

This section elaborates on why it matters that we cannot affirm that there is a global resettlement safeguard protecting people displaced by development projects – and ensuring that resettlement arrangements achieve the desired outcomes. First, the scope of displacement from homes, work, networks and resources on which people depend increases as pressures on land intensify, not just with escalating land conversion for development purposes, but also resulting from conflict, population growth, environmental change and conservation closures. To quantify this claim, the United Nations (UN) (2006) mentions millions of people displaced and forced into homelessness and inadequate housing and living conditions every year due to development projects. One report estimated that annually approximately 15 million people globally (IAP *et al.* 2010, p. 2) are forcibly evicted from their homes, communities and lands for a range of development projects: mines, oil and gas pipelines, urban renewal schemes, mega-dams, ports, transportation infrastructure. People may also lose their land or face restrictions on the use of land for resource management and agricultural projects. As well as direct impacts, indirect impacts escalate displacement effects, for example, from land and real estate speculation, changes in land use and environmental pollution (ibid.).

Meanwhile, non-DIDR forms of internal displacement are breaking records. The Internal Displacement Monitoring Centre (IDMC) estimates that, globally, 33 million people were internally displaced by conflict during 2013, a record high for the second year in a row (IDMC 2014a); while 143 million people from 124 countries were internally displaced from 2008–2012 by disasters including those arising from environmental and climate change causes.[4] The IDMC estimates that, in absolute terms, the risk of displacement has more than doubled since the 1970s (IDMC 2014b, p. 8).

Second, land acquisition or transfer is a risky undertaking, with multifaceted social, economic and cultural costs to affected people (Cernea 1997; Oliver-Smith 2009; de Wet, this volume) and with potential costs to the state through lost productivity and social instability. Corporations may suffer reputational risk for social costs that the market is unable to resolve and land conflicts can quickly jeopardize their social licence to operate. For example, Ruggie (2012) found cases of mining executives spending 50–80 per cent of their time resolving community protests that were delaying production – and a mining operation with start-up capital expenditures in the US$3–5 billion range suffers losses of roughly US$2 million per day of delayed or suspended production. Even with DIDR policies in place, evaluation studies have shown that resettlement efforts often fall short of restoring livelihoods and standards of living (World Bank 1994). While no borrower's standards fully match international standards, those projects in countries with DIDR regulation that is more aligned with international standards achieved better outcomes than those with lower standards (ibid.).

Third, lending flows take new, diverse forms and modalities. In the 1980s, when the World Bank first approved a DIDR policy guideline, IFIs worked with states through a model designed to fill financing gaps for public infrastructure projects, subjecting projects to a DIDR compliance check before project approval. The resettlement plan addressed the specific features and expectations of the potentially affected population, while responsibilities for DIDR were shared between the financier and the state. This type of investment has fallen to less than half of lending across the entire World Bank Group (World Bank 2010). Now, IFIs utilize a growing number of diversified financing modalities, including multipurpose financing facilities; lines of credit; financial intermediary projects; and projects with multiple subprojects such as sector loans – many of these modalities have displacement impacts that emerge only subsequently and cannot be appraised prior to project approval, the key point for a Resettlement Plan compliance check. Resettlement identification and planning is then undertaken post-approval – when leverage is significantly less – through limited project supervision resources (ibid.). The increasingly diverse financing modalities and growing use of intermediaries complicate responsibilities for DIDR outcomes between states, business and IFIs. There are special problems in regulating financial intermediaries, which often lack a legal obligation to the host country or direct contractual obligations with an IFI.

Many financial intermediaries lack the requisite DIDR experts and are unwilling to hire them for cost reasons.

Fourth, global financing flows are changing. New, or re-emerging, investors from emerging economies – including both public and private financiers – are steadily increasing their share of infrastructure investments globally, especially in the potentially displacing sectors of transport, power and telecommunications (World Bank 2013). In foreign aid, non-traditional donors are the fastest growing donor group. Non-DAC bilateral donors include Brazil; the People's Republic of China (PRC) (growing at the fastest rate); India; Taipei, China; Turkey; and Thailand. They are more likely to mix aid and trade through commercial deals, including loans prioritizing physical infrastructure development that may displace people, utilizing 'different transparency and safeguard standards than those governing traditional donors' (World Bank 2013, pp. 19–20). Private giving (by foundations, non-governmental organizations (NGOs), religious organizations, and private voluntary organizations) is increasingly significant. Multilateral agencies proliferate; thousands of new private organizations join the aid community, many of whom channel bilateral donor funds, taking on new roles with businesses, governments and IFIs.

Last, liberalization of land markets and bourgeoning FDI bring increasing foreign land ownership, partnerships or leasing to the developing world. This has led to claims by some of widespread 'land grabbing' with deleterious results for land-dependent communities (German *et al.* 2011). Land expropriation laws vary between countries, but the end results are often similar. The most vulnerable, including those without legal or legalizable title to land, lose out first without alternative livelihood means, while 'customary rights to vast areas of land are lost—often permanently, with limited to no compensation' (ibid., p. 28). Weak consultation processes have led to uncompensated loss of land rights especially by those without documented title to their land.

Cumulatively, these factors confirm the importance of understanding what is happening in implementation, especially of the vast majority of projects with DIDR being financed *outside* IFI frameworks. What resettlement outcomes eventuate for people's lives? This seemingly simple question involves an increasingly diverse array of actors.

The emerging international aid and investment architecture encompasses complex interactions between states, donors, financiers, transnational private sector entities and civil society actors that advocate on behalf of people displaced. For example, the limited ability of the public sector to support long-term investments means that, to scale-up infrastructure investments, governments must ensure that incentives, pricing and regulations are aligned to encourage private sector involvement (World Bank 2013). States are responsible for creating the conditions for private sector involvement in infrastructure projects – but, simultaneously, and in potential contradiction, states also have responsibility for the protection of people displaced by such projects. This means, for example, that states may offer corporations land that has been pre-cleared through the exercise of forced displacement instruments, raising concerns for impoverishment of those people as well as possible violations of their human rights (German *et al.* 2011). The next section briefly compares and contrasts risk- and rights-based DIDR strategies, and asks how well they are implemented in this increasingly complex terrain.

International resettlement policy guidelines

International policies for DIDR comprise two main groups, both with direct relevance to regulation of public and privately financed investments. First, risk-based DIDR policies of IFIs and other organizations apply when land is acquired or access to it is restricted involuntarily through the application of state legal powers, such as eminent domain, for IFI-financed projects. Second, rights-based approaches set standards that aim to prevent human rights violations arising through DIDR, whatever the financing source. This section briefly presents several salient characteristics of each group, focusing upon the scope for implementation as a necessary basis for determining resettlement outcomes.

Risk-based standards for DIDR

Risk-based approaches focus on the economics of rehabilitation for DIDR, with objectives to improve livelihoods and living standards (for example, World Bank 2004; EBRD 2008; ADB 2009; IFC 2012; among others). Whereas a compensation-only approach transfers all risk management to the affected persons, 'a focus on incomes and living standards, by contrast, requires careful delineation of responsibilities and elaborate risk management of financing the investment' (World Bank 2004, p. xxvi). Key operational elements, formulated over several decades of experience with resettlement planning, include socio-economic and census work to identify impacts; careful resettlement planning for time-bound, costed measures in close consultation with those people affected; grievance redress mechanisms; institutional frameworks; and monitoring and evaluation of benchmarks and outcomes.

Researchers highlight the importance of careful resettlement planning because of the impoverishment risks of displacement – without such planning investment projects potentially impoverish people even when land is acquired in accordance with the state (or sub-state) law. These risks go well beyond the direct loss of land, resources and other physical assets that the laws too often are mandated to compensate only in part. Downing (2002) estimated that the loss of land may address only 10–20 per cent of the risks arising from displacement. The Impoverishment Risks and Reconstruction (IRR) model (Cernea 1997) includes joblessness, homelessness, marginalization, food insecurity, loss of common lands and resources, increased health risks, social disarticulation, and, in later refinements, the disruption of formal educational activities, political tension and the loss of civil and human rights (Downing 2002).

Risk-based research produced a stronger notion of 'resettlement with development' than is included in IFI policies. It comprises three interlinked elements:

compensation alone, while essential, is insufficient to address the psychological, cultural, status-related and identity losses of displacement that too often result in unravelling patterns of social organization and social networks; project-related benefit sharing mechanisms can provide the additional resources; and resettlement objectives should aim to *improve* the post-project position of those displaced, rather than simply to *restore* what they have lost (Cernea 2003).

The IFC, the World Bank Group's lending arm for the private sector, broadened the World Bank policy principles into Performance Standards that shifted the emphasis from the lender's procedures to the client's social and environmental management systems (SEMS) – the 'client' in this case being the private sector project proponent. These standards are easier to apply for project finance, and more difficult for trade finance and equity investments in listed companies, which are not obligated to report annually to individual shareholders (World Bank 2010).

While the IFC is ultimately responsible for the due diligence conducted by IFC staff on its investments with information largely generated by the client, the client has a legal responsibility to meet the requirements of the Performance Standards through its own processes. But little is known about outcomes for people of the Performance Standards, a key report concluding that 'there is a need for greater disclosure and verification of monitoring reports by third parties and communities to ensure that desired environmental and social outcomes are achieved' (ibid., p. xviii).

Rights-based standards for DIDR

Human rights advocates, recognizing the potential for violations in the context of development displacement, seek to avoid rights violation in DIDR. For example, Rajagopal identified five 'human rights challenges' raised by DIDR: rights to development, self-determination, participation, life, livelihood and remedy, as well as challenges to the rights of vulnerable groups (cited in Robinson 2003, pp. 14–15).

Guidelines setting DIDR specifically into a human rights framework have, over the past decade, emerged with greater specificity. As also discussed in Morel's chapter in this volume, some of the major non-binding international standards include the United Nations' guide on internal displacement (UN 2004); on forced evictions (UN 2006); and on the rights of indigenous peoples. These rights-based standards permit development-induced displacement (DID) only in the case of compelling and overriding public interest, providing the rights of those displaced are not violated, and assign to the state 'principal obligations' for applying human rights in situations of DIDR. They require the full, prior informed consent to relocation options of those to be displaced, whether indigenous or not (ibid.). The last mentioned draft UN declaration proscribes relocation that takes place without the 'free and [prior] informed consent [FPIC] of the indigenous peoples concerned and after agreement on just and fair compensation and, where possible, with the option of return' (UN 2008, Article 10). A recent FAO report on risks to food security calls for transparent governance of land tenure documentation, recognizing and safeguarding a range of tenure rights – customary tenure, informal tenure and tenure of women – including those against arbitrary forced evictions (FAO 2012, p. 25).

While it contains no specific DIDR guideline, the UN's 2011 *Guiding Principles on Business and Human Rights* set out state duties to protect against human rights abuses by third parties, including business; corporate responsibilities to respect human rights and their remedies; and greater access by victims to effective remedy, judicial and non-judicial. The Principles rely on voluntary corporate reporting, with modalities still emerging around the central themes: that governments should provide greater clarity of expectations and consistency of rules for business in relation to human rights; while companies should 'know and show that they respect human rights, built around human rights due diligence and acting on its findings' (Ruggie 2012). This raises the question: what are the prospects for implementation of rights- and risk-based approaches – upon which rest outcomes for resettlement-affected people?

Implementing rights- and risk-based approaches

Certain differences mark the conceptualization and language of rights-based policies as compared to those of risk-based resettlement policies (UN 2013), but, significantly, both approaches depend upon state regulatory frameworks to facilitate procedural implementation, and require monitoring of outcomes. Extensive experience, primarily in public sector DIDR, revealed that policy intentions may unravel in implementation through: initial failure to identify the full range of potential impacts; neglect of broader development opportunities; failure to meaningfully consult people affected and elicit their engagement; weakness in capability, resources, and/or political clout of responsible agencies; or their immutability to changing circumstances (World Bank 2004). IFIs have some, albeit limited, capacity for supervision during the implementation period and upon completion, much of which is reported publicly on IFI websites.

Rights advocates consider human rights to be most effective when translated into national law – more than 20 countries have begun to develop policies and laws based on the aforementioned UN 2004 Guide and some have directly incorporated the Principles into their national law (Cohen 2013). In some countries this has resulted in clear benefits for internally displaced persons (IDPs), such as increased resources for food and shelter, assistance with returns, compensation for having been displaced and the right to vote in their current place of residence. Sometimes, national courts have cited the Guiding Principles in rulings to ensure that the displaced are provided with adequate material assistance. At the same time, governments have been slow to implement the policies and laws they have adopted, and some have failed to do so at all (ibid.).

In a growing convergence, some IFIs have adopted rights-based standards, for example, on improved housing, and on FPIC for relocation of indigenous peoples based upon good faith negotiation with the affected communities (IFC 2012). The IFC has, in collaboration with the International Business Leaders

Forum (IBLF) and the UN Global Compact, developed a non-mandatory tool for Human Rights Impact Assessment Management. The crystallization of human rights violations around DIDR means greater specificity for aggrieved stakeholders in articulating human rights grounds for bringing grievances against companies to such mechanisms as the OECD National Contact Points and the IFI's complaints procedures.

Responsibilities for implementation

Since both risk- and rights-based standards must be realized through state regulatory frameworks and, often, corporate self-regulation, we now look more closely at these frameworks.

State frameworks for DIDR

State law is generally considered to be the central instrument of regulatory governance, with business as key regulatees (Scott 2003). IFI policies and legal instruments generally differ from state legal instruments for involuntary land acquisition in three important ways: first, rather than just compensating for tangible, expropriated assets, IFIs aim to improve (or at least restore) living standards; second, IFIs recognize and assist people affected who are without title to assets, including land; and, third, they call for a specific resettlement planning phase with social analysis and participation of those affected (World Bank 2004). State legal instruments for land acquisition rarely articulate the outcomes expected for the lives of those people displaced. They have traditionally focused on expropriation for development purposes rather than providing a resettlement safeguard for the displaced, although this pattern is now changing as some states incrementally integrate selected international DIDR principles into law (Rew *et al.* 2006; Price 2008).

For example, in the Asia region, India's replacement of the colonial-era 1894 Land Acquisition Law – which forced land acquisition through the state's power without considering the impoverishing effects – with The Right to Fair Compensation and Transparency in Land Acquisition, Resettlement and Rehabilitation Act (LARR) (2013) introduces, among others, a partial 'prior consent' requirement; boosts compensation rates; creates new institutional frameworks; introduces social impact assessment (SIA) in planning resettlement; and extends entitlements to those without land title. Dealing with its own variant of the same 1894 Law, the Sri Lankan Cabinet in 2001 approved an international-standard National Involuntary Resettlement Policy (NIRP) – but, while helpful in clarifying objectives, incorporation of those policy principles into legal instruments is also vital to deliver clear instructions with legal force through the entire institutional framework to the point of face-to-face contact between local officials and people displaced.

Despite this progress, both rights- and risks-based DIDR principles are yet to be fully incorporated in the state legal instruments for land acquisition in most developing countries. Some IFIs allocate modest financing to build integrated country systems for environmental and social risk management including DIDR where requested – addressing policy, laws, regulations and administrative systems.[5] Even where the DIDR regulatory framework has moved towards international standards, gaps may open up in the chain of administrative responsibility from top to bottom. As Rew *et al.* (2006) have cogently argued, DIDR policy and laws are ultimately 'negotiated' between those people affected and local level administrators in multiple local spaces – this understudied process can mean some surprising results and variation in outcomes.

The sheer scale and structure of global production has challenged both global and government regulatory capacities. Globalization 'appears to have undermined both the willingness and capacity of governments to make global firms politically accountable' (Vogel 2010, p. 73). Social and environmental impacts have become particularly prominent – without adequate regulatory mechanisms they are externalized to vulnerable communities with often devastating consequences. Increasingly, frameworks for environmental impact assessment (EIA) are being adopted across the developing world – sometimes accompanied by an SIA. Identifying social losses or social risks, conducting sociological enquiry, formulating social reconstruction and capability building measures, and monitoring their realization or otherwise in outcomes for people affected, as required in DIDR planning and management, calls for skills often beyond the usual skill base of land acquisition officers.

Corporate self-regulation for DIDR

Proliferation of global investments from international capital markets translate into social and environmental costs for vulnerable communities that prominently feature in critiques from civil society (Oliver-Smith 2009). These, in turn, underline the adverse effects of regulatory failure on people and their DIDR communities. International public opinion has prompted businesses globally to adopt a range of 'soft law' self-regulatory mechanisms, including voluntary guidelines and codes of conduct, to fill governance gaps in the national and international regulatory frameworks for corporations. There are now 'soft law' mechanisms in more than 300 industry or product codes (Vogel 2010: 72). More than 3,000 global firms have developed their own codes and/or subscribe to one or more industry or cross-industry codes. More than 3,500 corporations support the UN Global Compact; more than 2,300 global firms have endorsed the International Chamber of Commerce's Business Charter for Sustainable Development. More than 70 major global financial institutions from 16 countries have signed the United Nations Principles for Responsible Investment (ibid.).

Consequently, state law while still important is no longer the exclusive regulatory control instrument (Scott 2003). A 'new global public domain' (Ruggie 2004, p. 8) does not replace the state but embeds 'systems of governance in broader global frameworks of social capacity and agency' in which civil society is also a key actor. Transnational business entities take on state roles through self-regulation (ibid., p. 6), which entails the creation of new transnational forms of managing their subsidiaries, suppliers and distributors. Institutional understandings, mandates and capacities become important right down the administrative chain to the front line of implementation with people affected.

Governments increasingly attract private investment through financial, informational, technical and bureaucratic support; by offering favourable investment frameworks with tax exemptions and minimal lease fees; or government-to-government diplomacy and tied aid. This can also entail 'widespread land expropriation by the state' as a 'precondition or means for transferring land to investors' whereby legal instruments intended for the public good benefit private interests (German *et al.* 2011, p. 4).

In view of its sensitivity and increasing scarcity, it is surprising that few voluntary codes of conduct address land issues specifically. The Equator Principles,[6] a notable exception, established for private banks and financial institutions – financiers of major development projects – comprise a voluntary, self-regulatory code of conduct designed to manage risk in investing in the developing world. The Principles utilize the IFC's Performance Standards for social and environmental risk management including land acquisition and resettlement. The Equator Principles have also been adopted by public financial institutions, such as the Danish Export Credit Agency, Export Development Canada, the Industrial Bank of China and the Arab African International Bank (Wright 2012).

The Principles claim significant influence through the spread of projects covered, reaching 70 per cent of international project finance debt in emerging markets.[7] Hence, signatories finance a significant proportion of capital-intensive, private sector infrastructure projects with generally large footprints in the developing world – which supporters claim represents significant progress in raising corporate performance in addressing social and environmental risks, processing steps and stakeholder engagement. Equator Principles coverage, effectiveness and reporting arrangements, however, are still emerging, relying solely on voluntary reporting and therefore sanctions to protect communities from known risks of displacement in weak regulatory or even non-democratic settings (ibid. 2012). Independent monitoring and auditing standards remain limited, with little known about the outcomes on people, because 'most financial institutions remain reluctant to disclose the project-specific information that is necessary for external actors to hold them accountable for their lending decisions' (ibid., p. 64). Contracting processes pay little attention to the possibility of DIDR and human rights violations – most 'fail to delineate the respective roles and obligations of governments and companies for when things go wrong' (Ruggie 2012). This means that detailed information about Equator Principle projects is based on local media stories and field reports gathered and disseminated by researchers and civil society in developing countries. The absence of enforcement mechanisms, coupled with minimal disclosure, raise the question: are these Principles more to do with reputation, trust, credibility, relationships with stakeholders and with access to new sites than with changing fundamental business practices and delivering improved outcomes for people whose lives have been affected?

Several voluntary sector-based DIDR codes exist. The ICMM's code has adopted ten principles on sustainable development that include resettlement. The Hydropower Sustainability Assessment Protocol, prepared by the IHA, also addresses affected populations, resettlement, social, economic, cultural and health impacts of hydropower plants. While these voluntary codes recognize the sensitivity of land access and expropriation, their DIDR arrangements are yet to reach international rights- and risks-based standards.

Conclusion

While DIDR rights- and risk-based strategies and remedies have brought understanding to a large new audience in public and, especially, private sectors over the past decade, these enhanced understandings have yet to translate into firm, transparent evidence that resettlement outcomes are improving – or at least, restoring – the lives of people affected. This chapter finds the absence of proof of a global DIDR safeguard is problematic – especially given the well-documented, multiple risks to those displaced. Understanding resettlement outcomes is vital not only in ensuring that people affected are not impoverished by the risky business of DIDR in specific cases. Such understandings also set an evidence-based framework for evaluating DIDR strategies for further action in public and private sectors more widely.

The numbers of the internally displaced from conflict and disasters are breaking global records – but there is no global monitoring of DIDR numbers, processes and outcomes. Evolving global aid and investment architecture highlights the growing importance of private sector agents, diverse new financing modalities, and new donors and financiers. This creates new DIDR risks and ambiguities, heightening the need for a better understanding of both resettlement scope – the numbers affected, processes through which they are impacted and outcomes of resettlement policies for people – as well as the impact of private sector negotiations, contracting and management practices on DIDR. That some states are taking steps towards enacting DIDR concerns into policy and legal frameworks is a positive step – follow-through into implementation is also important for realizing outcomes. The absence of a global effort to understand the scale, scope, dimensions, impacts and outcomes of development displacement, however, leaves people vulnerable to chance. A global institutional mandate and responsibility for monitoring DIDR would help to build a more credible DIDR knowledge base – for better, more participative monitoring, reporting and analysis, particularly on outcomes for people's lives and living standards, as an essential basis both for immediate action and for future policy making and practice.

Notes

1 IFIs, as discussed here, encompass the World Bank Group including its private sector arm, the International Finance Corporation (IFC), and the regional Multilateral

Development Banks including the European Investment Bank (EIB); Asian Development Bank (ADB); European Bank for Reconstruction and Development (EBRD); Inter-American Development Bank Group (IADB); African Development Bank (AfDB); and Islamic Development Bank (IsDB).

2 The Equator Principles Development Assistance Committee (DAC) of the Organisation for Economic and Social Development (OECD).

3 International Council on Mining and Metals (ICMM) website www.icmm.com (accessed 7 July 2014). International Hydrosector Association (IHA) website is at www.hydrosustainability.org (accessed 17 July 2014). For a critique of the IHA protocol Sustainability Assessment Protocol see International Rivers www.internationalrivers.org/files/attached-files/ngo_critique_final_iha_protocol.pdf (accessed 17 July 2014).

4 According to the IDMC, disasters includes environmental and climate change disasters (www.internal-displacement.org [accessed 20 July 2014]). The estimates of the number of people newly displaced by disasters are related to both weather-related and geophysical hazard events during a year, including floods, storms, earthquakes, volcanic eruptions and wildfires. The figures do not include slower-onset type events such as droughts, as well as technological hazards (such as nuclear or industrial accidents) and biological hazards (such as epidemics). The IDMC's disaster-related displacement data for each year from 2008 to 2012 covers only 124 countries, so 'many more countries are likely to have disaster displacement events that have not been captured in identified reports' (www.internal-displacement.org/global-figures#natural [accessed 20 July 2014]).

5 For example, see ADB's Technical Assistance since the 1990s, with expenditure of some US$23.875 million since 2009 alone towards strengthening and effectively implementing environmental and social safeguards in country safeguard systems; see www.adb.org/site/safeguards/country-safeguard-systems (accessed 15 July 2014).

6 See the website at www.equator-principles.com (accessed 2 January 2014).

7 Op. cit.

References

Asian Development Bank (ADB), 2009, *Safeguard Policy Update*. ADB, Manila.

Bugalski, N. and Pred, D., 2014, *World Bank Safeguards: Pushing More Money out the Door at the Expense of the Poor?* in Devex, 5 August. Available at https://www.devex.com/news/world-bank-safeguards-pushing-more-money-out-the-door-at-the-expense-of-the-poor-84060#.U-Dve1XUpTc.gmail [accessed 8 September 2014].

Cernea, M., 1997, 'The Risks and Reconstruction Model for Resettling Displaced Populations', *World Development* 25 (10), 1569–1588.

Cernea, M., 2003, 'For a New Economics of Resettlement: A Sociological Critique of the Compensation Principle', *International Social Science Journal*, 175. UNESCO, Paris: Blackwell.

Cernea, M., 2005, 'The Ripple Effect in Social Policy and its Political Context: Social Standards in Public and Private Sector Development Projects', in Likosky, M.B. (ed.), *Privatising Development: Transnational Law, Infrastructure and Human Rights*, 65–103. Martinus Nijhoff, Leiden.

Cohen, R., 2013, *Lessons Learned from the Development of the Guiding Principles on Internal Displacement*. Working Paper, The Crisis Migration Project, Institute for the Study of International Migration, Georgetown University.

Downing, T.E., 2002, *Avoiding New Poverty: Mining-induced Displacement and Resettlement*. Mining Minerals and Sustainable Development No. 58, World Business Council for Sustainable Development, International Institute for Environment and Development.

European Bank for Reconstruction and Development (EBRD), 2008, *Environmental and Social Policy*. London: EBRD.

Food and Agriculture Organisation (FAO), 2012, *Voluntary Guidelines on the Responsible Governance of Tenure of Land, Fisheries and Forests in the Context of National Food Security*. World Committee on Food Security, Rome.

German, L., Schoneveld, G., and Mwangi, E., 2011, Processes of Large-Scale Land Acquisition by Investors: Case Studies from Sub-Saharan Africa. Paper presented at the *International Conference on Global Land Grabbing 6–8 April*, Land Deal Politics Initiative.

Internal Displacement Monitoring Centre (IDMC), 2014a, *Global Overview 2014. People Internally Displaced by Conflict and Violence*. Geneva: IDMC.

International Accountability Project (IAP), Housing and Land Rights Network, Habitat International Coalition, International Network for Displacement and Resettlement (INDR), 2010, *Key Issues for Upholding Housing, Land and Property Rights in the International Finance Corporation's Review of the Environmental and Social Policy and Standards*. Available at: http://allthingsaz.com/wp-content/uploads/2012/01/Downing-et-al-IAP-HLRN-INDR-briefer-on-housing-rights-_-the-IFC.pdf (accessed 24 March 2014).

——, 2014b, *Global Estimates 2014. People Displaced by Disasters*. Geneva: IDMC.

International Finance Corporation (IFC), 2011, *International Financial Institutions and Development through the Private Sector*. A joint report of 31 multilateral and bilateral development finance institutions. Washington, DC: IFC.

——, 2012, *Performance Standard 5 on Land Acquisition and Involuntary Resettlement*. Washington, DC: IFC.

Oliver-Smith, A., 2009, *Development and Dispossession: The Anthropology of Displacement and Resettlement*. School for Advanced Research Press, Santa Fe, NM.

Price, S., 2008, 'Compensation, Restoration and Development Opportunities: National Standards on Involuntary Resettlement', in Cernea, M.M. and Mathur, H.M. (eds), *The Resettlement Dilemma: Can Compensation Prevent Impoverishment?*, 147–179. Oxford University Press, New Delhi.

Rew, A., Fisher, E., and Pandey, B., 2006, 'Policy Practices in Development-Induced Displacement and Resettlement', in de Wet, C. (ed.), *Development-Induced Displacement: Problems, Policies and People*, 38–69. Berghahn, Oxford.

Robinson, W.C., 2003, *Risks and Rights: The Causes, Consequences, and Challenges of Development-Induced Displacement*. An Occasional Paper. The Brookings Institution-SAIS, Project on Internal Displacement, Washington, DC.

Ruggie, J., 2004, *Reconstituting the Global Public Domain: Issues, Actors and Practices*. CSR Initiative, Working Paper No. 6. John F. Kennedy School of Government, Harvard University, Cambridge, MA.

——, 2012, Keynote Remarks at Association of International Petroleum Negotiators Spring 2012 Conference, Washington, DC.

Scott, C., 2003,'Regulation in the Age of Governance: The Rise of the Post- Regulatory State', *National Europe Centre Paper No. 100*, Australian National University, Canberra.

United Nations, 2004, *Guiding Principles on Internal Displacement*. Office for the Co-ordination of Humanitarian Affairs. Available at: http://www.ifrc.org/Docs/idrl/I266EN.pdf (accessed 14 September 2013).

——, 2006, Statement by Mr Miloon Kothari, Special Rapporteur on adequate housing as a component of the right to an adequate standard of living. Appendix *Basic Principles and Guidelines on Development-Based Evictions and Displacement*. E/CN.4/2006/. Vancouver: United Nations Economic and Social Council, Commission on Human Rights.

——, 2008, *Declaration on the Rights of Indigenous Peoples*. Available at: www.un.org/esa/socdev/unpfii/documents/DRIPS_en.pdf [accessed 26 March 2013].

——, 2011, *Guiding Principles on Business and Human Rights: Implementing the United Nation's Framework for Protect, Respect and Remedy*. Geneva: Human Rights Officer of the High Commissioner.

——, 2013, *Report of the Special Rapporteur on Adequate Housing as a Component of the Right to an Adequate Standard of Living, and on the Right to Non-Discrimination in this Context*. Raquel Rolnik, Addendum Mission to the World Bank, A/HCR/22/46/Add.3. Geneva: United Nations.

Vogel, D., 2010, 'The Private Regulation of Global Corporate Conduct Achievements and Limitations', *Business and Society* 49 (1), 68–87.

World Bank, 1994, *Resettlement and Development: Bankwide Review of Projects Involving Involuntary Resettlement 1986–1993*. Report No. 12971. Washington, DC: World Bank.

——, 2004, *Involuntary Resettlement Sourcebook*. Washington, DC: World Bank.

——, 2010, *Safeguards and Sustainability Policies in a Changing World*: An Independent Evaluation of World Bank Group Experience. Available at: http://siteresources.worldbank.org/EXTSAFANDSUS/Resources/Safeguards_eval.pdf [accessed 3 July 2012].

——, 2013, *Financing for Development Post 2015*. Washington, DC: World Bank.

Wright, C., 2012, 'Global Banks, the Environment, and Human Rights: The Impact of the Equator Principles on Lending Policies and Practices', *Global Environmental Politics* 12 (1), 56–77.

9 Protection against development-induced displacement in international law

Michèle Morel

Introduction

Development and displacement often go hand in hand. Practice reveals that large-scale development projects, such as the construction of dams, ports, mines, railways, highways, airports, irrigation canals and urban infrastructure, almost always entail involuntary, forced displacement of people. Development projects therefore raise important legal issues as well as ethical questions: do benefits of development ever outweigh the resulting displacement? If so, under what conditions does a development project, usually benefitting a significant number of people, justify the negative consequences that follow for a usually (but not necessarily) more limited number of individuals? What is owed to those displaced?

From an ethical point of view, three theoretical perspectives have been suggested to test the justification of development-induced displacement (DID), namely: the public interest perspective, the perspective of self-determination and the egalitarian perspective (Penz, 2002 p. 4). The public interest perspective uses a cost–benefit analysis and treats displacement as a cost. Where the benefits of the project exceed the costs, the project is justified and displacement is considered a sacrifice for the good of the country:

> In decades past, the dominant view of those involved in the 'development' of traditional, simple, Third World societies was that they should be transformed into modern, complex, Westernized countries. Seen in this light, large-scale, capital-intensive development projects accelerated the pace toward a brighter and better future. If people were uprooted along the way, that was deemed a necessary evil or even an actual good, since it made them more susceptible to change. In recent decades, however, a new development paradigm has been articulated, one that promotes poverty reduction, environmental protection, social justice, and human rights. In this paradigm, development is seen as both bringing benefits and imposing costs. Among its greatest costs has been the displacement of millions of vulnerable people.
>
> (Robinson, 2004)[1]

While the public interest (in development) has long been considered to prevail over the interest of the individual (in not being displaced), in recent times more attention has been placed upon the latter. An expression of this shift in thinking is the second perspective, which has self-determination as its central value.[2] According to this perspective, displacement is viewed as intrinsically immoral because it is imposed upon the people involuntarily. Public interest considerations are not viewed as a sufficient justification for displacement. However, where the people affected by the project are offered adequate compensation through fair negotiation – negotiation that addresses asymmetries in bargaining power and information – that they accept, and subsequently move voluntarily, they are not considered to be involuntarily displaced.

Finally, the perspective of egalitarianism accepts DID when the project decreases social inequalities by primarily benefitting the poor and thus reducing global poverty. Whichever perspective is preferred, it is clear that DID is an ethically complex issue with much room for balancing different interests.

Although the fate suffered by victims of DID may be as bad as the fate of people displaced by other forces, such as conflict, persecution or natural disasters (and sometimes worse, given that development evictees are usually unable to return to their homes unlike many other displaced persons), they seem to receive less attention from the media and international aid agencies compared to other types of forced migrants.[3] Just like the latter, people displaced as a result of development projects find themselves compelled to face the challenge of starting a new life in an unfamiliar environment.

> Like becoming a refugee, being forcibly ousted from one's land and habitat by a dam, reservoir or highway is not only immediately disruptive and painful, it is also fraught with serious long-term risks of becoming poorer than before displacement, more vulnerable economically, and disintegrated socially.
>
> (Cernea, 1996 p. 304)

The relatively little interest in DID may be related to the fact that where persecution, conflict or natural disasters are never considered to be a 'good cause' in and of themselves, development is by many considered to be a right and thus, at least in some cases, as justifying displacement.

Parallel to the shifting ethical thinking on the subject, normative evolutions have taken place at the international level in order to regulate development activities leading to the displacement of people. Legal protection standards specifically dealing with DID have been developed, mostly with non-binding character. These standards are based on general human rights law. After highlighting the specific standards, this chapter will therefore explore the international human rights framework relevant to DID, thereby examining the extent to which human rights law guarantees protection against 'unjust forms' of displacement, or, differently stated, identifying the conditions under which states – bearing the primary responsibility for securing their citizens' human rights – can lawfully carry out the displacement of a part of their population. Based on this analysis, the chapter finds that international law currently contains an emerging, qualified 'right not to be displaced', meaning a non-absolute right that is only partially developed.

Legal protection standards on DID

A number of normative instruments at the international and regional level contain standards specifically relating to DID. While some of these instruments are legally binding, most of them are sets of legally non-binding guidelines and principles.

According to the Guiding Principles on Internal Displacement (GPID),[4] which are a set of principles formulated in 1998 by the former UN Secretary-General's Representative on internally displaced persons (IDPs) to guide states on the protection of IDPs against, during and after displacement, displacement in cases of large-scale development projects that are not justified by compelling and overriding public interests constitutes a prohibited – because arbitrary – form of displacement.[5] In other words, DID is only permissible when it can be considered to be strictly necessary and proportionate to the public interest (Kälin, 2008 p. 33). In addition, the GPID, as well as the Convention for the Protection and Assistance of Internally Displaced Persons in Africa (Kampala Convention)[6] and the Protocol on the Protection and Assistance to Internally Displaced Persons,[7] the latter of which was adopted by states of the Great Lakes Region in Africa in the context of the 2006 Pact on Security, Stability and Development in the Great Lakes Region[8] (IDP Protocol to the Great Lakes Pact), prescribe that states must ensure that all feasible development alternatives are explored, with full information and consultation of persons likely to be displaced by the project, in order to avoid DID where possible. Socio-economic and environmental impact assessments must be carried out prior to undertaking a development project. Where no feasible alternatives exist, states must take all measures necessary to minimize displacement and mitigate its adverse effects, including through the provision of proper accommodation for displaced persons where practicably possible. States must ensure that the displacement takes place in satisfactory conditions of safety, nutrition, health and hygiene. Displacement must be mandated and carried out in accordance with domestic law. Adequate compensation for the displacement and any lost property and possessions must be guaranteed and legal remedies must be made available.[9] Special attention is paid to the situation of people who are particularly attached to their lands, such as indigenous peoples, minorities, peasants and pastoralists. States have a 'particular obligation' towards these people to protect them against displacement.[10]

In addition to these instruments on internal displacement, a number of other normative documents contain similar standards on protection against DID. These are the Guidelines for Aid Agencies on Involuntary Displacement and Resettlement in Development Projects of the Organisation for Economic

Co-operation and Development (OECD),[11] the Report of the (former) UN Special Rapporteur on Human Rights and Population Transfer,[12] the Comprehensive Human Rights Guidelines on Development-Based Displacement,[13] the World Bank Operational Policy Statement on Involuntary Resettlement[14] and the UN Basic Principles and Guidelines on Development-Based Evictions and Displacement.[15]

The underlying idea of all of these standards and the conditions stipulated therein under which development-based evictions can take place in a lawful, non-arbitrary way, are essentially inspired by and in full accordance with certain provisions of international human rights law, which will now be closely examined. While development projects may significantly contribute to a country's development and the realization of economic and social human rights of the people, and therefore must not be prohibited per se, sufficient legal safeguards must ensure 'that development cannot be used as an argument to disguise discrimination or any other human rights violation' (Kälin, 2008, p. 32).

The international human rights framework for the protection against arbitrary displacement

The phenomenon of DID is characterized by conflicting interests and conflicting human rights. On the one hand, there is the right to development of people benefitting from the project, according to which 'every human person and all peoples are entitled to participate in, contribute to and enjoy economic, social, cultural and political development, in which all human rights and fundamental freedoms can be fully realised'.[16] On the other hand, there are the human rights of the potential and actual victims of DID. Various rights are at stake here, including the right to housing, the right to livelihood, the right to self-determination, the right to participation and the right to remedy (Leckie, 1995; Langford and Plessis, 2005 pp. 11–21). Neither the right to development nor the rights of the displaced persons have an absolute character. These rights must be balanced against each other and, depending on the particular circumstances of each case, one interest will outweigh the other. This chapter focuses on the international legal protection of persons against being displaced in a non-justified way as a result of development projects and processes. The right to development will not be examined in depth but comes into play in the balancing exercise between the individual's interest not to be displaced and the public interest to develop.[17] While this chapter exclusively deals with the international and regional legal level, it should be noted that victims of displacement generally first resort to domestic legal frameworks and judicial bodies before seeking redress at the international level.

The right to adequate housing

Victims of arbitrary displacement and non-governmental organizations (NGOs) defending the interests of the former usually condemn cases of arbitrary displacement with reference to the human right to adequate housing before any other human right. Certain other human rights, such as the right to freedom of movement and residence, the right to private life and home, and the right to property (classified as civil rights), may offer more effective protection from a judicial point of view, because the international enforcement mechanisms for these rights are more developed than those for socio-economic rights (generally requiring higher levels of investment by the state). Nevertheless, the right to adequate housing, a socio-economic right, is indeed seen by many as the most obvious human rights concern in relation to displacement, and therefore considered to be the principal legal framework for assessing the (un)lawfulness of evictions.[18]

The right to adequate housing is guaranteed at both the international and the regional (continental) level. This chapter will limit itself to a discussion of the explicit recognition of the right to housing in article 11 of the International Covenant on Economic, Social and Cultural Rights (ICESCR).[19] The Committee on Economic, Social and Cultural Rights (CESCR), the monitoring body for the ICESCR, has clarified the content of the right to housing under article 11(1) ICESCR in relation to evictions and displacement in its General Comments No. 4 and No. 7.[20] The Committee has identified several aspects of adequate housing that constitute the conditions that must be met before a certain form of shelter can be regarded as 'adequate'. These aspects include legal security of tenure; availability of services, materials, facilities and infrastructure; affordability; habitability; accessibility; location; and cultural adequacy.[21] Legal security of tenure is thus one of the core aspects of adequate housing. In this regard, the Committee stated:

> Tenure takes a variety of forms, including rental (public and private) accommodation, cooperative housing, lease, owner-occupation, emergency housing and informal settlements, including occupation of land or property. Notwithstanding the type of tenure, all persons should possess a degree of security of tenure which guarantees legal protection against forced eviction, harassment and other threats.[22]

Thus, forms of tenure are diverse, and legal security of tenure goes beyond legal ownership or land use rights. It is the legal right to protection from arbitrary eviction or displacement from one's home or land. Hence the right to housing includes such protection. Indeed, the CESCR is of the view that 'instances of forced eviction are prima facie incompatible with the requirements of the Covenant and can only be justified in the most exceptional circumstances, and in accordance with the relevant principles of international law'.[23]

While article 2(1) ICESCR states that each state party is under the obligation 'to take steps ..., to the maximum of its available resources, with a view to achieving progressively the full realization of the rights recognized in the present Covenant by all appropriate means, including particularly the adoption of legislative measures', the right to housing entails certain obligations that have immediate effect, regardless of the state of development of a country.[24] In relation to evictions, the Committee itself has phrased it as follows:

> In essence, the obligations of States parties to the Covenant in relation to forced evictions are based on article 11.1, read in conjunction with other relevant provisions. In particular, article 2.1 obliges States to use 'all appropriate means' to promote the right to adequate housing. However, in view of the nature of the practice of forced evictions, the reference in article 2.1 to progressive achievement based on the availability of resources will rarely be relevant. The State itself must refrain from forced evictions and ensure that the law is enforced against its agents or third parties who carry out forced evictions.[25]

In General Comment No. 7, the Committee has defined 'forced eviction' as 'the permanent or temporary removal against the will of individuals, families and/or communities from the homes and/or land which they occupy, without the provision of, and access to, appropriate forms of legal or other protection.'[26] The Committee links the phenomenon in particular to heavily populated urban areas, but also considers the connection with forced population transfers, internal displacement, forced relocations in the context of armed conflict, mass exoduses and refugee movements.[27]

The Committee emphasizes that '[t]he prohibition on forced evictions does not, however, apply to evictions carried out by force in accordance with the law and in conformity with the provisions of the International Covenants on Human Rights.'[28] The core question arising here is thus under what circumstances evictions are permissible.[29] In this regard, the Committee has stated that where it may be necessary to impose limitations on the right to adequate housing and the right not to be subjected to forced eviction, article 4 ICESCR must be fully complied with. According to this article, economic, social and cultural rights may be subjected to limitations 'as are determined by law only in so far as this may be compatible with the nature of these rights and solely for the purpose of promoting the general welfare in a democratic society.' Thus, limitations to the right to housing are only permissible if they are proportionate to the promotion of general welfare.[30]

To be in accordance with the right to housing under article 11(1) ICESCR, an eviction must be in accordance with domestic law, have a substantive and proper justification (such as the public interest),[31] and be reasonable and proportionate.[32] The requirements of reasonability and proportionality entail the following elements: states must explore all feasible alternatives before carrying out an eviction; evictions must not violate the prohibition of discrimination; adequate compensation must be provided for affected property; adequate alternative housing, resettlement or access to productive land must be made available where reasonably possible; and the following procedural guarantees must be afforded:

> (a) an opportunity for genuine consultation with those affected; (b) adequate and reasonable notice for all affected persons prior to the scheduled date of eviction; (c) information on the proposed evictions, and, where applicable,

on the alternative purpose for which the land or housing is to be used, to be made available in reasonable time to all those affected; (d) especially where groups of people are involved, government officials or their representatives to be present during an eviction; (e) all persons carrying out the eviction to be properly identified; (f) evictions not to take place in particularly bad weather or at night unless the affected persons consent otherwise; (g) provision of legal remedies; and (h) provision, where possible, of legal aid to persons who are in need of it to seek redress from the courts.[33]

Procedural justice, the aim of these safeguards, is a critical value and as crucial as other requirements for achieving displacement and resettlement situations that respect the interests and rights of the affected people.[34] This is especially so given the broad notions of 'general welfare' and 'public interest', and the delicate judgement exercise as regards the proportionality condition.

It is thus important to understand that the right to housing does not prohibit evictions altogether, but imposes conditions and procedural limits on it.[35] Hence it would be a misconception to think that the right to housing absolutely prohibits major development projects that could displace people from their homes. Safeguarding the right to adequate housing, however, comes before a discussion of eviction.

Other human rights

In addition to the right to adequate housing, a number of other human rights offer legal protection against being arbitrarily displaced. These are in particular the right to freedom of movement and residence, the right to private life and home, and the right to property. While much can be said about each of these human rights and their 'protective capacity' with regard to evictions, space restrictions do not allow thorough analysis.[36] The following concise discussion, however, suffices to indicate that significant protection from arbitrary displacement derives from, in addition to the right to adequate housing, several civil human rights.

Freedom of movement and residence, laid down in each of the main international and regional human rights instruments,[37] includes the right, subject to lawful restriction, for every person who is residing lawfully in the territory of a state to move freely and to choose his or her place of residence within the whole territory of that state.[38] According to the Human Rights Committee (HRC), the monitoring body for the International Covenant on Civil and Political Rights (ICCPR),[39] the right to reside in a place of one's choice within the territory 'includes protection against all forms of forced internal displacement'.[40] Indeed, the right to move freely implies the right *not* to move – the right to remain or stay in the place of one's choice. Thus, subject to permissible limitations, the freedom of movement implicitly guarantees protection from being displaced or evicted.[41] In the case of *Yanomami Community v. Brazil* (1985),[42] for example, the Inter-American Commission on Human Rights (IACmHR) found that the displacement of the Yanomami Indians from their ancestral territory, in the context of a plan of exploitation of natural resources in and development of the Amazon region, amounted to a violation of several human rights, including the right to residence and movement (article VIII of the American Declaration of the Rights and Duties of Man).[43]

The rights to private (and family) life and home,[44] which must be guaranteed against all arbitrary interference and attack, whether emanating from state authorities or other (natural or legal) persons,[45] are other human rights offering a considerable extent of legal protection from arbitrary displacement. Although these human rights have historically not been understood by the HRC in the first place as 'a bulwark against forced movement' but rather as 'a component of a wider "right to privacy"' (McFadden, 1996 p. 39), the case law of international and regional human rights bodies indicates that these rights, particularly the right to respect for the home, offer legal protection against various forms of displacement and forced eviction, including state-conducted searches and raids, and destruction of housing.[46] The term 'home' indicates the 'place where a person resides or carries out his usual occupation'.[47] In 2005, the HRC explicitly clarified in its Concluding Observations on Kenya that the practice of forcible eviction of thousands of inhabitants from informal settlements, in Nairobi and elsewhere in the country, without proper consultation and notification 'arbitrarily interferes with the Covenant rights of the victims of such evictions, especially their rights under article 17 [rights to private and family life and home] of the Covenant'.[48]

The right to property, laid down in regional human rights treaties only,[49] guarantees protection against arbitrary forms of displacement and eviction where such situations involve the formal or de facto expropriation (or deprivation) of property, including property destruction. Indeed, it is clear that the forced eviction of people from their homes renders the property in question useless, in particular when the housing is destroyed.[50] This reasoning is affirmed in the case law of the regional human rights bodies.[51] For example, in a case concerning the Endorois indigenous community in Kenya (2009),[52] the African Commission on Human and Peoples' Rights was of the opinion that the displacement of the pastoralist community from their ancestral homeland in central Kenya by the Kenyan government, for the creation of a national reserve and tourist facilities, violated a number of human rights enshrined in the African Charter on Human and Peoples' Rights (ACHPR), including the right to property (article 14). In the view of the Commission:

> [T]raditional possession of land by indigenous people has the equivalent effect as that of a state-granted full property title …, the Endorois community has a right to property with regard to its ancestral land, the possessions attached to it, and their animals.[53]

The Commission subsequently noted that 'access roads, gates, game lodges and a hotel have all been built on the ancestral land of the Endorois community around Lake Bogoria and imminent mining operations also threaten to cause irreparable damage to the land'.[54] While any limitations on the right to property must be proportionate to a legitimate need, and should be the least restrictive measures possible, the Commission found that in the present case, the Kenyan government unlawfully evicted the Endorois from their land and destroyed their possessions in the pursuit of creating a game reserve. The displacement of the Endorois and the denial of their property rights was considered disproportionate to any public need served by the reserve.[55] Even if the game reserve was a legitimate aim and served a public need, according to the Commission this aim could have been accomplished by alternative means: 'from the evidence submitted both orally and in writing, it is clear that the community was willing to work with the Government in a way that respected their property rights, even if a game reserve was being created.'[56] No effective participation was allowed for the Endorois, they did not enjoy any reasonable benefit, and no environmental and social impact assessment was carried out prior to the displacement.[57] The Commission concluded that the right to property had been severely encroached upon. It called on the Kenyan government to recognize rights of ownership to the Endorois, to restore their historic land and to pay adequate compensation to the community for the loss suffered.[58]

A similar view with regard to the right to property in relation to indigenous people and DID can be found in Latin America. In various cases, including *Mayagna (Sumo) Awas Tingni Community v. Nicaragua* (2001),[59] *Yakye Axa Indigenous Community v. Paraguay* (2005),[60] *Sawhoyamaxa Indigenous Community v. Paraguay* (2006)[61] and *Saramaka People v. Suriname* (2007),[62] the IACmHR found violations of the right to property (article 21 of the ACHR) of indigenous communities, who were forced to abandon their ancestral lands because the state authorities granted concessions to third parties for the exploration and exploitation of natural resources.[63]

As these property cases indirectly indicate, the greatest weakness of the right to property as a protection mechanism against forced movement lies in the requirement of house or land ownership. Although the concept of property has been interpreted in a broad way by the regional human rights bodies, a large part of the world's population lacks legal or legalizable property ownership. The unequal distribution of property within and among nations means that it is often the most marginalized and vulnerable groups of society who cannot rely on the protection offered by the property right and therefore bear the greatest risk of becoming victims of displacement.[64]

The human right not to be arbitrarily displaced

Important legal protection against arbitrary forms of displacement and eviction is guaranteed by the right to adequate housing, the right to freedom of movement, the right to respect for private life and home, and the right to property. These human rights, the right to property excluded because of the aforementioned ownership requirement, are automatically interfered with in every displacement situation irrespective of the particular circumstances. It should be noted that an 'interference' with a human right does not necessarily amount to a 'violation' of that right, since interferences are lawful if they respect the conditions and procedural limitations determined in the law. Because of this automatic interference, it can be concluded that these human rights, with their respective protective capacities, jointly imply a free-standing or autonomous 'human right not to be arbitrarily displaced', which protects every person from being compelled to leave his or her home in an *arbitrary* way, meaning in violation of domestic law, in the absence of a legitimate aim (such as the public interest), when not necessary to achieve the legitimate aim pursued or when not proportionate to that aim. A free-standing or autonomous right means a right that exists independently from other, underlying rights.

Indeed, the right not to be arbitrarily displaced has been explicitly recognized in several international and regional legal instruments, most of which, however, have no legally binding character.[65] In other words, the right not to be displaced can be considered as an *emerging* right in terms of international law, implicitly grounded in hard law (legally binding) and explicitly recognized in soft law (not strictly legally binding). It exists 'to some extent' in the law without being fully developed.[66]

Since the right not to be displaced is derived from other, well-established human rights, its substance is already covered by those rights. Nevertheless, the recognition of displacement as an independent phenomenon through a free-standing human right laid down in a legally binding instrument may effectively enhance the protection of people against forced movement in practice. Its added value would essentially be brought about by the 'naming effect': restating and clarifying a legal norm in a legally binding or otherwise authoritative instrument, thereby defining explicitly what is implicit in international law, is likely to significantly strengthen existing protection.

At the preventive level, the explicit recognition in hard law of the right not to be displaced would have a considerable symbolic value. It would give a clear signal to state and non-state actors actively involved in the displacement of people by explicitly affirming that arbitrary displacement is a gross violation of international human rights law, therefore is strictly prohibited, and can under no circumstances be tolerated. In addition, it would serve as a solid legal frame guiding responsible actors on their various duties in relation to the prevention of arbitrary displacement. It may encourage the international community and individual states to renew efforts to prevent displacement where possible, and pressure states to translate the right into specific obligations and responsibilities, in legislation, policy and practice.

The express recognition of the right not to be displaced may also contribute to raising international awareness about the illegality of many displacement situations. Certainly, potential victims of arbitrary displacement would be empowered by its existence: it would serve as a useful tool in their relations with state authorities and may thereby alleviate their struggle against unlawful state conduct or policy decisions.

At the remedial level, the right not to be displaced may provide victims of arbitrary displacement wishing to hold their states accountable with a stronger legal basis to plead their case. Both at the national and at the international level, it may lessen the effort required to bring successful claims for remedy and reparation before judicial or quasi-judicial bodies, since a 'detour' through other human rights would no longer be necessary.

The existence and promotion of an explicit, legally binding right not to be displaced, which takes into account the full complexity of displacement, may overall lead to increased international attention for the underlying basic aspiration – to remain in one's home. It would highlight a global issue that is still too often ignored at the national level, thereby helping to identify governmental conduct as illegal and potentially contributing to constraining state behaviour.

Conclusion

The existing international legal framework for the protection of people against arbitrary forms of DID is well developed. Several well-established human rights guarantee legal protection against unjust displacement. In particular the right to adequate housing, the freedom of movement and residence, and the right to private life and home offer significant legal protection and can moreover be said to imply a 'right not to be arbitrarily displaced'. In addition, several guidelines on DID spell out the circumstances under which displacement can be carried out in a lawful way.

International human rights law does not prohibit evictions necessitated by development projects altogether nor does it consider such evictions per definition as sacrifices for a good cause. Human rights law instead distinguishes between arbitrary or unlawful evictions on the one hand, and non-arbitrary or lawful evictions on the other. In order to be in accordance with human rights law, an eviction must not be carried out before all feasible alternatives are explored. Adequate compensation must be provided for affected property and where reasonably possible the people affected must be provided with adequate alternative housing. In addition, a number of procedural guarantees, for example relating to information, consultation and legal remedies, must be complied with.

In sum, the law at the international level is clear and can reasonably be said to offer decent protection against arbitrary forms of displacement caused by development projects. Nonetheless, this protection could be further reinforced by the explicit recognition of an autonomous human right not to be displaced in a legally binding international instrument.

Notes

1 See also Kanbur, R., 2003. Development economics and the compensation principle. *International Social Science Journal*, 55(1), pp. 27–35.

2 See in this regard Penz, P., Drydyk, J. and Bose, P.S., 2011. *Displacement by development: ethics, rights and responsibilities*. Cambridge: Cambridge University Press, pp. 142 and following.

3 See on this point Ferris, E., 2012. Development and displacement: hidden loser from a forgotten agenda. *World disasters report 2012: focus on forced migration and displacement*. Geneva: IFRC.

4 Guiding Principles on Internal Displacement (GPID), E/CN.4/1998/53/Add.2.

5 Principle 6(2)(c) of the GPID.

6 Kampala Convention, African Union, 23 October 2009.

7 The text of the Protocol on the Protection and Assistance to Internally Displaced Persons is available at www.refworld.org/pdfid/52384fe44.pdf [Accessed 1 July 2014].

8 The text of the Pact on Security, Stability and Development in the Great Lakes Region is available at www.refworld.org/pdfid/52384fe44.pdf [Accessed 1 July 2014].

9 Principle 7 of the GPID; article 10 of the Kampala Convention; and article 5 of the IDP Protocol to the Great Lakes Pact. Regarding compensation, see also Principle 16 of the Pinheiro Principles on Housing and Property Restitution for Refugees and Displaced Persons, E/CN.4/Sub.2/2005/17, 28 June 2005, pleading for a similar treatment of customary owners (as well as tenants and other non-owners) as people possessing formal ownership rights.

10 Principle 9 of the GPID; article 4(5) of the Kampala Convention; and article 4(1)(c) of the IDP Protocol to the Great Lakes Pact.

11 OECD, adopted in Paris in 1992. See in particular Policy Objectives, first policy consideration, 6:

> Involuntary population displacement should be avoided or minimized whenever feasible by exploring all viable alternative project designs. In every case, the alternative to refrain from carrying out the project (the 'non-action' alternative) should seriously be considered, and people's needs and environmental protection must be given due weight in the decision-making process.

12 Report of the (former) UN Special Rapporteur on Human Rights and Population Transfer, Mr Al-Khasawneh, E/CN.4/Sub.2/1997/23, 27 June 1997, on the freedom of movement and population transfer. See in particular para. 68:

> In the context of development programmes, population transfers are lawful if they are non-discriminatory and are based upon the will of the people, and do not deprive a 'people' of their means of subsistence. The general consent of the population sought to be transferred must be obtained by means of dialogue and negotiation with the elected representatives of the population on terms of equality, fairness and transparency, and equivalent land, housing, occupation and employment, in addition to adequate monetary compensation, must be provided. Moreover, such transfers are justified by the public interest.

13 Expert seminar on the practice of forced evictions, Geneva, 11–13 June 1997. *The practice of forced evictions: comprehensive human rights guidelines on development-based displacement*. See in particular para. 17:

> States should refrain, to the maximum possible extent, from compulsorily acquiring housing or land, unless such acts are legitimate and necessary and designed to facilitate the enjoyment of human rights through, for instance, measures of land reform or redistribution. If, as a last resort, States consider themselves compelled to undertake proceedings of expropriation or compulsory acquisition, such action shall be: (a) determined and envisaged by law and norms regarding forced eviction, in so far as these are consistent internationally recognized human rights; (b) solely for the purpose of protecting the general welfare in a democratic society; (c) reasonable and proportional; and (d) in accordance with the present Guidelines.

14 World Bank OP 4.12, December 2001, revised February 2011. See in particular para. 2(a): 'Involuntary resettlement should be avoided where feasible, or minimized, exploring all viable alternative project designs.'

15 Annex 1 of the report of the Special Rapporteur on adequate housing as a component of the right to an adequate standard of living, A/HRC/4/18, 5 February 2007. See in particular para. 21:

> States shall ensure that evictions only occur in exceptional circumstances. Evictions require full justification given their adverse impact on a wide range of internationally recognized human rights. Any eviction must be (a) authorized by law; (b) carried out in accordance with international human rights law; (c) undertaken solely for the purpose of promoting the general welfare; (d) reasonable and proportional; (e) regulated so as to ensure full and fair compensation and rehabilitation; and (f) carried out in accordance with the present guidelines. The protection provided by these procedural requirements applies to all vulnerable persons and affected groups, irrespective of whether they hold title to home and property under domestic law.

See also paras 37–44.

16 UN General Assembly, A/RES/41/128, 1986, Declaration on the right to development, article 1(1).

17 On the right to development, see Kirchmeier, F., 2006. The right to development – where do we stand? State of the debate on the right to development. *Dialogue on Globalization Occasional Papers*, 23; Marks, S., 2004. The human right to development: between rhetoric and reality. *Harvard Human Rights Journal*, 17, pp. 137–168.

18 See Leckie, S., 1995. *When push comes to shove: forced evictions and human rights*. Geneva: Habitat International Coalition, pp. 33–60; Leckie, S., 1999. New United Nations regulations on forced evictions. *Third World Planning Review*, 21(1), p. 41, arguing that housing NGOs should invest more energy in the human rights domain; COHRE, 2007. *Fair play for housing rights – mega-events, Olympic Games and housing rights*. Geneva: COHRE, pp. 30–39 and 58–62. See also UN Commission on Human Rights, 2004/28, 16 April 2004, Resolution on the prohibition of forced evictions, para. 1: 'that the practice of forced eviction that is contrary to laws that are in conformity with international human rights standards constitutes a gross violation of a broad range of human rights, in particular the right to adequate housing.'

19 ICESCR, 16 December 1966, 993 UNTS 3. Article 11(1) reads: 'The States Parties to the present Covenant recognize the right of everyone to an adequate standard of living for himself and his family, including adequate ... housing.' This human rights provision has been often referred to by researchers in the field of development-induced displacement and resettlement (DIDR). See, for example, Robinson, W.C., 2003. *Risks and rights: the causes, consequences, and challenges of development-induced displacement*. Washington, DC: The Brookings Institution–SAIS Project on Internal Displacement; Barutciski, M., 2006. International law and development-induced displacement and resettlement. In: C.J. de Wet, ed. 2006. *Development-induced displacement: problems, policies and people*. Oxford/New York: Berghahn, p. 75; Norwegian Refugee Council, 2011. *Beyond squatters' rights: durable solutions and development-induced displacement in Monrovia, Liberia*. Oslo: Norwegian Refugee Council, p. 14; Terminski, B., 2012. *Development-induced displacement and resettlement: theoretical frameworks and current challenges*. Geneva: University of Geneva, p. 93.

20 CESCR, 13 December 1991, General Comment No. 4: the right to adequate housing (Art. 11(1)); CESCR, 20 May 1997, General Comment No. 7: the right to adequate housing (Art. 11(1)): forced evictions.

21 CESCR, General Comment No. 4, para. 8.

22 Ibid., para. 8(a).

23 Ibid., para. 18.

24 See ibid., para. 10. See also CESCR, 14 December 1990, General Comment No. 3: the nature of states parties obligations (Art. 2(1)), para. 9: 'the fact that realization over time, or in other words progressively, is foreseen under the Covenant should not be misinterpreted as depriving the obligation of all meaningful content.'
25 CESCR, General Comment No. 7, para. 8.
26 Ibid., para. 3.
27 Ibid., paras 5–7.
28 Ibid., para. 3.
29 See ibid., para. 2.
30 See in this regard, Kälin, W. and Künzli, J., 2009. *The law of international human rights protection*. Oxford: Oxford University Press, pp. 114–120.
31 The Committee gives the examples of persistent non-payment of rent and damage to rented property without reasonable cause. On the other hand, no such proper justification exists where evictions are carried out as a punitive measure: CESCR, General Comment No. 7, paras 11–12. The question has been raised whether the 'opaqueness' of the formulation of the justification requirement is satisfactory. The Committee indeed does not provide an (exhaustive) list of justifications. While this vagueness or generality does not offer much guidance to states wishing to comply with the provisions, it might on the other hand be the appropriate mechanism for preventing abuse. It also enhances the importance of the conditions of reasonability and proportionality. See Langford, M. and Plessis, J. du, 2005. Dignity in the rubble? Forced evictions and human rights law. *COHRE Working Paper*, June 2005, pp. 15–16.
32 For a detailed discussion of the elements of reasonability and proportionality, see Morel, M., 2014. *The right not to be displaced in international law*. Antwerp/Cambridge: Intersentia, pp. 294–299.
33 CESCR General Comment No. 7, para. 15, and more generally, paras 10–16. See UN Habitat and Office of the UN High Commissioner for Human Rights (OHCHR), 2009. *Fact Sheet No. 21/Rev.1: the right to adequate housing*. Geneva: United Nations, pp. 5–6; Langford, M. and Plessis, J. du, 2005. Dignity in the rubble? Forced evictions and human rights law. *COHRE Working Paper*, June 2005, p. 14: the requirement of procedural due process implies that collective evictions may be presumed to be arbitrary and therefore in violation with the right to housing.
34 On the importance of consultation and participation of the affected people, see World Commission on Dams, 2000. *Dams and development: a new framework for decision-making*. London: Earthscan, pp. 208–211.
35 See UN Habitat and OHCHR, 2009. *Fact Sheet No. 21/Rev.1: the right to adequate housing*. Geneva: United Nations, p. 7.
36 See Morel, M., 2014. *The right not to be displaced in international law*. Antwerp/Cambridge: Intersentia, pp. 103–201.
37 Article 12 of the International Covenant on Civil and Political Rights (ICCPR), 16 December 1966, 999 UNTS 171; article 2 of Protocol 4 to the European Convention on Human Rights (ECHR), 4 November 1950, 213 UNTS 222; article 22 of the American Convention on Human Rights (ACHR), 22 November 1969, 1144 UNTS 123; article 12 of the African Charter on Human and Peoples' Rights (ACHPR), 27 June 1981, 21 ILM 58.
38 Article 12(1) ICCPR; article 2(1) of Protocol 4 ECHR; article 22(1) Asian Human Rights Commission (AHCR); and article 12(1) ACHPR. Whether a person resides 'lawfully in the territory of a State' is a matter of domestic law and therefore depends on the national access and residence criteria. See Human Rights Committee (HRC), 2 November 1999, General Comment No. 27: freedom of movement (Art. 12), para. 4.
39 ICCPR, 16 December 1966, 999 UNTS 171.
40 HRC, General Comment No. 27, para. 7.

41 This has been affirmed by judicial and quasi-judicial bodies in individual cases. See, for example, Inter-American Commission on Human Rights (IACmHR) 16 October 1996, *María Mejía v. Guatemala*, Case 10.553, Report No. 32/96; Inter-American Court of Human Rights (IACtHR) 15 September 2005, *Mapiripán Massacre v. Colombia*, (ser. C) No. 134; IACtHR 1 July 2006, *Ituango Massacres v. Colombia*, (ser. C) No. 148; African Commission on Human and Peoples' Rights (ACmHPR) 11 May 2000, *Malawi African Association and Others v. Mauritania*, Comm. Nos. 54/91, 61/91, 98/93, 164/97–196/97 and 210/98; ACmHPR 29 May 2003, *D.R. Congo v. Burundi, Rwanda and Uganda*, Comm. No. 227/99; ACmHPR 27 May 2009, *COHRE v. Sudan*, Comm. No. 296/05. In the latter case, the African Commission expressly made the link between the freedom of movement and displacement:

> The right to protection from displacement is derived from the right to freedom of movement and choice of residence contemplated in the African Charter and other international instruments. Displacement by force, and without legitimate or legal basis, as is the case in the present Communication, is a denial of the right to freedom of movement and choice of residence.
>
> (para. 189)

42 IACmHR 5 March 1985, *Yanomami Community v. Brazil*, Case No. 7615.

43 For more details see Morel, M., 2014. *The right not to be displaced in international law*. Antwerp/Cambridge: Intersentia, pp. 122–124.

44 The right to private life and home is laid down in article 17 ICCPR; article 8 ECHR; and article 11 ACHR. No provision on the right to privacy can be found in the ACHPR.

45 HRC, 8 April 1988, General Comment No. 16: the right to respect of privacy, family, home and correspondence, and protection of honour and reputation (Art. 17), para. 1.

46 See, for example, HRC 20 July 2009, *Maral Yklymova v. Turkmenistan*, Communication No. 1460/2006; European Commission on Human Rights (ECmHR) 10 July 1976, *Cyprus v. Turkey*, 6780/74 and 6950/75; European Court of Human Rights (ECtHR) 30 August 1996, *Akdivar and Others v. Turkey*, 21893/93; ECtHR 28 November 1997, *Mentes and Others v. Turkey*, 23186/94; ECtHR 24 April 1998, *Selçuk and Asker v. Turkey*, 23184/94, 23185/94; ECtHR 12 July 2005, *Moldovan and Others v. Romania*, 41138/98, 64320/01; ECtHR 27 May 2004, *Connors v. The United Kingdom*, 66746/01; ECtHR, 18 November 2004, *Prokopovich v. Russia*, 58255/00; ECtHR 13 May 2008, *McCann v. The United Kingdom*, 19009/04; ECtHR 9 October 2007, *Stanková v. Slovakia*, 7205/02; IACtHR 1 July 2006, *Ituango Massacres v. Colombia*, (ser. C) No. 148; ACmHPR 27 May 2009, *COHRE v. Sudan*, Comm. No. 296/05. The latter case involved an interference with the right to family life under article 18(1) ACHPR. The Commission held: 'Ensuring protection of the family also requires that States refrain from any action that will affect the family unit, including arbitrary separation of family members and involuntary displacement of families' (para. 214). The eviction of the victims from their homes and the displacement of a large number of civilians constituted a threat, according to the Commission, to 'the very foundation of the family and renders the enjoyment of the right to family life difficult' (para. 216).

47 HRC, General Comment No. 16, para. 5.

48 HRC, CCPR/CO/83/KEN, 24 March 2005, Concluding Observations on Kenya. Concluding Observations are the outcome of the consideration by the HRC of reports submitted by state parties under article 40 of the ICCPR.

49 Article 1 Protocol 1 ECHR; article 21 ACHR; and article 14 ACHPR.

50 See Thiele, B., 2003. Litigating against forced evictions under the American Convention of Human Rights. *Netherlands Quarterly on Human Rights*, 21(3), pp. 463–477. This article was adopted from an *amicus curiae* brief submitted to the IACmHR with respect to Report No. 75/01, Case 12.266, *El Aro, Ituango – Colombia* (10 October 2001), 5–6.

51 See, for example, ECtHR 30 August 1996, *Akdivar and Others v. Turkey*, 21893/93; ECtHR 28 November 1997, *Mentes and Others v. Turkey*, 23186/94; ECtHR 24 April 1998, *Selçuk and Asker v. Turkey*, 23184/94, 23185/94; ECtHR 16 November 2000, *Bilgin v. Turkey*, 23819/94; ECtHR 30 January 2001, *Dulas v. Turkey*, 25801/94; ECtHR 18 June 2002, *Orhan v. Turkey*, 25656/94; ECtHR 24 July 2003, *Yöyler v. Turkey*, 26973/95; ECtHR 8 January 2004, *Ayder and Others v. Turkey*, 23656/94. In these cases, the Court systematically stated that the deliberate destruction of houses resulting in the displacement of the villagers constituted 'particularly grave and unjustified interferences' with their right to peaceful enjoyment of possessions as guaranteed by article 1 of Protocol 1 ECtHR (for example, *Selçuk and Asker v. Turkey*, para. 86; *Bilgin v. Turkey*, para. 108; *Ayder and Others v. Turkey*, para. 119); IACtHR 1 July 2006, *Ituango Massacres v. Colombia*, (ser. C) No. 148; ACmHPR 4 June 2004, *Bah Ould Rabah v. Mauritania*, 197/97; ACmHPR 29 July 2010, *COHRE v. Sudan*, Comm. No. 296/05.

52 ACmHPR 25 November 2009, *Centre for Minority Rights Development (Kenya) and Minority Rights Group International on behalf of Endorois Welfare Council v. Kenya*, 276/2003. See Morel, M., 2014. *The right not to be displaced in international law*. Antwerp/Cambridge: Intersentia, pp. 193–196.

53 ACmHPR, 25 November 2009, *Centre for Minority Rights Development (Kenya) and Minority Rights Group International on behalf of Endorois Welfare Council v. Kenya*, 276/2003, paras 184 and 209.

54 Ibid., para. 210.

55 Ibid., para. 214.

56 Ibid., para. 215.

57 Ibid., para. 228.

58 Ibid., Recommendations (a), (b) and (c).

59 IACtHR 31 August 2001, *Mayagna (Sumos) Awas Tingni Community v. Nicaragua*, (ser. C) No. 79.

60 IACtHR 17 June 2005, *Yakye Axa Indigenous Community v. Paraguay*, (ser. C) No. 125.

61 IACtHR 29 March 2006, *Sawhoyamaxa Indigenous Community v. Paraguay*, (ser. C) No. 146.

62 IACtHR 28 November 2007, *Saramaka People v. Suriname*, (ser. C) No. 172.

63 For more details see Morel, M., 2014. *The right not to be displaced in international law*. Antwerp/Cambridge: Intersentia, pp. 190–193.

64 See in this regard UN Habitat, 2011. *Forced evictions: global crisis, global solutions*. Nairobi: UN Habitat, p. 64.

65 Principle 6 of the GPID, E/CN.4/1998/53/Add.2; article 4(1) of the London Declaration of International Law Principles on Internally Displaced Persons, adopted by the 69th Conference of the International Law Association, 25–29 July 2000; article 4(4) of the Convention for the Protection and Assistance of Internally Displaced Persons in Africa (Kampala Convention), African Union, 23 October 2009; and principle 5(1) of the United Nations Principles on Housing and Property Restitution for Refugees and Displaced Persons (Pinheiro principles), E/CN.4/Sub.2/2005/17, 2005, endorsed Sub-Com. res. 2005/21, E/CN.4/Sub.2/RES/2005/21. See also UN Sub-Commission on Prevention of Discrimination and Protection of Minorities, 1998/9, 20 August 1998, Resolution on forced evictions, Preamble; and UN Commission on Human Rights, 2004/28, 16 April 2004, Resolution on prohibition of forced evictions, Preamble, proclaiming that 'every woman, man and child has the right to a secure place to live in peace and dignity, which includes *the right not to be evicted* unlawfully, arbitrarily or on a discriminatory basis from their home, land or community' (own emphasis).

66 On the right not to be displaced more extensively, see Morel, M., Stavropoulou, M. and Durieux, J.-F., 2012. The history and status of the right not to be displaced. *Forced Migration Review*, 41, pp. 5–7; Morel, M., 2014. *The right not to be displaced in international law*. Antwerp/Cambridge: Intersentia.

References

Cernea, M., 1996. Bridging the research divide: studying development oustees. In: T. Allen, ed. *In search of cool ground: war, flight and homecoming in Northeast Africa*. London: James Currey, pp. 293–317.

Kälin, W., 2008. *Guiding principles on internal displacement: annotations*. Washington, DC: The American Society of International Law.

Langford, M. and Plessis, J. du, 2005. Dignity in the rubble? Forced evictions and human rights law. *COHRE Working Paper*, June 2005.

Leckie, S., 1995. *When push comes to shove: forced evictions and human rights*. Geneva: Habitat International Coalition.

McFadden, P., 1996. The right to stay. *Vanderbilt Journal of Transnational Law*, 29(1), pp. 1–44.

Penz, P., 2002. Development, displacement and ethics. *Forced Migration Review*, 12, pp. 4–5.

Robinson, W.C., 2004. Minimizing development-induced displacement. *Migration Information Source*, 1 January 2004. Available at www.migrationinformation.org/feature/display.cfm?ID=194 [Accessed 1 July 2014].

10 Destroying a way of life

The Forest Rights Act of India and land dispossession of indigenous peoples

Indrani Sigamany

Introduction

This chapter contains a narrative that is not new. The story concerns land displacement of indigenous peoples, some of whom are nomadic, and whose occupations such as hunting and gathering and herding animals are a continuation of ancient lifestyles. Land dispossession of indigenous peoples is a story that is occurring globally, and has been happening for centuries, resulting in impoverishment: 'While indigenous peoples make up around 370 million of the world's population (some five percent) they constitute around one third of the world's 900 million extremely poor rural people' (UN, 2010, no page number). When examining the issues of land rights of indigenous peoples, it rapidly becomes apparent that this area is riddled with contradictions and anomalies. The laws of land ownership for example presume private individual ownership, and indigenous peoples, especially mobile indigenous peoples, traditionally use land collectively not individually, and do not necessarily possess titles to the land they use, making land rights law relatively inaccessible for them. In this chapter I argue that true access to justice requires more than merely enacting new legislation.

Access to justice is defined by the United Nations Development Programme (UNDP) as 'much more than improving an individual's access to courts, or guaranteeing legal representation. It must be defined in terms of ensuring that legal and judicial outcomes are just and equitable' (UNDP, 2004, p. 6). For indigenous peoples struggling against dispossession of their lands and livelihoods, access to justice not only ensures their tenurial rights, but also contributes positively to poverty alleviation (Anderson, 2003, p. 23). This study critically examines the internal displacement debate in the context of human rights legislation and explores whether access to justice is improved by social justice legislation such as the Forest Rights Act 2006 (FRA) of India. This chapter is divided into three sections. In the first section I begin with a description of indigenous peoples, and explore the particular problem of displacement that they are faced with by the emergence of the land conservation movement and the development of extractive industries. In the second section I trace the evolution of human rights norms, which, since the 1970s, has been the foundation for 'the elimination of extreme poverty as a moral imperative' (Gauri and Gloppen, 2012, p. 486). I posit that these norms have created positive change for indigenous rights and have led to development of legal architecture based on principles of social justice and human rights. In the third section, using two contemporary case studies of land displacement of two groups of forest people in Odisha and in Madhya Pradesh, I examine empirically how the FRA of 2006, which is social justice legislation in India, affects indigenous forest peoples. Applying a UNDP typology for Access to Justice (UNDP, 2004) as a theoretical framework, I analyse socio-legal indicators for positive change resulting from the FRA. I compare these indicators to evidence that the FRA's requirements are being ignored by both the Indian government and the corporate sector, who are prioritising economic development over indigenous livelihoods and land rights. This in turn could be propelling forest peoples into vulnerability and further impoverishment. I conclude the chapter with a discussion of whether this legislation offers indigenous peoples a tool with which to advocate for their rights against displacement, or whether in reality it makes this community more vulnerable.

Indigenous peoples and displacement

Indigenous peoples were ancient inhabitants of the land before the land was either colonised or had been established as separate Nation States (Gilbert and Doyle, 2011, p. 5). There are around 370 million indigenous peoples, comprising 5,000 groups, living in about 70 countries (Impe, 2011, p. 12). Among indigenous peoples, mobile indigenous peoples comprise a sub category, who earn their livelihoods from activities that require a nomadic way of life (Dana Standing Committee, 2002). Examples of mobile indigenous peoples are pastoralists who herd animals; hunters and gatherers; and coastal nomads who sail and fish, though an increasing number of them are resorting to either semi nomadic or completely settled lives. In India, indigenous peoples are ancient communities who reside in the hills and forests. The government uses the word Adivasi or tribal to refer to them. Kurup (2008, p. 91) reports that, according to the 2001 Government of India Census, 8.2 per cent of India's population is considered as tribal.

During and after the colonial period in India, tribal communities had an unfortunate history of land dispossession and impoverishment. Initially, under colonial rule, their lands were converted to state property as a source of revenue in the 1850s (Gadgil, 1992, p. 102; Veron and Fehr, 2011, p. 285). Excluded from their forest-based livelihoods, and from their lands, which were being 'eroded by the penetration of market forces, Adivasis were increasingly engulfed in debt and lost their land to outsiders, often being reduced to the position of agricultural labourers, sharecroppers and rack rented tenants' (Chandra *et al.*, 2008, p. 135). The most detrimental legislation, passed by the British in 1871, was the Criminal Tribes Act that 'notified about 150 tribes around India as criminal, giving police wide powers to arrest them and monitor their movements' (D'Souza, 1999, p. 3576). Though the criminal Tribes Act was annulled in 1952 several years after independence (Radhakrishna, 2009), the attitudes of police and the general mainstream population have retained an anti tribal prejudice, often perceiving indigenous peoples as inferior and criminal. D'Souza (1999, p. 3576) points out that Adivasis, who were traditional hunters and gatherers, when excluded from the forests were forced to forage elsewhere, and if found by the police were charged with 'stealing'. Furthermore, their culture was being undermined by missionaries and colonists. Legislation such as the Indian Forest Act 1927 (Lim and Anand, 2004) displaced traditional forest dependents and dwellers from forest lands reserved for economic timber harvesting for the colonial government, and legalised the expropriation of forest lands from tribal and other forest peoples. The 1927 law is not to be confused with the FRA of 2006, which legislates the restoration of land rights of forest peoples and forest workers.

Pressure from growing populations, their need for food and therefore more demand for agricultural land, often encroaches on forest lands. Growing extractive industries such as mining for economic development in mineral rich forest lands have been a threat to forest peoples in India both before and after independence. In addition to extractive industries, biodiversity conservation as a movement has unintentionally displaced forest peoples. In many parts of the world including India, efforts at community conservation are often impeded by processes of development, and competition between human beings and wildlife (Pathak, 2009). This process of destruction of habitats has happened universally and not only in India. For the world of conservation, this connotes the disappearance of flora, fauna and competition for shrinking space between human beings and wildlife (Chatty and Colchester, 2002, p. 3; Chatty, 2002).

The Wildlife Protection Act of 1972 in India, which created 'inviolate protected areas', excluded forest dwellers, and aimed at protecting wildlife. It was amended in 2002, to permit tribal peoples who were dependent on the forests to have usufruct rights. The amendments also introduced the concept of participative community management of buffer zones outside the forests, and of 'Community Reserves'. This decentralised governance created new powers for local village decision making in the form of governance committees called *gram sabhas*. The amendments extended the *gram sabha* remit to 'safeguard and preserve the traditions and customs of the people, their cultural identity, community resources and the customary mode of dispute resolution' (Government of India, 2011). This was the start of more rights-based norms to land rights in India, inclusive of greater participative and democratic policies, paving the way for a more just social legislation in the form of the FRA of 2006.

This normative progression reflected the universal evolution of rights-based jurisprudence, which offered indigenous peoples a legal tool to counter displacement, to rectify historical injustices and lost territories. This new awareness of the need to develop protective human rights norms grew dramatically after the Second World War, strengthening the rights of indigenous peoples. It included both international and national human rights instruments, aspects of which can be used to advocate legally for land rights of indigenous peoples. These human rights instruments 'establish principles and minimum rules for administration of justice and offer fairly detailed guidance to states on human rights and justice' (Galligan and Sandler, 2004, p. 24). In the section below, I do not comprehensively list all legislation that comprises a normative framework for land rights, but highlight a few of the most important enactments pertaining to land rights that are used by indigenous peoples.

A human rights normative framework

The Universal Declaration of Human Rights (UN, 1948) recognises equality, dignity and respect for all individuals, and these rights are 'inalienable' and absolute (UN, 1948). Revolutionary for marginalised communities such as indigenous communities, its basic principles have informed subsequent international and national legislation. The Convention on the Elimination of Racial Discrimination (CERD) of 1965 applies to all indigenous individuals and groups and resolves 'to adopt measures to eliminate racial discrimination in all its forms' (OHCR, 1965). In its General Recommendation 23 on indigenous peoples, the CERD urged States to make sure 'that no decisions directly relating to [indigenous] rights and interests are taken without their informed consent' (Gilbert, 2007, p. 222). Signatory states must submit a report to the UN Office of the High Commissioner for Human Rights (OHCHR) on the status of discrimination in their country.

The International Labour Organisation (ILO) Convention on Indigenous and Tribal Peoples of 1989, No. 169 (ILO, 2003) contains a substantial component on land rights. The ILO Convention used the term 'self management' which was incorporated into newer legal standards such as the 2007 UN Declaration of the Rights of Indigenous Peoples, and the national FRA of 2006 in India, and has been used by indigenous and tribal peoples to fight against displacement and for self management of forest lands. The Dana Declaration of 2002 emerged as a response to increasing problems of displacement of mobile indigenous peoples (Dana Standing Committee, 2002). It was the first declaration unique to mobile indigenous peoples, and therefore constituted a milestone. Though not legally binding, it established the context for mobile indigenous peoples' rights, and it also raised international awareness of a group that has been marginalised through history. Once a government ratifies a treaty recognising rights of indigenous and tribal peoples, it has a responsibility to protect these rights, and to implement the legal principles fully (ILO, 2003). Since nomadic peoples use land and property collectively, the question of property rights is complicated. Their particular rights were expanded in the 2007 UN Declaration of Rights for Indigenous Peoples (The Declaration) which has been a landmark for indigenous peoples and especially for pastoralists, since it refers to communal land rights, collective usufruct rights and also customary land laws (Gilbert and Doyle, 2011). One of the most significant international legal norms has been Free and Prior Informed Consent (FPIC) found in The Declaration. This specifies a very definite obligation of the state, requiring governments to inform and obtain the consent of indigenous and tribal peoples before taking any action involving their lands and giving indigenous peoples veto rights to decisions concerning their lands.

Consistent with this international human rights normative development, a series of other social justice laws were passed in India including the National

Rural Employment Guarantee Act, 2005; Right to Information Act, 2005; Protection of Women From Domestic Violence Act, 2005; Right of Children to Free and Compulsory Education Act, 2009 (Sircar, 2012, p. 545), and the Forest Rights Act: Scheduled Tribes and Other Forest Dwellers (Recognition of Forest Rights) Act 2006 also known as the FRA (Government of India, 2012; Indian Tribal Heritage, 2013). The FRA, enacted by the Parliament of India, recognised usufruct and habitat rights of tribal and indigenous peoples. It was framed in progressive, rights-based language, and was the result of long and vigorous advocacy by forest dwellers and activists.

Case studies and socio-legal analysis

The FRA grants community and individual forest rights to forest tribes and other forest dwellers. It is a revolutionary land rights law in India, because it includes local democratic forest governance, and gives the community the right to conservation of their lands, and rights to minor forest produce which has been the basis of their traditional livelihoods. A crucial aspect of this law is that forest dwellers cannot be evicted from the forests over which they have claimed rights, especially 'till the recognition and verification procedure is completed' (Government of India, 2012). In India there have been many recent examples of clear violations of the FRA, however. The national newspaper *The Hindu* reported on 18 February 2013, that government officials destroyed 30 huts of the very isolated Baiga tribe leaving about 200 people homeless. They lived near the Bhoramdeo Reserve Forest, in the state of Orissa, sometimes known as Odisha. The Nehru government in 1947 records the Baiga community's presence for centuries in Odisha and the surrounding hills. The tribe had not been told that they would be evicted. The eviction, any potential plans of resettlement without prior land allocation and a lack of *gram sabha* consent, were all violations of the FRA. No reason was given by the Administration for the destruction of the community's homes, other than ensuring the 'safety of wildlife' (Sambhav, 2012).

On 15 February 2013, the Central government of India filed an affidavit in the Vedanta case, in which it took the position that it can acquire forest lands for the 'public interest' by 'extinguishing' tribal rights. Vedanta is a global mining company, planning to mine for bauxite in the Niyamgiri hills, which is sacred to the Dongria Kondh tribes in Odisha (Saikia, 2014, p. 18). This violated the provision in the FRA that maintains forest dwellers and tribal communities have the final say in allowing forest land diversion for mining and other projects. Furthermore, the affidavit sought to dilute the powers of the *gram sabha* who also had veto rights under the FRA (Natural Justice, 2013, p. 161). According to the FRA, forest dwellers cannot be resettled without the consent of the *gram sabha*. Furthermore, the affidavit claimed that consent is only necessary in cases in which 'displacement of large numbers of people' was involved, and which affected their 'quality of life' (Sambhav, 2012), though the text of the law itself contained no such exception.

In each of these cases the FRA was violated. I will concentrate only on the Vedanta case, in which the government diverted forest lands for non forest purposes. In doing so, the government circumvented the authority of the *gram sabha* and its eviction of the community under these circumstances was illegal. It also overrode the law's requirement for FPIC. Activists and the tribal populations were extremely concerned that this was the beginning of the erosion of the FRA, and everything that it was meant to protect (Dash and Khotari, 2013, p. 156; Natural Justice, 2013, p. 160).

When discussing a typology of fundamental elements of 'access to justice' below, I list the capacities that advance access to justice for marginalised communities such as indigenous peoples. This typology was developed by the UNDP (2004), and includes legal protection, legal awareness, legal aid and counsel, adjudication, enforcement, civil society and parliamentary oversight, which I define below. I support this list with a discussion of the Indian government's response to the FRA.

The first element identified in this typology is *legal protection*, referring to enactment of the law and provision of mechanisms to implement it, including entitlement to remedies for violations of the law. The FRA fulfils the first element of the typology by providing a comprehensive framework for identifying those who are protected, and establishing procedures under which rights may be asserted.

The second element of the typology is *legal awareness* on the part of disadvantaged people. This includes their understanding of their right to seek redress, to know which individuals and institutions are entrusted with the protection of their rights, and the procedures for claiming their rights. In the Vedanta case, the community began a protest that drew the support of civil society activists. The activists helped raise their awareness of rights and the procedures under the FRA. The FRA requires the government to educate the community about the law. The government has failed to educate both the applicable communities and its own government officials about the FRA (Sarin and Springate-Baginski, 2010), as is shown in the Vedanta case, in which the government also ignored the substance of the law by forwarding a proposal to divert forest lands in Odisha for the mining of bauxite (Dash and Khotari, 2013, p. 159). One of the particular challenges of providing access to justice through the FRA is that 85 per cent of the Adivasi population live below the poverty line (Bhengra *et al.*, 1999, p. 7), with lower literacy levels, making the formal legal system even more unfamiliar to them in comparison to their indigenous dispute resolution traditions. In addition, Adivasis, impoverished through land displacement, have fewer resources to pursue claims.

Legal aid and counsel is the third component and includes legal representation in formal legal proceedings. The constitution of India requires that free legal aid be provided to all those needing such services (Indian Constitution Part 4, article 39A). However, as with many of the promises embodied in the constitution, this is a right that is available more in theory than in practice. Galanter and Krishnan (2004, p. 793) point out that public interest litigation programmes in India have contributed to social change by raising 'public awareness of many issues, energised citizen action, ratcheted up governmental accountability, and enhanced the legitimacy of the judiciary'. However, the vast majority of poor people in India have no legal representation and lack resources, rendering them unable to claim their legal rights under either the FRA or any other law (Galanter, 1983. p. 8).

The fourth component is *adjudication*, which refers to the fora in which disputes are resolved and compensation determined. India has courts and other less formal bodies such as *lok adalats* which are people's courts. These are, however, expensive, overcrowded and slow.

> [T]he courts and tribunals where ordinary Indians might go for remedy and protection [of their rights] are beset with massive problems of delay, cost and ineffectiveness. Potential users avoid the courts; in spite of a long standing reputation for litigiousness, existing evidence suggests that Indians avail themselves of the courts at a low rate and the rate seems to be falling.
>
> (Galanter and Krishnan, 2004, p. 789)

India does have procedures in place for appeals, and for implementation of final court orders, which constitute *enforcement*, the fifth element for the access to justice typology. If it is possible to overcome the barriers discussed in relation to the above four components of access to justice, and obtain a court order, the element of enforcement should not be a significant barrier to realising rights. In India, however, research shows a 'failure of the government to enforce court orders' even when a courtroom victory has been secured. 'The High Court of Bangalore, for example, had 11,500 contempt of court proceedings before it in 1996 – most relating to the failure of government officers to enforce court orders' (Anderson, 2003, p. 17). For indigenous peoples seeking court action to force government officials to comply with the FRA, this creates further barriers to accessing justice.

The last element for access to justice comprises the monitoring and watchdog capacities of *civil society and parliamentary oversight* in order to strengthen accountability of the justice system. Civil society organisations and the media are effective watchdogs. India has a robust and activist civil society, and a 'largely uncensored' media (Drèze and Sen, 2013, p. 12), both of which carefully highlight transgressions and lack of compliance on the part of the government. The Baiga and Vedanta cases discussed in this chapter are contemporary and have been reported extensively by the media, which contributes to public awareness of issues related to the law. India's vibrant civil society has generated non-governmental organisations (NGOs), such as AWARE, CERC and Anand Niketan Ashram, which run legal support programmes for the poor (Galanter, 1983, p. 13). Given the large numbers of potential claimants under the FRA, these resources are probably inadequate. National social justice activist NGOs such as Kalpavriksh, Vasundhara and Campaign for Survival Dignity to name just a few, have been instrumental in passing and monitoring the legislation, and creating nationwide networks such as Community Forest Rights Learning and Advocacy (CFR-LA) to share information, problems and updates about efforts to fully implement the FRA across India. Governmental accountability mechanisms include the Parliamentary Standing Committee on Social Justice and Empowerment, Forest Advisory Committee and the MoEF-MoTA (Ministry of Environment and Forests and Ministry of Tribal Affairs) Joint Committee set up in 2010 to examine the implementation of the FRA.

Conclusion

Since independence in 1947, a number of promises have been made to the people of India through constitutional and legislative enactments. The implementation of some of these laws has been inadequate, leading to laws making very little practical difference in the lives of the people. The caste system, child labour and bonded labour, have all been abolished in theory. However, in spite of human rights norms dominating social legislation for about three decades, a lack of access to justice for marginalised peoples ensures the existence of each of these outlawed practices. For the sake of a balanced view, we need to draw attention to the fact that under the FRA, many claims have been made, some of which have been successful in restoring land rights to indigenous peoples. The fact that social justice legislation such as the FRA exists also means that legal protection is established in principle. The issue is that these successes are neither uniform nor are they guaranteed, as illustrated above by the socio-legal analysis using the UNDP typology on access to justice. Indigenous peoples are still faced with threats to their forest lands and livelihoods, in spite of the FRA having been in existence since 2006.

To some extent, it may be expected that a law will rarely solve all the problems its proponents hoped it would address. 'Sociolegal studies now assume that an inevitable gap exists between black letter law and law in action' (Halliday and Schmidt, 2004, p. 7). One of the reasons for this gap is those who work to pass a law and those who are responsible for its implementation are always members of different branches of the government: in India the Parliamentary and Executive branches. The different groups may have radically different levels of commitment to the purposes of the law, which impacts on whether the law is successful in contributing to social justice. In the case of the FRA, those who fought for its passage were members of the indigenous communities and civil society organisations who shared a fervent commitment to improving the lives of tribal peoples. However, those responsible for implementing the law and honouring its intent when dealing with forest lands are largely members of the Forest Department of the MoEF. The Forest Department has for many years had territorial responsibility over forest lands. The FRA radically changed their responsibilities and removed a good deal of power from them. Perhaps not surprisingly, they have been reluctant to relinquish the power they previously enjoyed. Studies on the implementation of the Act paint a sobering picture of government violations, heavy handed and unjust administration, and of community forest rights being withheld (Agarwal, 2011; Dash and Khotari, 2012). This has led to 'the alienation of tens of millions of forest dwellers from their surroundings, constant harassment and suffering, and the erosion of their own customs, institutions and knowledge related to forests' (Dash and Khotari, 2013, p. 155). The Council for Social Development (CSD, 2010), in its report on the Implementation of the Forest Rights Act, warns:

> [U]nless immediate remedial measures are taken, undoing the historical injustice to tribal and other traditional forest dwellers, the Act will have the opposite outcome of making them even more vulnerable to eviction and denial of their customary access to forests.

The implementation of the FRA, albeit imperfect, provides a tool for progress and legitimate hope for forest peoples that this legislation will correct historical injustices and begin to give forest peoples a greater voice in decisions. Changes, however, will be needed for the purposes of the law to be fully realised. These changes would include a sincere commitment to abide by the letter of the law, accountability including consequences for those who fail to abide by the law, increased awareness and education about the law for both community and government administrators, and provision of greater resources for legal services. The capacity to be able to use legal processes would have many positive repercussions. Besides legal empowerment it would increase the political power of indigenous communities, which is 'a prerequisite to the elimination of extreme poverty' (Gauri and Gloppen, 2012, p. 486).

References

Agarwal, R. 2011. Five years of forest rights law. *Civil Society Online*. Available at: http://www.civilsocietyonline.com/pages/Details.aspx?4

Anderson, M. R. 2003. Access to justice and legal process: making legal institutions responsive to poor people in LDCs. *IDS Working Paper*.

Bhengra, R., Bijoy, C. R. and Luithui, S. 1999. *Report on the Adivasis of India*. London: Minority Rights Group.

Chandra, B., Mukherjee, M. and Mukherjee, A. 2008. *India Since Independence*. New Delhi: Penguin Books.

Chatty, D. 2002. Mobile peoples and conservation. *Anthropology Today*, 18, 1–30.

Chatty, D. and Colchester, M. 2002. *Conservation and Mobile Indigenous Peoples: Displacement, Forced Settlement, and Sustainable Development*. New York, Berghahn.

CSD 2010. *State of Implementation of the Forest Rights Act: Summary Report*. India: Council for Social Development. Available at: www.forestrightsact.com/component/k2/item/15

Dana Standing Committee 2002. *Dana Declaration on Mobile Peoples and Conservation*. Refugee Studies Centre, Oxford University, WCPA, WWF and DICE (eds). Jordan: Wadi Dana.

Dash, T. and Khotari, A. 2012. Grabbing: dangers of the Green India Mission. In: Kohli, K. and Menon, M. (eds) *Banking on Forests: Assets for a Climate Cure?* Delhi/Pune: Kalpavriksh and Heinrich Boll Stiftung.

Dash, T. and Khotari, A. 2013. Forest rights and conservation in India. In: Jonas, H. J. and Subramanian, S. M. (eds) *Right to Responsibility: Resisting and Engaging Development, Conservation, and the Law in Asia*. Natural Justice and UNU-IAS Institute of Advanced Studies.

Drèze, J. and Sen, A. 2013. *An Uncertain Glory: India and its Contradictions*. London: Penguin.

D'Souza, D. 1999. De-notified tribes: still criminal? *Economic and Political Weekly*, 34, 3576–3578.

Gadgil, M. 1992. Conserving biodiversity as if people matter: a case study from India. *Ambio – Economics of Biodiversity Loss*, 21, 102.

Galanter, M. 1983. Making law work for the oppressed. *The Other Side*, lll, 8–13.

Galanter, M. and Krishnan, J. 2004. 'Bread for the poor': access to justice and the rights of the needy in India. *Hastings Law Journal*, 55, 789–834.

Galligan, D. and Sandler, D. 2004. Implementing human rights. In: Halliday, S. and Schmidt, P. (eds) *Human Rights Brought Home: Socio-Legal Perspectives on Human Rights in the National Context North America (US and Canada)*. Oxford: Hart Publishing.

Gauri, V. and Gloppen, S. 2012. Human rights-based approaches to development: concepts, evidence and policy. *Polity*, 44, 486.

Gilbert, J. 2007. Indigenous rights in the making: the United Nations Declaration on the Rights of Indigenous Peoples. *International Journal on Minority and Group Rights*, 14, 207–230.

Gilbert, J. and Doyle, C. 2011. A new dawn over the land: shedding light on collective ownership and consent. In: Allen, S. and Xanthaki, A. (eds) *Reflections on the UN Declaration on the Rights of Indigenous Peoples*. Oxford: Hart Publishing.

Government of India 2011. Sustainable development in India: stock-taking in the run up to Rio+20. In: Forests, M. O. E. A. (ed.) *Sustainable Development in India: Stock-taking in the Run up to Rio+20*. India: Government of India.

Government of India 2012. The Forest Rights Act. In: Notification, M. O. T. (ed.) *The Forest Rights Act*. New Delhi: Government of India, Controller of Publications, 6 September.

Halliday, S. and Schmidt, P. 2004. Introduction: socio-legal perspectives on human rights in the national context. In: Schmidt, P. and Halliday, S. (eds) *Human Rights Brought Home: Socio-Legal Perspectives of Human Rights in the National Context. Human Rights Law in Perspective*. Portland, OR: Hart Publishing.

ILO 2003. ILO Convention on Indigenous and Tribal Peoples. 1989 (No. 169). *A Manual Project to Promote ILO Policy on Indigenous and Tribal Peoples*. Geneva: UN.

Impe, A.-M. 2011. A convention to fight discrimination. *Union View*. IUTC International Trade Union Confederation.

Indian Tribal Heritage 2013. The scheduled tribes and other traditional forest dwellers (Recognition of Forest Rights) Act, 2006 Reports and Articles. Available at: www.indiantribalheritage.org

Kurup, A. 2008. Tribal law in India: how decentralised administration is extinguishing tribal rights and why autonomous tribal governments are better. *Indigenous Law Journal*, 7, 91.

Lim, L. A. and Anand, R. 2004. Confronting discrimination: nomadic communities in Rajasthan and their human rights to land and adequate housing. In: Kothari, M. (ed.) *Nomadic Communities in Rajasthan and their Human Rights to Land and Adequate Housing*. India: Housing and Land Rights Network Habitat International Coalition.

Natural Justice 2013. *The Right to Responsibility: Resisting and Engaging Development, Conservation, and the Law in Asia*. Malaysia: Natural Justice and United Nations University – Institute for Advanced Studies.

OHCR 1965. International convention on the elimination of all forms of racial discrimination. In: UN (ed.). Geneva: UNOHCHR. Available at: www.ohchr.org/Documents/ProfessionalInterest/cerd.pdf

Pathak, N. 2009. *Community Conserved Areas in India: A Directory*, Pune/Delhi: Kalpavriksh.

Radhakrishna, M. 2009. Hunger among PTG and non-PTG nomadic communities. *Mukt – Saad*, 8, 1–6.

Saikia, S. 2014. Govt rejects Vedanta's Niyamgiri mining project. *The Hindu*, 12/1/2014.

Sambhav, K. S. 2012. Centre set to dilute tribal rights over forestland. *Down to Earth*. Available at: http://www.downtoearth.org.in/content/centre-set-dilute-tribal-rights-over-forestland

Sarin, M. and Springate-Baginski, O. 2010. India Forest Rights Act: the anatomy of a necessary but not sufficient institutional reform. In: Papers, I. D. (ed.) *Research Programme Consortium for Improving Institutions for Pro-Poor Growth*. Manchester: IDPM School of Environment and Development, University of Manchester.

Sircar, O. 2012. Spectacles of emancipation: reading rights differently in India's legal discourse. *Osgoode Hall Law Journal*, 49(3), 527.

UNDP 2004. *Access to Justice Practice Note*. New York: Democratic Governance Group, Bureau for Development Policy UNDP.

United Nations 1948. Universal Declaration of Human Rights. Available at: www.un.org/en/documents/udhr

United Nations 2010. State of the World's Indigenous Peoples. Available at: www.un.org/indigenous

Veron, R. and Fehr, G. 2011. State power and protected areas: dynamics and contradictions of forest conservation in Madhya Pradesh, India. *Political Geography*, 30, 285–293.

11 Patterns in arbitrariness

Resettlement experiences of the unrecognized urban poor in Chennai

Priti Narayan

Introduction

These are interesting times in Chennai, India. While 30,000 resettlement houses are being built for evicted slum dwellers, the state is also planning interventions under the Rajiv Awas Yojana (RAY), a housing scheme that aims to create slum-free cities by developing both officially recognized and unrecognized slums *in situ*. The time is ripe for examining what large-scale displacement and resettlement has meant for the urban poor in Chennai so far.

Approaches to slum intervention in the city of Chennai have undergone paradigm shifts over the years. The state's politics in the 1960s were rooted in patronage: shelter policies in specific were aimed at satisfying slum dwellers who formed a large part of the vote bank. This meant that the Tamil Nadu Slum Clearance Board (the TNSCB or the Board henceforth) was oriented mainly towards *in situ* slum improvements and tenement construction, rather than eviction and resettlement (Raman, 2011). Raman argues that it was the intervention of the World Bank into city-level shelter policies that partly shifted the government's approach from *in situ* tenement construction to the Sites and Services approach, which involved selling plots of land to beneficiaries in integrated sites with basic facilities in the peripheries of the city.

Today, development projects are putting immense pressure on land inside the city, causing the TNSCB to evict slums on a large scale, and repeatedly claim that it is the paucity of land within the city that has led to the construction of resettlement colonies far away (Transparent Chennai, 2012). Ghertner (2011) details how a logic of aesthetics led to the sanction of many illegal structures in New Delhi, thus causing widespread evictions of city slums. In Chennai city, Coelho and Raman (2010) establish how strategies to make world class cities, such as "development," "beautification," and "eco-restoration," end up ensuring that the poor have no place in the city, leading to mass forced relocation. When occupancy in the constructions in progress is complete, over 50,000 families will have been resettled in Chennai's resettlement colonies.[1] Living conditions at resettlement colonies have garnered a lot of media attention (see Lakshman, 2009; Ramakrishnan, 2009; Staff Reporter, 2012 for instance). Fact-finding reports by civil society organizations such as the People's Union for Civil Liberties, the Forum for Securing Land and Livelihood Rights of Coastal Communities (FLLRC), and the Citizens' Rights Forum (CRF) also detail the eviction experiences of some evictees.

Unrecognized slums in the city are most vulnerable to being evicted because they fall in a legal grey area without protections offered by the law (Transparent Chennai, 2012). Many of these unrecognized slums have been evicted without any resettlement housing, while some have been provided monetary compensation in addition to housing. Our research at Transparent Chennai[2] has also been unable to reveal whether a standard procedure for evictions and resettlement exists at all in Chennai, especially in the absence of formal status for most slums. Roy (2009) argues that the state in India itself is a deregularized entity whose law is often arbitrary and open to multiple interpretations. In addition, the deregularized state uses the flexibility offered by informal settlements and structures to acquire land and undertake various development projects.

This paper is an effort to examine eviction and resettlement experiences to understand the workings of the state. It attempts to document and understand the process of resettlement in Chennai by cataloguing and comparing the experiences of eviction and relocation of different slum communities now living in two different resettlement sites. First, a brief legislative context for slums, evictions, and resettlement in the state and city is provided. After defining the research methodology, the experiences of 14 slum communities across the various stages of eviction and resettlement are compared and analyzed for consistency across communities and adherence to existing policy.

Legal framework for evictions, resettlement, and rehabilitation

Some legislation exists on evictions, resettlement, and rehabilitation processes, in the national and state level contexts. However, existing legislation is inadequate and ambiguous.

At the national level, a rehabilitation and resettlement policy was formulated in 2007. However, after being approved by the Cabinet, the bill, along with the new Land Acquisition Bill, lapsed in the Parliament since it was opposed for being "anti-farmer" and for its problematic definition of public purpose (Menon, 2009). In January 2014, the Right to Fair Compensation and Transparency in Land Acquisition, Rehabilitation and Resettlement Act came into force. This legislation mandates a social impact assessment (SIA) survey for land acquisitions and mandatory rehabilitation and resettlement for all those affected by any acquisition. However, this legislation was not in place when the evictions studied in this chapter occurred.

Only three states in India have rehabilitation laws (Fernandes, 2004) and Tamil Nadu is not one of them. The primary legislation that exists for dealing with slums is the Tamil Nadu Slums (Improvement and Clearance) Act that was passed in 1971 (Transparent Chennai, 2012). The Act lays down a clear procedure for interventions into slums in the city: identify, declare (or officially recognize) as a slum, and improve. However, the Act is weak as it does not stipulate the act of declaration of slums to be undertaken on a regular basis (Nagasaila, 2013). As a result, slum declaration has occurred only once, in 1971, with 1,202 slums being officially recognized, and around 17 slums added to that list in 1985. No further declaration has been taken up, leading to very poor access to basic services in undeclared slums, possible underestimations of slum populations, and, thus, of service needs in the city as a whole (Transparent Chennai, 2012).

The Slums Act also states a slum can be cleared only for improving life conditions for the slum dwellers, and not for improving infrastructure of the city.

Since the Act only stipulated the eviction of declared slums, the government has perpetuated the informal status of many low income settlements in the city by not declaring them. Thus, undeclared slums, which are more vulnerable to evictions, fall under different legal jurisdictions.

In matters of land, the state has eminent domain—it can acquire any land that it does not own for governmental activities. Most of the evictions in the city invoke the Tamil Nadu Land Encroachment Act of 1906 (Nagasaila, 2013). This Act declares all public land (public roads, bridges, ditches, rivers, streams, and lakes) the property of the government and confers on the government the right to summarily evict anyone "unauthorizedly" occupying taxable land.

While state legislation provides some explanation of *who* can be evicted, there seems to be no mention of resettlement processes, the basic services that need to be provided at resettlement sites, and who is to provide these services. Minimum rehabilitation packages and compensations have not been mandated. The exact roles and jurisdictions of the various city agencies—the Revenue Department, the landowning body, the TNSCB and the Chennai Metropolitan Development Authority (CMDA)—have also not been defined clearly. Thus, it is evident that there are several gaps in the existing laws and policies that are constantly negotiated, manipulated, or disregarded by the state, so that informal settlements may be evicted for the "development" of the city.

Research methodology, selected communities, and the resettlement sites

Fourteen communities were selected for the study by convenience sampling, based on the availability of sufficient people from a community for focus group discussions and their referrals to other communities for discussion. A "community" in the context of this chapter constitutes the residents of a slum who articulate a shared experience of eviction and resettlement. Even after moving to the resettlement site, these residents continue to identify themselves by the names of the areas or roads where they lived before eviction, thus distinguishing themselves from other communities residing in the resettlement colony, and addressing civic issues together as members of that specific community. One focus group discussion, running for up to 90 minutes, was held with each community. Each focus group had anywhere between ten and 30 participants. There were male and female respondents in each focus group spanning different age groups and occupations. The discussions were semi-structured and the data obtained from them were coded and catalogued for easy comparison of eviction experiences between various communities. Follow-up interviews with individual members of communities were used to complement missing information in the tables.

Twelve of the 14 communities studied resided in Kannagi Nagar, the largest occupied tenemental resettlement colony in Chennai so far (with 15,656 tenements). Discussions were also held with two communities evicted from peri-urban areas (Ambattur Eri and Thiruverkadu), who experienced a different kind of resettlement. Instead of being relocated to concrete homes in a large-scale "integrated" tenemental resettlement site such as Kannagi Nagar (as is usually the case with most evictees in the city), they were moved to empty plots of land in New Kanniyamman Nagar village outside the city. The study targeted communities that had experienced evictions differently, in order to allow for comparisons between them (these differences are detailed later in this chapter). Table 11.1 summarizes the profile of these communities. The chapter also uses interviews with officials from the TNSCB, activists, lawyers, and with the communities, to understand the evictions and to identify best practices for resettlement in the city upon which a better and more consistent resettlement policy can be built.

Findings

The study reveals that existing legislation concerned with evictions and resettlement is weak and inadequate. Resettlement practices also do not seem to map onto the existing policy. These are discussed in detail below.

The eviction decisions

An interview with an ex-employee of the TNSCB (2013) revealed that no legal government order is passed to enable or facilitate an eviction. Decisions to evict are taken at interdepartmental meetings, with decisions to evict often approved on paper *after* the evictions have already occurred.

The reasons for evictions are contentious. The TN Slums Act explicitly states that evictions of a slum community must be taken up only in the interest of improving the living conditions for slum dwellers. However, only in four cases out of 14 in this study can evictions be considered as undertaken for the safety and improved living conditions of the poor: in the case of the community affected by the tsunami, the one affected by flooding, and the two where slum fires took place. All the other evictions examined in this city have been caused by what could be best described as "development projects." Moreover, one could argue that relocation of slum dwellers to resettlement sites has not improved their living conditions, due to the lack of basic services and social infrastructure at these resettlement sites.

Interviews found that coercive evictions were common. All communities except Thideer Nagar, affected by the tsunami, were evicted and moved against their will.

Table 11.1 Summary of the communities studied

Slum/community name	*Reason why the slum was evicted*	*Project implementing body*	*Location of original slum: within city boundaries?*	*Legal recognition as slum?*	*Objectionable (on road margins, pavements, railway track margins and river margins)?*	*Year of eviction; resettlement site to which they were relocated*	*Number of families evicted*
Slaterpuram	The Chennai Mass Rapid Transit System (MRTS) project	Ministry of Railways, Government of India	✓		✓	2003; Kannagi Nagar	Over 2,000
St Mary's Road (SM Nagar)	MRTS project	Ministry of Railways, Government of India	✓	✓		2000; Kannagi Nagar	43
Taramani	MRTS project	Ministry of Railways, Government of India	✓			2000; Kannagi Nagar	210
LG Road	Slum fire (people also claim they were evicted so that the waterway they lived next to, the Cooum river, could be rejuvenated)	City Corporation/local government body	✓		✓	2009; Kannagi Nagar	1500
Adyar	Construction of a park nearby	City Corporation/local government body	✓			2000; Kannagi Nagar	100
1000 Lights	Construction of a flyover	City Corporation/local government body	✓		✓	2000; Kannagi Nagar	40
Ayanavaram	Replacing water pipelines on which the slum lay	City Corporation/local government body	✓			2009; Kannagi Nagar	1,500

Slum/community name	*Reason why the slum was evicted*	*Project implementing body*	*Location of original slum: within city boundaries?*	*Legal recognition as slum?*	*Objectionable (on road margins, pavements, railway track margins and river margins)?*	*Year of eviction; resettlement site to which they were relocated*	*Number of families evicted*
Ambattur	Flooding of the slum, and for preservation of the adjoining lake	City Corporation/local government body			✓	2008; New Kanniyamman Nagar	1,000
Thiruverkadu	Water harvesting project	City Corporation/local government body			✓	2009; New Kanniyamman Nagar	1,000
Saidapet	Chennai Metro Rail Project	Chennai Metro Rail Limited (CMRL) a joint venture of the Government of India and the Government of Tamil Nadu	✓		✓	2010; Kannagi Nagar	225
Thideer Nagar	Tsunami	City Corporation/local government body	✓			2005; Kannagi Nagar	1,350
Samiyar Thottam	Widening of adjoining railway track	City Corporation/local government body	✓		✓	2000; Kannagi Nagar	110
Reserve Bank	Expansion of nearby playground. In addition, huts caught fire later	City Corporation/local government body	✓			2000; Kannagi Nagar	Over 500
Zoo Maidanam	Expansion of nearby grounds for the Asian Athletics Championship	City Corporation/local government body	✓			2013; Kannagi Nagar	150

Only one of 14 communities studied was a formally recognized slum with some security of tenure, but that slum was treated no differently from the other unrecognized slums despite the fact that residents in declared slums are protected from eviction without due process under the TN Slums (Improvement and Clearance) Act, 1971. In accordance with the law, residents of this "recognized" slum had been paying rents to the TNSCB and were on the road to obtain property title for their homes before being evicted for the Chennai Mass Rapid Transit System (MRTS). According to residents, they had been resisting evictions for a month before officials suddenly arrived one morning and started demolishing their homes.

The eviction procedures

A common thread that ran through all evictions was the lack of any advance notice given to the occupants in the area before they were asked to leave, presumably to prevent concerted resistance. Even though evictions were imminent in most cases, the exact date of eviction was only known in two cases out of the total 14 cases.

An ex-employee of the TNSCB (2013) revealed that a due process used to be followed in eviction and resettlement: an enumeration of the affected families, a large period of community interaction and consensus building followed by allotment at the resettlement site. But over time, the process was corrupted, with politicians and political party members demanding houses for their friends and family. Today, there is often ambiguity of authority and jurisdiction between departments in the case of local projects, leading to inefficiencies in the process. The Community Development Wing of the TNSCB, which was set up specifically to liaise with communities during slum interventions, is often not even involved in the process, leading to friction and even violence in some evictions.

Implementation of the evictions

In six cases out of the total of 14, there was violence during evictions, with damage to, and loss of, property. Loss of property occurred also because people were often not being given adequate time to pack their belongings before they were forced to move. For example, in the Reserve Bank case, residents claimed fires were set in the slum by the party in power in order to free the land the huts were located on. People lived on the streets for months awaiting the judgment of the court, while facing violence and coercion to leave.

Terms of resettlement

The eligibility criteria for getting houses in the resettlement site and the allotment process seem to be entirely discretionary. In over 70 percent of the cases, people reported that not all those evicted received houses or plots in the resettlement sites. They claim that the reasons range from inadequate identity proof to families not being around at the time of eviction and the officials' irritation at people's attempts to hoodwink them to obtain more than one house. The arbitrary nature of allotment was confirmed in an interview with an ex-employee of the TNSCB (2013), who revealed that houses are randomly allotted to displacees without any systematic procedure. There is no government order that mandates procedure, and no supervision over the allotment procedure either.

On the other hand, all those displaced by the MRTS project, which was jointly implemented and funded by the central and state governments, have been allotted homes in Kannagi Nagar. Eligibility criteria for allotments were so lenient for the MRTS that even tenants and those without ration cards were given houses in the resettlement colony. This is true of the Chenai Metro Rail Limited (CMRL) project as well, where eligibility criteria were more flexible than in other projects. Most of the families evicted for these projects were provided allotments in the resettlement colony—according to residents, this was mostly due to administrative oversight, and not narrow eligibility criteria. All displacees were immediately allotted homes after eviction as well.

Some local projects have not fared too badly either. Initially, about 50 families, mainly tenants, living in the tsunami-hit Thideer Nagar were left out of resettlement in Kannagi Nagar. But eventually even these families were resettled in Semmenchery. Displacees of other local projects such as in the Reserve Bank slum have also been resettled without any eligibility criteria, possibly due to urgency and pressure in completing the project.

Overall, local-level projects seem to be less planned and more ad hoc in nature in matters of eviction and resettlement. At least 20 percent of the families in the evicted slums did not get housing in the resettlement colony after eviction, with eligibility criteria being ambiguous or at least inconsistent among different families. People from the LG Road slum reported that officials demanded bribes for providing them allotments in Kannagi Nagar. In the Samiyar Thottam case, residents stated that after months of living on the streets post evictions, most residents in the original slum were not given allotments in Kannagi Nagar. The officials reportedly "got irritated" and stopped allotment altogether because some individuals were trying to deceive them into allotting additional homes in the resettlement colony. Interaction with officials has also generally been unpleasant.

Transparent Chennai's analysis of slum policy in Chennai (2012) had suggested that projects with central government involvement have been more inclusive at the resettlement stage as compared to local projects—this study confirms it.

All those resettled felt deceived about the terms of resettlement. Many respondents claimed that they were told that their new houses would be given for free. It was upon arrival that they discovered that they needed to pay high down payments and monthly rents.

Kannagi Nagar residents receive hire purchase agreements from the TNSCB, under which they are required to pay monthly rents to the Board for 20 years before being given paperwork signifying ownership. From discussions with residents, it was understood that down-payment and rents paid to the TNSCB have risen over the years. The People's Union for Civil Liberties (PUCL) fact finding report (2010) confirms that beneficiaries of the earlier scheme at Kannagi Nagar paid Rs. 600

(7.5 EUR) as down-payment and Rs. 150 (1.9 EUR) as rent every month, while the beneficiaries of the later scheme paid at least Rs. 1,000 (12.4 EUR) as down-payment, and a government order in 2003 increased the monthly rents to Rs. 250 (3.1 EUR) for those who benefited after a certain date (FLLRC and CRF, n.d.), presumably to account for rising costs of land and inflation. In effect, early arrivals at Kannagi Nagar are paying lower rents than those who arrived later although many people told us that they are now required to pay much more than their monthly rents due to penalties for late payment thus far. Across the board, irrespective of the year in which they were evicted, people complained of rents being unaffordable, especially when they have been unable to access regular jobs.

However, later arrivals have received a better deal than those who arrived early. House size has increased over the years if only by a few square feet (FLLRC and CRF, n.d.). The earlier scheme at Kannagi Nagar allowed for one toilet to be shared by two households, while the later scheme had a toilet built for every house. Our discussions revealed that sharing a toilet has proved to be a major inconvenience and cause for hostility between households.

Resettlement and rehabilitation processes

Adequate arrangements for resettlement of displacees were not made before evictions. In four cases, allotment in the resettled area was not immediate. People had to live on the streets for a month or more and stage protests before being allotted homes elsewhere. Displacees from Ambattur Eri and Thiruverkadu arrived to barren thorn fields with not even the semblance of a house and no basic facilities (water, drainage, toilets, or electricity) in New Kanniyamman Nagar. Thirteen out of the total 14 communities arrived at their new houses to find that tap water was not available, so they had to fetch it from a fair distance or buy water from private providers. Eleven communities reported having no formal electricity connections when they first came to the resettlement site; some coped by drawing illegal lines from streetlights, some survived with no electricity at all.

In most cases, the evictees did not receive any monetary compensation for their losses. Only in the case of the CMRL eviction in Saidapet was there a monetary compensation called "shifting allowance" and subsistence allowance for 12 months totaling about Rs. 50,000 (about 828 EUR at the time) to each displaced family. According to the published project information there were also some other benefits such as skills training to meet livelihood requirements (Chennai Metro Rail Limited, n.d.). In all other cases, allotments in resettlement colonies alone were considered sufficient, even though this was not provided to all residents. An ex-employee of the TNSCB (2013) cited the CMRL eviction as a positive turning point in the resettlement era in the city. The project had a strong relief and rehabilitation (R&R) policy that kept the people at the forefront and detailed the due process to be followed. Among all the communities interacted with for this study, the CMRL evictees from Saidapet seemed least dissatisfied. However, this needs to be attributed to the relative strength of the R&R policy of the particular project, and not to the policy or practices of the state.

Tenure security has been provided to displacees by means of allotments in resettlement colonies. However, the status of tenure security for households in Kannagi Nagar and other resettlement colonies continues to be unclear, mostly due to inadequate documentation. Three of the communities do not have allotment papers at all. In two cases, communities were told upon their arrival that their housing in Kannagi Nagar was only a temporary arrangement before other accommodation was arranged for them. A lot of people interviewed during the study revealed that they felt insecure in their current homes, and wondered whether they would be evicted from there as well. Their fears were not baseless: in March 2013, about 32 families who had been living in Kannagi Nagar were indeed evicted because they did not have allotment papers (Special Correspondent, 2013).

Resettlement site facilities

"Completion" of a resettlement site in government-speak simply refers to the completion of the construction of the housing structures, and not to the provision of all physical infrastructure and basic services. In Kannagi Nagar, barely any amenities were in place for those who arrived in 2000. Regular water supply by their community hand pumps and formal electricity connections are fairly recent developments. Discussions revealed that fights over limited resources broke out between the host population and the resettlers, and also among different groups of settlers. Schools, ration shops, buses to the city, and livelihood opportunities have, over time, become available and accessible. Crime (and fear) has reduced in recent years.

At the New Kanniyamman Nagar resettlement site, the displacees were allotted plots of land in barren fields with absolutely no amenities at the time. People have built houses over time, and any access to amenities they have now (such as water supply and electricity) has been due to piecemeal efforts undertaken by the village local body to accommodate the sudden influx of residents. Having been moved to a village from the city, they have lost the benefits of urban service provision (such as improved transportation, health and education services) and livelihood opportunities.

Residents of Kannagi Nagar and New Kanniyamman Nagar seem to value the benefits of their mostly secure tenure and concrete houses, yet are unable to access livelihood opportunities where they live now. Bus services continue to be inadequate in these highly dense sites. Neither site has a public hospital in the neighborhood where they can access immediate medical care at low costs. Garbage accumulation and sewage stagnation are burning issues in the site today. House sizes in Kannagi Nagar tenements have proved to be prohibitively small with no scope for expansion, resulting in complete lack of privacy for growing families. Construction quality is visibly poor in the tenements: leaking roofs, cracked buildings, and broken steps are common sights.

Evictions often happened in the middle of the academic year, and people reported having stayed back in the city as tenants or in huts they put up, so the kids could complete that academic year in the school they were going to. People claimed that educational facilities at the resettlement site were inadequate and poor, and so some children continued to commute to schools in their old neighborhoods, while others dropped out because of the difficulties in commuting long distances. Early arrivals described both sites as being akin to "forests" when they came there: difficult circumstances where they felt a sense of danger. The Reserve Bank community, one of the first arrivals in Kannagi Nagar, reported having eaten insects for a few days because there were no grocery stores or ration shops in the vicinity.

Unanimously, the discussions revealed that people would move back to their old neighborhoods to live in their huts if they could. These, along with the fact that about 50 per cent of Kannagi Nagar's beneficiaries do not live in the tenements anymore (Lopez, 2012), suggest that resettlement, as it has been implemented so far in these colonies, has been an abject failure.

Discussion

Findings reveal that evictions caused by development projects have mostly been coercive, sometimes violent. The absence of transparency and accountability in eviction processes is notable, with many communities not receiving advance notice about evictions, and not being told clearly or correctly about their terms of resettlement. Eligibility criteria for resettlement have been inconsistent across different projects. Sometimes, evictees of the same development project have been treated differently due to bureaucratic arbitrariness. Even as the government considers resettlement housing as adequate compensation for eviction, there continues to remain some tenure insecurity due to inadequate, vague documentation.

This study is evidence that slum dwellers in Chennai, especially those living in unrecognized settlements, are subject to processes of eviction and resettlement that are, de facto, arbitrary and inconsistent across different development projects. The state seems to thrive on the informality of unrecognized slums by using it as a basis to subject slum dwellers to arbitrary processes, thereby fitting into Roy's (2009) theory of the deregularized state in Indian cities.

However, certain patterns are visible in the examination of the evictions across slum communities. There seem to be certain factors that determine how a community is treated during evictions and resettlement and these patterns are detailed below:

1. *In the absence of an all-encompassing policy, different kinds of development projects offer different kinds of resettlement experiences.*

The study reveals that in the absence of adequate legislation concerning evictions and resettlement, the kind of development project causing the eviction influences the way evictees are treated. Projects with central government involvement (the MRTS and the Metro Rail projects in this study) have largely been able to provide more humane, inclusive resettlement experiences than smaller, local, ad hoc projects. Their sizeable budgets have ensured a semblance of a rehabilitation package, especially in the Metro Rail project. The Metro Rail project even has its own resettlement and rehabilitation policies, while at the local level, adequate policy guidance is not usually available even on an ad hoc or project to project basis. These factors play a large part in determining how a certain community is treated in eviction and resettlement, and on a larger level, demonstrate the arbitrariness of the state in the way it treats its subjects.

2. *Those living on the peripheries of the city have been further peripheralized and marginalized by development projects: they have been subject to counter-urbanization.*

The research indicates that those living in the peripheries of the city, when evicted, are further peripheralized from the city and suffer from lack of access to proper housing, basic amenities, and social infrastructure. These evictees have been subject to counter-urbanization by being moved from semi-urban local bodies to rural local bodies, and this move has perpetuated their marginalization and adversely impacted their access to livelihoods, education, and basic services.

3. *Formal status of a slum does not offer additional protection against evictions, or a better resettlement package.*

Although only one of the 14 communities identified for this paper was "declared" or officially recognized by the Tamil Nadu government, its status did not offer additional protection against evictions, or better treatment during the process of resettlement and rehabilitation compared to the unrecognized slums studied. A large-scale development project (the MRTS in this case) seems to be able to override in a short time the legitimacy and tenure security that poor communities have been inching towards for many years.

4. *Even in the same resettlement site, evictees have received different resettlement deals depending on when they moved in.*

Early arrivals in the resettlement site paid lower rents but also had to struggle to access basic services and social infrastructure upon arrival. Later arrivals, on the other hand, have not had to struggle for amenities upon arrival, because over time, facilities have improved on the site. However, they pay higher rents. This means that even within the same site, different communities have experienced different resettlement outcomes.

Conclusion

This study is significant in that the patterns reveal the existence of inequities even among evicted slum communities. Residents of a particular slum are subject to worse treatment than those of another, for reasons that are completely out of their control. The complete lack of human agency in the actual events and the processes involved is illustrative of coercion and arbitrariness exercised by the state. Situated at a vantage point in time, the study points to evident policy gaps ahead of what promises to be a massive eviction drive of almost 30,000 slum households in the city to fill up the new tenements in Ezhil Nagar and Perumbakkam.

The state has acted against its own rules to serve the interests of the development of the city (Roy, 2009). However, unlike Ghertner's New Delhi (2011) where an overarching logic of aesthetics was applied to facilitate evictions in the city, in Chennai, a more humane eviction and resettlement experience has been provided in certain circumstances. Future research can point to how these circumstances can be leveraged to push the state towards inclusive and considerate resettlement practices.

The RAY may also be that critical point in the history of slum interventions that can steer the focus back on to a services-based approach to slums in Chennai city. In that context, the study offers new evidence of inhuman, extra-legal, and ad hoc procedures followed by the government in evictions and relocation that only strengthen the argument in favor of better policy that is pro *in situ* development and anti coercive evictions.

Notes

1 Numbers of tenements in the various large-scale resettlement colonies—Kannagi Nagar, Semmenchery, and Perumbakkam—as mentioned by Lopez (2012), Jothilakshmy and Malar (2010), and the JNNURM Cell (2012) were added to arrive at this figure.

2 An action research group working on issues concerning the urban poor. Transparent Chennai analyzes slum policy and its impacts on the urban poor. It works closely with a local network of slum-based organizations, civil society groups, students, academics, and activists to push for more humane policies and practices.

References

Chennai Metro Rail Limited, n.d. *Frequently Asked Questions*. Available at http://chennaimetrorail.gov.in/faq.php [Accessed 25 August 2014].

Coelho, K. and Raman, N.V., 2010. Salvaging and Scapegoating: Slum Evictions on Chennai's Waterways. *Economic and Political Weekly*, Vol. XLV, No. 21, pp. 19–23.

Ex-employee of the TNSCB (requested anonymity), 2013. Personal interview conducted on January 24, 2013.

Fernandes, W., 2004. Rehabilitation Policy for the Displaced. *Economic and Political Weekly*, Vol. 39, No. 12, March 20–26, pp. 1191–1193.

FLLRC and CRF, n.d. *Information for the Fact Finding Report on the Relocation Settlements of Kannagi Nagar and Semmencherry*. Chennai: FLLRC and CRF.

Ghertner, A.D., 2011. Rule by Aesthetics: World-Class City Making in Delhi. In A. Roy and A. Ong, eds, *Worlding Cities: Asian Experiments and the Art of Being Global*. Oxford: Wiley-Blackwell.

JNNURM Cell—National Buildings Organization, 2012. *Status of DPRs Received under Basic Services for the Urban Poor from Mission Cities*. Available at https://jnnurmmis.nic.in/jnnurm_hupa/jnnurm/DPR_BSUP-status.pdf [Accessed 25 August 2014].

Jothilakshmy, N. and Malar, R.A., 2010. Inclusive Planning Processes and Institutional Mechanisms for the Urban Poor: Innovations and Lessons Learnt from Different Schemes in Chennai City. *Institute of Town Planners, India Journal*, Vol. 7, No. 2, April–June, pp. 50–62.

Lakshman, N., 2009. Grim Prospects for Kannagi Nagar. *The Hindu*. Available at www.hindu.com/2009/12/07/stories/2009120757970300.htm [Accessed 25 August 2014].

Lopez, A.X., 2012. 50% Beneficiaries Missing from Tenements. *The Hindu*. Available at www.thehindu.com/news/cities/chennai/50-beneficiaries-missing-from-tenements/article4006818.ece [Accessed 25 August 2014].

Menon, S., 2009. Land Acquisition, R&R Bills Lapse. *Business Standard*. Available at www.business-standard.com/article/economy-policy/land-acquisition-r-r-bills-lapse-109022800054_1.html [Accessed 25 August 2014].

Nagasaila, D., 2013. Personal interview conducted on February 14, 2013.

People's Union for Civil Liberties (PUCL), 2010. *Forced Eviction and Rehabilitation of Slum Dwellers in Chennai: Fact Finding Report*. Chennai: People's Union for Civil Liberties.

Ramakrishnan, D.H., 2009. Kannagi Nagar Demands its Due. *The Hindu*. Available at www.hindu.com/2009/06/15/stories/2009061558030300.htm [Accessed 25 August 2014].

Raman, N., 2011. The Board and the Bank: Changing Policies towards Slums in Chennai. *Economic and Political Weekly*, Vol. XLVI, No. 31, pp. 74–80.

Roy, A., 2009. Why India Cannot Plan its Cities: Informality, Insurgence and the Idiom of Urbanization. *Planning Theory*, Vol. 8, No. 1, pp. 76–87.

Special Correspondent, 2013. Evicted, this time from Kannagi Nagar. *The Hindu*. Available at www.thehindu.com/news/cities/chennai/evicted-this-time-from-kannagi-nagar/article4505855.ece [Accessed 25 August 2014].

Staff Reporter, 2012. Poor Quality Water Sparks Protests among Kannagi Nagar Residents. *The Hindu*. Available at www.thehindu.com/news/cities/chennai/poor-quality-water-sparks-protests-among-kannagi-nagar-residents/article3675688.ece [Accessed 25 August 2014].

Transparent Chennai, 2012. *Draft of the Summary Analysis of Slum Policy in Chennai and Their Implementation*. Chennai: Transparent Chennai.

Part IV

Voice and power of people

12 Forging new avenues for rights-claiming

Community responses to development-induced displacement and resettlement in rural Myanmar

Jill Kavanagh

'It is enough for me if I have land to work on. I don't need any other things.'[1]

The Salween River remains the longest free-flowing river in south-east Asia and marks the border between Thailand and Myanmar for approximately 120 km (75 miles) before it turns west and empties into the Gulf of Martaban. Along the length of the Salween River basin from where it rises in the Chinese Himalayas, communities rely on it both for irrigation and fishery. In November 2012, while travelling along one of its more remote stretches in Myanmar's eastern Kayin state, I spotted a large sign tacked up on the opposite side of the bank. It was incongruously written in English, red painted on white, its elevated bankside location prominently intended to capture the attention of any foreign journalists, non-governmental organisation (NGO) staff or missionaries venturing here. On the rough-hewn wood, it simply said: 'No Dam', with a skull where the 'O' should have been.

The purpose of such a sign is clear: it is a shout and a protest against development-induced displacement (DID) where there are no formal channels through which to vent grievances; where recent experience with violence deters complaint and where orders to relocate are accompanied by threats. Rural Kayin state is heavily militarised, the setting for a long-running, low-intensity conflict between government troops and various armed Karen factions since 1948. Villagers' collective experience of decades of conflict-induced displacement (CID), arbitrary arrests, executions, clashes and counter-insurgency efforts by government troops has instilled the values of remaining silent and unseen. Common sayings reveal the caution with which people speak freely: 'If you're talking during the day, check who's behind you. If you're talking at night, check under the house.'[2] Another belies the ingrained distrust between communities, often on the basis of ethnic or religious[3] distinctions: 'For Karen people, before you finish your plan, don't let the Burmese see.'[4]

These traditional reservations against open communication contribute to the wholesale exclusion of local communities from project planning and the lack of advance notification that a new project will necessitate their relocation. If it does come, the notification is often framed by threats, explicit or implicit. While some in Myanmar laud the increased 'space' for engagement with policy makers since the advent of civilian government in March 2011,[5] the reality is that the Myanmar government has only just begun to address land compensation and expropriation complaints. Instead, it is the informal rights-claiming measures – such as negotiation, media complaint, protest and non-compliance – that predominate of necessity, when it comes to village-level grievance-airing during business and development projects.

Throughout 2012, villagers in upland areas of eastern Myanmar interviewed by the Karen Human Rights Group (KHRG)[6] described their forced displacement by both government and non-state actors without any (in some cases) or adequate (in all cases) compensation, to make way for *inter alia* eight hydropower dams, five sites targeted for military or transport infrastructure, four logging projects, eight gold, coal and antimony mining sites and ten commercial plantations, as well as a highway connecting to the new developments around the Dawei deep-sea port project area. Newly displaced villagers join the ranks of those long-displaced by 60 years of conflict between armed groups and the government, where generations of counter-insurgency efforts have created a population of internally displaced which is estimated by The Border Consortium (TBC), a network of humanitarian service providers, at around 400,000. New infrastructure and industrial projects threaten to swell this population, while some 143,000 refugees from ten camps along the Thailand border may be repatriated to the same areas within the coming years. Long-displaced communities still living in these areas describe overcrowding and increased pressure on shrinking areas of land that are cultivated using the traditional slash-and-burn rotational cropping system of swidden agriculture.

It should come as no surprise that, given the closed nature of political and legal structures in Myanmar, and their lack of legislative protection, villagers are accustomed to pursuing informal rights-claiming strategies with a wide variety of actors, particularly through negotiation, in an attempt to secure some form of redress to their immediate problems. What is surprising, however, is the ongoing assumption that the State should play the crucial role in enforcing human rights norms and thereby preventing unilateral and uncompensated development-induced displacement and resettlement (DIDR). This is inherent in the way that prevention, mitigation and compensation of harm are perceived to be a job for the 'harming' party – often the state or corporate actors – to manage, rather than a process in which the harmed party takes an active role. Underpinning this is the understanding – enshrined in the 2011 Guiding Principles on Business and Human Rights – that the claiming of rights vis-à-vis business will predominantly be shaped by the internalisation of international norms into domestic laws and the sound exposition of principles in corporate charters.

This monolithic portrayal of social rights-claiming movements in relation to the state is fundamentally flawed since it does not apply to non-democratic or transitional contexts and ignores rights-claiming directed not at states or political institutions but at corporate actors or non-state armed groups (NSAGs) with financial stakes in business. For this reason, it is timely to take a closer look at the informal rights-claiming strategies emerging in the non-democratic and transitional context of Myanmar, particularly in areas where State institutions continue to play only a marginal role and other factors shape or hinder their success. The chapter seeks to show that opportunities exist for well-crafted programmatic measures that go far beyond institutional capacity-building to support community rights-claiming in response to DIDR.

Complaint to and negotiation with local or State authorities

In July 2012, in the northernmost part of Kayin State, villagers complained to local authorities from the non-State political body, the Karen National Union (KNU) during a community meeting about new gold-mining projects in that area implemented by a domestic Myanmar company. Their expressed intention was to enlist the support of these influential local elites to help them to build informal leverage for compensation. Where there exist no viable channels to engage with project developers, response strategies may play into local oppositional politics and provide a rallying cause for non-State armed or political groups vis-à-vis the State.

Across large areas of eastern Myanmar, there exist varying degrees of state control and often numerous non-State authorities. This creates an uncertain environment in which villagers may not know who is sanctioning the project that is displacing them, let alone to whom they can apply to seek redress. Villagers are traditionally extremely hesitant when it comes to complaining openly to government actors. Similarly, they may suspect, but be afraid to confirm, that local authorities from NSAGs have sanctioned the project. Given the diverse areas of state and/or armed group control, permission may be granted in one quarter and denied in another, further complicating the channels through which villagers can complain.

A prime example concerns the forced displacement in June 2012 of villagers from a site in southern Hpapun for the construction of a military barracks by Tatmadaw Border Guard troops.[7] The troops told villagers in the area that the KNU had sanctioned and been paid to provide permission for the project. In this area of mixed administration, in which KNU, Border Guard and government troops all maintain road travel checkpoints, the KNU also operates an unofficial regional land registration system in contrast to the State registration system and communities rely heavily on this system to mediate property disputes, rather than on the institutions of the State. Upon hearing that the project had been sanctioned by the KNU, some villagers vacated their land in exchange for a nominal fee. When they sought subsequently to complain to the KNU, a commander in the KNU's armed wing, the Karen National Liberation Army (KNLA), told the villagers that the KNU had not given permission for the project or met with the Border Guard and that the villagers had been duped by the Border Guard's lies.

In such cases where local elites are complicit in securing or facilitating a project, where the process for securing permission is unclear, or where there is simply a lack of transparency as to who the project implementers are, individuals and communities face stark uncertainty as to how they can protect their land in a way that will be recognised vis-à-vis external actors. In a context of multiple authorities and competing unofficial praxis, effective channels of complaint and negotiation are achieved by pursuing other strategies simultaneously, such as reporting or even just threatening to make reports to independent media and to document community losses or damages.

In some cases, collective community action is also facilitated by the high-profile nature of a particular project. This was true in the case of the Dawei deep sea port project implemented by Italian-Thai Development (ITD). The highway from the port is still under construction on the Andaman Sea in Myanmar to Kanchanaburi in Thailand but has already bisected villages, displaced residents and damaged agricultural land en route. In response to their concerns that they would not receive compensation for their lost assets, villagers formed a group called the 'Village and Public Sustainable Development Committee' to represent collective interests and lobby for compensation. Twenty-five committee members signed a letter in July 2011 outlining the values of lost or damaged properties. This committee approached local government and ITD representatives to negotiate compensation for the damage, using a list that documented property description, damaged acreage and an estimate of the damage cost. While the compensation requested and received in this case (less than US$4,000 in total) failed to accurately reflect either fair market value or cyclical agricultural losses flowing from the one-time loss of property, it is crucial that community pressure in this case did result in redress, illustrating that there is abundant opportunity for programmatic measures to build on and strengthen these nascent rights-claiming operations.

These case studies underline the fact that the greatest challenge facing villagers attempting to register grievances is the absence of any mechanism, either domestic or international, into which complaints can be submitted and of which villagers are aware. At the domestic level, the Myanmar government has only just begun to address land compensation and expropriation complaints. Recent developments include the creation of a Land Investigation Commission by the lower house of Parliament which came to Hpa-an and Thandaung towns at the end of September and early October 2012. The Rule of Law and Stabilisation Committee has also received hundreds of complaints that deal with land, and the Land Allotment Scrutiny Committee provides information to Parliament on the social and environmental impact of investment sites, and is tasked to review the national land-use policy and make recommendations to central government. Some members of Parliament have expressed willingness to receive complaints, but lacked the mandate to follow up on them. These new initiatives nonetheless demonstrate, at a minimum, the desire in powerful spheres to appear to be addressing land complaints. This form of official condemnation at the highest levels can, at the very least, give local commanders and business actors reason to pause and so create space at the grassroots level for villagers to engage with and confront armed perpetrators and other actors seeking to force them off their land.

Reporting to independent media

In April 2012, residents of five villages in a remote area of eastern Myanmar where the Salween River turns west on its way to the Gulf of Martaban were informed that a newly surveyed dam site at Hat Gyi was going to necessitate their relocation and the abandonment of schools on both sides of the river. Villagers in this area separately reported to local human rights defenders that the Myanmar military arranged a meeting regarding the relocation of villages before January 2012 in Myaing Gyi Ngu, a large town on the Salween, which also served as the former base for the DKBA. During the meeting, the Myanmar military officers gave each of the villagers in attendance one solar panel, one solar LED lantern and one battery, while explaining that the villages would have to move from the new dam site. A male villager in attendance at the meeting explained that: 'This gift does not benefit our villagers, but we accepted it when they gave it to us. The situation will be worse if we have to move our place and leave our village than if we can stay in our own village' (KHRG 2013).

The decision to report an incident of attempted displacement or relocation to local media or human rights groups is part of a proactive rights-claiming strategy for villagers across eastern Myanmar, accustomed to prolonged armed conflict. Villagers in the Hat Gyi case reported to media at the first hints of a dam survey in January 2012 and some intrepid souls painted the 'No Dam' sign that I saw later that year. Since then, protests at the dam site have drawn coverage from leading domestic media outlets inside Myanmar. Local armed groups have issued strongly worded warnings that uncompensated DIDR at the Hat Gyi site carries with it the strong potential to disrupt existing ceasefires and reignite ethnic conflict.

In such cases, reporting to independent media is used to bolster other rights-claiming strategies, to draw attention to public protests or even as a last-ditch attempt to secure redress after exhausting more diplomatic strategies such as negotiation or complaint. For example, during the 2012 protests at the Letpadaung copper mine against relocation to what was deemed to be unsatisfactory housing, several villagers travelled four hours to Mandalay to purchase camera and video equipment to do their own documentary reporting and so stimulate wider media coverage of their protests. In contrast, in remoter Kayin state, a large dam along the Shwegyin River in Bago Region was completed in December 2008. The area was, at that time, an active conflict zone. Villagers described fears of violent retribution from armed actors that prevented them from negotiating with or complaining to project developers following the inundation of more than 18,000 acres of farmland and 300 structures without compensation or provision of alternative housing. Nonetheless, many affected villagers chose to report covertly their specific losses and the indirect consequences of their displacement to media in an attempt to secure redress. One 58-year-old man reported his acreage that had been inundated and noted that the opportunity for more open complaint and negotiation was decidedly limited: 'They [the government] ordered us to leave. We were not happy to leave ... They just ordered us to go to town' (KHRG 2013).

This reliance in some cases on the media for grievance-airing reflects the lack of opportunity for formal complaint or meaningful negotiation with project implementers. Where legal channels are closed and fears or language barriers prevent overt engagement, the media may serve as the only means of vocalising complaints or demands. At another dam site 400 miles south, near Myitta town in Tanintharyi Region, which is the spur of Myanmar that juts south along the Malay peninsula next to Thailand, a 23-year-old villager described the typically scant opportunities for engagement: 'The company never discussed it with me ... They did it on their own' (KHRG 2013).

Reporting and subsequent media coverage may draw public attention to a case, but this is no guarantee of redress. In the case of the Hat Gyi dam, for example, the project still remains officially on the table and, while construction has not yet begun, this is far more likely due to the conflict sensitivities around the project than a direct effect of the villagers' response strategies. In any case, media access for project-affected communities in rural areas of Myanmar is patchy at best and the permissible flow of information often depends on the nature and extent of militarisation in the local area, the military actors' financial stake in projects, and the local history of violence and impunity. Central areas under hegemonic state military control are enjoying greater media freedom recently, contributing to the publicity surrounding rights-claiming protests at sites such as the Letpadaung copper mine and the controversial Myitsone dam on the Ayeyarwaddy River. In contrast, in many rural ethnic areas, armed actors continue to regulate media access and the outflow of information, particularly in cases where their own valuable business or commercial projects are concerned. Reports written by local human rights defenders are frequently read and checked for 'factual accuracy' by military office staff, which prevents the reporting of sensitive cases that impact business interests of local elites. These case studies illustrate the urgent need for further research and support for existing human rights reporting endeavours, as well as the ample space that exists for donors to support and strengthen community documentation of DIDR incidents and build on existing covert information-gathering and media networks.

Public protest

On 25 September 2012, villagers stood in the Day Loh River upstream from the as-yet-uncompleted Toh Boh dam to protest the flooding of land and the inundation of residential structures and bridges. Residents of affected villages organised the public protest, coordinating with local civil society organisations and media. Protesters held signs that read 'Free River' in English and 'Let the river flow freely' in Burmese to maximise publicity. When the project began in 2005, residents of 15 villages displaced from the dam site attempted to complain about their displacement by forming a committee and approaching local military commanders. However, they were threatened with arrest if they continued to seek compensation after being informed that the orders were not local and there was nothing that could be done. Speaking in April 2011, a 37-year-old KNU Township Secretary official interviewed by the KHRG described the formation of the 30-person committee back in 2005:

> They went to the Tantabin office and the people in charge said: 'This is not a Tantabin project. The project comes from headquarters, so we can't do anything. If you want compensation, you have to go to the Division … Even if you go to them, they won't give you compensation. Furthermore, they will arrest you and put you in prison.'
>
> (KHRG 2013)

Seven years later, following an unprecedented ceasefire between the Myanmar military and the KNU, villagers organised protests, covered by local media, as the dam threatened to uproot additional communities in the area without compensation. Although they could not guarantee redress, new protests such as this serve to illustrate that the cessation of hostilities in some areas and new regulations around public demonstrations are creating new space for DIDR-affected communities' rights-claiming strategies today.

Public protests have only recently been legalised in Myanmar when new legislation was introduced in December 2011 to regulate peaceful public protest for which permission must be granted at least five days in advance. As pointed out immediately by Human Rights Watch (HRW), the legislative phrasing lends itself to repressive over-interpretation, its provisions making it a criminal offence to give speeches deemed to contain false information, do anything that could harm the state, or that causes fear, disturbance or blocked roads. What has yet to be pointed out though is the Act's centrality for venting grievances of all kinds in the absence of formal complaints mechanisms. This is aptly demonstrated not just by the Toh Boh dam case, but by other protests newly cropping up and breaking the silence surrounding other long-established projects. The Letpadaung copper mine protests received a write-up in the *New York Times*, focusing on the organisational efforts of two local women spearheading the protest movement. Subsequent statements from the implementing companies disavowed plans to force villagers to relocate, although controversy has since erupted again over the violent dispersal of the protests in November 2012.

Numerous less publicised cases of protest in response to long-standing projects have also emerged, with villagers seeking retrospective redress. As described above, the Shwegyin dam in Bago Region flooded large tracts of land and the displaced villagers have been left without compensation since 2008. The villagers were reticent when it came to complaining openly about their plight. In March 2012, however, residents of five affected villages organised a large-scale protest along the banks of the Shwegyin River, again coordinating with local media, to call for the water to 'flow freely', as well as demanding retrospective compensation for inundated homes and agriculture. In Myanmar, new displacements without compensation are continuing apace and villagers do not have time to wait for the institutionalisation of norms into domestic policy. The kind of informal rights-claiming that garners media attention – and the attention of a central administration that is determined to deliver 'quick wins' and demonstrate tangible positive results from Myanmar's reform process – still serves as an important interim option for villagers seeking to secure some tangible remedy at the community level in the interim.

Non-compliance

In the T'Nay Hsah area to the east of Hpa-an, the capital of Kayin State, villagers were long accustomed to cultivating their own land and paying a profit-percentage fee to local Border Guard troops. In March 2012, they were suddenly confronted with wholesale eviction to make way for new rubber plantations. Border Guard troops informed villagers who had lived and worked on the land for generations that they were now required to sign a document certifying that the military authorities had legal ownership of the land. A 60-year-old man whose grandparents had worked the same land described the situation: 'They will completely take our farms and we will become like people who rent and work on their land. To let their leaders know, they asked us to sign … It will become their farm. We have to sign' (KHRG 2013). The same man went on to elucidate the difficulty facing villagers attempting to avoid complying with such coercive expropriations undertaken among multiple armed actors accustomed to exerting their will with easily realised threats of violence. 'Now, they pressure us and they said if we don't sign, they will report us to the police, the Democratic Karen Buddhist Army and the Peace Council who will arrest the villagers.' The likelihood of violent reprisal in remote areas in which numerous armed groups operate makes non-compliance a dangerous option.

Despite the very real threat of violent retribution, other villagers in this area expressed a steadfast refusal to sign the documents or to give up their land. A local human rights defender described villagers' refusals to comply with the relocation order for the military barracks in K'Taing Tee:

> The powerful groups that came … were the Border Guard and Tatmadaw. … The villagers responded in some ways … they replied that they could not give the land because they earn their livelihoods by farming flat fields and hill fields.
>
> (KHRG 2013)

A 54-year-old woman in T'Nay Hsah also described how, in the face of displacement without alternative land or housing, villagers refused to sign the documents:

> We asked him: 'If the battalion confiscates our land, then where are we going to live?' He said that the leaders from the State gave orders: 'You villagers have to leave. You have to sign.' I told him: 'We will not sign … The battalion will confiscate our land and we will not get it back, so we will not sign.'
>
> (KHRG 2013)

This type of officially sanctioned displacement, to which villagers in the T'Nay Hsah case responded with non-compliance, has been facilitated across Myanmar by a series of new laws passed in March 2012. These build upon the already restrictive legal environment in which government expropriation of 'waste' land is permissible. The new laws appear, on their face, to clarify land registration and bolster individual property rights by granting farmers who register their agricultural land the right to sell, transfer, mortgage or lease it. The new framework, however, is weighted heavily towards the highest bidder and the quickest off the mark, and is fraught with institutional corruption and insurmountable expense for those few villagers who do attempt to register their title. In any case, certification is no guarantee against displacement as land belonging to the certificate-holder can still be confiscated legally for a variety of reasons, including if it is left fallow, even during rotational cropping, or for any project deemed – without any clear guidelines – to be in the long-term national interest of the State or the public.

This restrictive legal framework curtails engagement with perpetrators who have no reason to listen to complaints. It also limits, but does not eradicate, the scope for non-compliance. In contrast to complaints or negotiation attempts, which recognise and respond to an order, non-compliance or civil disobedience take the form of any action that constitutes ignoring or defying an order for displacement. The act itself may take many forms, including refusing to vacate, relocate or authenticate with signature a coercive land expropriation – clear acts of resistance to an order. For example, in July 2012, farmers in Pandaung, Bago Region, ignored an order for land confiscation and walked together to plough their confiscated fields. On the other side of the country in Meiktila, south of Mandalay, three farmers lay in front of tractors that arrived to plough their contested lands. The tractor drivers in that case abandoned their attempt to plough the confiscated field.

Despite villagers' non-compliance with orders, the sheer immoveable nature of land means that the scope for effective rights-claiming to emerge from non-compliance alone is limited. Land can be forcibly taken, guarded, fenced, flooded, planted or built upon, and land use, once altered, is difficult to undo. Media coverage of non-compliance contributes to notifying NGO and civil society groups capable of providing legal or technical assistance and pressure groups able to lobby for changes in policy. In this way, non-compliance is akin to protest in terms of its capacity to draw media attention to a cause and stimulate additional rights-claiming measures and support. In cases such as T'Nay Hsah and Hpapun, where media access and NGO activities are strictly curtailed, and the prospect exists of violent retribution by an armed group or government troops – either of which may be motivated to protect valuable business interests – the fact that non-compliance manifests at all is in itself remarkable. It demonstrates the potentially rich rewards that community empowerment, land documentation and grassroots legal-support schemes might reap in combatting unjust and exploitative DIDR, even in the restrictive legal environment that persists across Myanmar.

Conclusion

The cases described above begin to illustrate the over-emphasis, both within the literature and current practice in Myanmar, on State institutions as rights enforcers, rather than on the non-institutional ways in which communities attempt rights-claiming responses to DIDR. They illustrate the pressing need for further research and for research-driven programmes that seek not merely to build the capacity of institutions but also to bolster and support informal responses to DIDR. Shaped by complex local power dynamics, these types of response are already forging viable avenues for rights-claiming in some cases. This chapter seeks to counter the assumption that well-framed legal and political institutions are the sole prerequisite from which effective rights-claiming will flow. Programmatic measures undertaken by donors in the interim must not confuse informal rights-claiming strategies with political demands, nor ignore such strategies as inherently 'political' and therefore untouchable. Rather, they should capitalise on the integral role such strategies can play in securing interim recognition for rights norms in eastern Myanmar, where State institutions may remain shaky, and their enforcing role peripheral, for many years to come.

Notes

1 Fifty-five-year-old male villager displaced by the Shwegyin dam, Bago Region, eastern Myanmar (unpublished interview by Karen Human Rights Group, March 2011).

2 *Ne pyaw nauk kyi, nya pyaw auk kyi.* (Translation: 'Talking during the day, look behind you. Talking at night, look under.')

3 Due to extensive Christian missionary work, populations of ethnic Karen Christians exist across southern Myanmar. In contrast, the vast majority of ethnic Burmans are Theravada Buddhists.

4 *Ka-yin ma pyi kin Ba-ma ma myin se nè.* (Translation: 'Before Karen finish, don't let the Burmese see.')

5 Myanmar's November 2010 elections were the first election permitted by the military government since the 1990 elections in which Aung San Suu Kyi's National League for Democracy (NLD) party famously won a majority but was later prevented from forming a government. The 2010 elections – viewed by many in the international community as flawed due to the lack of monitors, improper advance voting procedures and allegations of ballot-stuffing – saw the military-backed Union Solidarity and Development Party (USDP) unsurprisingly secure the majority of seats in the Union Parliament. Thein Sein, former Prime Minister under the previous military government, was nominated to the position of President, in a process regarded by some Myanmar political analysts to have been engineered by former Senior-General Than Shwe. Despite these inauspicious origins, Thein Sein's government, which took effect from 31 March 2011, has since initiated some momentous political and economic reforms in the intervening three years since coming into power. The next general elections are slated to take place in late 2015 or early 2016.

6 Founded in 1992, the Karen Human Rights Group (www.khrg.org) is an independent local organisation committed to improving the human rights situation in Burma by projecting the voices of villagers and supporting their strategies to claim human rights. The KHRG trains community members in eastern Burma to document individual human rights abuses using a standardised reporting format. This chapter was written during the course of my two years with the KHRG and was a product especially of my work on the

thematic report *Losing Ground: Land conflicts and collective action in eastern Myanmar*, published in March 2013. Available through the KHRG website at: www.khrg.org/2013/03/losing-ground-land-conflicts-and-collective-action-eastern-myanmar

7 During the run-up to the 2010 elections, a number of ethnic armed ceasefire groups in Myanmar were formally incorporated into Myanmar military command structure, becoming what were known as 'Border Guard' battalions. These included most battalions of the Democratic Karen Buddhist Army (DKBA) battalions, which had long operated as a government-allied ceasefire group.

Bibliography

Asian Human Rights Commission (AHRC). (2011, November 1). *Burma: draft land law denies basic rights to farmers*. Available at: www.humanrights.asia/news/ahrc-news/AHRC-STM-163-2011/?searchterm=

Barta, P. (2012, September 24). Mine protests challenge Myanmar reforms. *The Wall Street Journal*. Available at: http://www.wsj.com/articles/SB10000872396390444083304578016000561897778

Cassel, J. (2007). Enforcing environmental human rights: selected strategies of US NGOs. *Northwestern Journal of International Human Rights*, 6(1), 104–127.

De la Vega, C., Mehra, A. and Wong, A. (2011, July). Holding businesses accountable for human rights violations: recent developments and next steps. Friedrich Ebert Stiftung (FES) International Policy Analysis. Available at: http://library.fes.de/pdf-files/iez/08264.pdf

Fuller, T. (2012, September 26). In battling mine project in Myanmar, two 'iron ladies' rise. *New York Times*. Available at: http://www.nytimes.com/2012/09/27/world/asia/27iht-myanmar27.html?pagewanted=all

Fuller, T. (2012, November 29). Violent raid breaks up Myanmar mine protest. *New York Times*. Available at: http://www.nytimes.com/2012/11/30/world/asia/myanmar-security-forces-raid-protest-camp.html

Goldstone, J. A. (2003). Bridging institutionalized and non-institutionalized politics. In Jack Goldstone (ed.), *States, parties and social movements*, pp. 1–12. London: Cambridge University Press.

Hull, S. (2009). The 'everyday politics' of IDP protection in Karen State. *Journal of Current Southeast Asian Affairs*, 28(2), 7–21.

Human Rights Watch (HRW). (2012, October 2). *Burma: peaceful protest organizers charged*. New York: HRW.

Karen Human Rights Group (KHRG). (2013, February). *Losing ground: land conflicts and collective action in eastern Myanmar*. Chiang Mai: KHRG.

Karen National Union (KNU). (2009). *Land policy* (Burmese language). Available at: www.kesan.asia/index.php/publication-and-media/policy/finish/6-policy/72-knu-s-land-policy

Kavanagh, J. (2012, November). *Myanmar Field Notes* (unpublished).

Knight, R., Adoko, J., Siakor, A., Salomao, A., Auma, T., Kaba, A. and Tankar, I. (2012). *Protecting community lands and resources: evidence from Liberia, Mozambique and Uganda*. Rome: Namati and International Development Law Organisation (IDLO).

Koenig, D. (2001, July). *Toward local development and mitigating impoverishment in development-induced displacement and resettlement*. University of Oxford: Refugee Studies Centre. Available at: http://r4d.dfid.gov.uk/PDF/Outputs/Mis_SPC/R76442.pdf

Kriesi, H. (1999). The impact of social movements on political institutions. In Marco Giugni, Doug McAdam and Charles Tilly (eds), *How social movements matter*, pp. 42–65. Minneapolis, MN: University of Minnesota Press.

Myanmar Food Security Working Group (FSWG). (2012, November). *Legal review of recently enacted farmland law and vacant, fallow and virgin land management law*. Yangon: FSWG.

Myanmar Land Core Group of the Food Security Working Group (FSWG). (2012). *Land tenure security in Myanmar's uplands*. Yangon: FSWG.

Prosterman, R. and Vhugen, D. (2012, June 13). Land to the tillers of Myanmar. *New York Times*. Available at: http://www.nytimes.com/2012/06/14/opinion/land-to-the-tillers-of-myanmar.html

Rootes, C. A. (1999). Political opportunity structures: promise, problems and prospects. *La lettre de la maison Française d'Oxford*, pp. 75–97. Available through Centre for the Study of Social and Political Movements, Darwin College University of Kent at Canterbury at: www.kent.ac.uk/sspssr/staff/academic/rootes/pos.pdf

Schaefer-Caniglia, B. and Carmin, J. (2005). Scholarship on social movement organisations: classic views and emerging trends. *Mobilization: An International Journal*, 10(2), 201–212.

Siusue, M. (2012). How civil society can engage with policy-making in Myanmar's transitional context. *Journal of International Affairs*, Columbia School of International and Public Affairs. Available at: http://jia.sipa.columbia.edu/how-civil-society-can-engage-policy-making-myanmar's-transitional-context

Smith, M. (1999, October). *Burma: insurgency and the politics of ethnicity* (2nd edn). *Politics in Contemporary Asia* series. London: Zed Books.

Somayaji, S. and Talwar, S. (2011). *Development-induced displacement, rehabilitation and resettlement in India: current issues and challenges*. Abingdon: Routledge.

Steiner, H. J. and Alston, P. (2008). *International human rights in context: law, politics, morals*. London: Oxford University Press.

The Border Consortium (TBC). (2012, October 31). *Changing realities: poverty and displacement in south-east Myanmar*. Available at: http://www.theborderconsortium.org/media/10374/report-2012-idp-en-1-.pdf

13 Speaking through the silence

The role of literature in development-induced displacement and resettlement activism

Christine Gilmore

Introduction

Recent studies within the field of development-induced displacement and resettlement (DIDR) suggest the need to develop suitable methodologies grounded in sound social theory in order to further our understanding of why oustee communities resist displacement and the strategies they employ to achieve their political objectives (World Commission on Dams 2000; McCully 2001; Nixon 2011; Oliver-Smith 2011; Bennett and MacDowell 2012).

Using the literature of the Nubian minority in Egypt displaced by successive dam construction on the Nile at Aswan in 1902, 1912, 1933 and 1964 respectively, this chapter seeks to add value to the field of DIDR studies by examining how literature constitutes a crucial nexus for agency, activism and resistance in a situation of radical power imbalances between governments, development agencies and corporate interests on the one hand, and marginalised, oustee groups on the other.

Whether in illustrating the impact of DIDR on displaced communities or articulating the voices and political demands of those most affected by development, this chapter will argue that the intervention of writer-activists such as Muhammad Khalil Qasim in the public sphere through the publication and distribution of subversive literary texts such as *The River Gauge* (Qasim 2011 [1968]) can help generate momentum for reform and redress by speaking through the institutional silence to enhance the visibility of oustee voices.

Resistance to development and DIDR activism

Recent decades have witnessed a spike in what Rob Nixon has termed 'resource rebellions' (Nixon 2011, pp. 17–19) whereby communities slated for displacement have sought to resist large-scale development schemes such as megadams, mines, oil pipelines or infrastructure projects. Resistance to development has partly been fuelled by the forced removal, environmental degradation, impoverishment, social disarticulation and multidimensional stress that have characterised some development-induced displacement (DID) operations in the past, particularly in the absence of democratic checks and balances (McCully 2001, p. 77).

However, resistance to development has also been ascribed to a failure to ensure that oustees participate in the process of DIDR planning, and consent to the proposed scheme (Oliver-Smith 2011). Under current DIDR guidelines, oustees are rarely questioned about their own development priorities and application of the principle of free and prior informed consent (FPIC) is restricted in practice to cases dealing with the rights of indigenous peoples (World Commission on Dams 2000, p. 112).

Even though it is widely acknowledged that the cooperation of displaced peoples is a key factor in achieving a positive long-term outcome to resettlement operations, the World Bank's requirement for planners to undertake 'meaningful community consultation' (World Bank 2001) is too often regarded as a box-ticking exercise. Failure to acknowledge oustee perspectives may also be due to the fact that, statistically speaking, the displaced tend to be members of marginalised minority groups not considered to have 'the social and cultural tools necessary for executive or even advisory forms of decision-making, planning and execution that pertain to development projects' (Oliver-Smith 2011, p. 97).

Perhaps for these reasons, a paternalistic tendency has developed on the part of governments and resettlement planners to treat the displaced as passive objects of analysis or abstract individuals endowed with identical needs and wants rather than as active participants in the development progress endowed with agency, vision and a capacity to act in defence of their individual and communal interests (Scott 1998, pp. 346–348).

Resistance to DIDR, then, can be seen as the by-product of widespread failure by governments, planners and development agencies both to take seriously and address the multiple fears, apprehensions, reservations, concerns and conditions of communities slated for resettlement who feel that the only way for their voices to be heard is through material and symbolic acts of protest that, taken together, constitute DIDR activism.

Varying from overt public displays of resistance such as violent insurrection, civil disobedience, public protest and political lobbying to 'everyday acts of resistance' such as foot-dragging, disrespect and non-compliance in the face of authority, DIDR activism is typically incremental, turning violent primarily when more peaceful strategies to resolve the concerns of oustee communities through debate and negotiation have failed (Oliver-Smith 2011).

At a symbolic level, discursive opposition to DIDR typically emerges from clandestinely expressed complaints and grievances against authority that circulate within oustee communities that constitute what Scott has termed their 'hidden transcript' (Scott 1990, pp. 4–8). Derived and elaborated from the collective acknowledgement of a violated sense of order, justice and meaning by those undergoing the same experience of oppression, this dissenting discourse is rarely articulated openly or publicly for fear of retribution, particularly in contexts where freedom of speech and political association are repressed.

Rather, it tends to be expressed obliquely, through euphemisms, symbols and images that subvert the established discursive order without directly challenging it (Scott 1990). However, on those occasions when the hidden transcript enters the public domain, be it through writing, music, art, folk culture, polemic or political speech, it constitutes a powerful form of symbolic resistance, even rebellion, against hegemonic political and development discourses.

Once culture is mobilised as an axis of resistance to development, therefore, the literary sphere often becomes one of the key battle grounds for DIDR activism where it can have the iterative force of 'a symbolic declaration of war' (Scott 1990, p. 8) by providing a public platform for challenging hegemonic development discourses; expressing dissenting perspectives and priorities; and articulating political demands that ordinary individuals within the oustee community may be afraid of voicing publicly.

The role of literature in DIDR activism

Whereas past conversations about development typically took place among élites, a counter-discourse is now emerging in the internet age that is much more broad based and democratic, enabled by the emergence of global civil society, social media and an international public sphere in which debates over social and environmental justice and minority rights can be played out. In the increasingly global context for DIDR activism, writer-activists play a mediating role in resource conflicts by amplifying the voices of communities whose voices might not otherwise be heard and advocating, however indirectly, on their behalf in the international public sphere.

By tapping into potentially global audiences, writer-activists such as Abdulrahman Munif, Ken Saro-Wiwa, Indra Sinha and Arundhati Roy – who acted as unofficial porte-parole for the 'Save the Narmada' movement founded in opposition to construction of the Sardar Sarovar Dam in Gujarat, India (Roy 1999) – have deployed their cultural capital and iterative authority to raise awareness of the human and environmental impact of issues ranging from petroleum extraction, construction of oil pipelines and outsourced toxicity to megadams.

In acting as the symbolic representatives or iconic figureheads for social movements and indeed oustee communities, writer-activists become 'lightning rods' for controversy by deflecting the political repercussions for oustees of voicing their 'hidden transcript' of dissent openly (Nixon 2011, pp. 23–30). Partially shielded by their elevated public status, writer-activists typically enjoy greater discursive freedom to intervene in the public sphere to articulate the views and demands of marginalised oustee communities and advocate on their behalf, harnessing the power of transnational alliances that provide a common platform from which oustee groups can 'speak to and for others and themselves' (Chaturvedi 2000, p. 200) to highlight injustice and advocate for change.

By testifying against injustice, representing the lived experience of displacement and supplying a dissenting voice in the face of radical power imbalances between oustees, the state and development agencies, writer-activists not only resist symbolic domination by hegemonic discourses equating 'big development' with modernity and nation-building but can help generate political change by enhancing the visibility and effectiveness of those campaigning against DIDR (Said 2002).

Through the affective pull of their imaginative testimony, writer-activists aim to bring the socio-cultural and environmental threats posed by DIDR emotionally to life by communicating and humanising oustees' fears and apprehensions. As such, literary displacement narratives are not simply 'tales' whose value is primarily aesthetic or literary but politicised discourses that aim, whether explicitly or implicitly, to motivate public action and influence policy by drawing public attention to the alternative perspectives and demands of those Cernea (1999) has described as 'the people in the way' of big development schemes.

Moreover, because displacement literature is often written in response to the failure of outsiders to adequately represent the oustee community's interests and concerns, it explicitly articulates the oustee experience of displacement *in their own terms*, using organising principles from their culture's own symbolic universe instead of being refracted through the mediating lens of expert 'others', whose interpretational authority has long been privileged over those most affected by the DIDR process (Chaturvedi 2000, p. 184). As such, literature can provide an intimate insight into private histories, experiences and perspectives that might otherwise remain unrecorded or hidden from the public domain (Bennett and MacDowell 2012).

Similarly, because of the long time frame and multiple perspectives literary texts encompass, they can help reveal the complex, contradictory and often shifting responses to involuntary displacement across ethnic, class and gender lines that may provide greater insight into the communal perceptions of oustee groups towards DIDR and help explain why resistance to development occurs. While not always strictly objective or historically accurate, therefore, literature's long lens, which encompasses the periods before, during and post-resettlement, makes it a suitable medium to reflect on what Nixon has called the 'long dyings' of minority cultures that exceed the bounds of individual human memory (Nixon 2011, p. 3).

However, despite literature's clear role in DIDR activism, literary and cultural studies have yet to be fully integrated into the field. As with cognate disciplines such as disaster studies (Carrigan 2013), a literary approach may prove useful in furthering our understanding of both why communities resist development and the discursive strategies deployed by writer-activists to amplify oustee voices and demands in the political domain in order to enhance the effectiveness of grassroots DIDR activism.

Egyptian Nubians and the Aswan am case

The importance of literature as a vehicle for both articulating and advancing DIDR activism can be observed in the case of writer-activists connected to the revivalist cultural movement known as *Ṣaḥwa Nubiyya* or 'Nubian Awakening' from 1968 to the present. Their writing represents the voices, experiences and demands of the Egyptian Nubian community displaced by four successive waves of involuntary displacement and resettlement over the course of the twentieth century to make way for dams on the river Nile.

The Aswan Low Dam was constructed in 1902 and subsequently raised in 1912 and 1933 respectively, displacing 11 villages within a relatively small geographical area, although exact number of displacees was not recorded. In 1964, the Aswan High Dam flooded all that remained of ancient Nubia on either side of the Egyptian/Sudanese border, as a result of which an estimated 50,000 Egyptian Nubians were resettled to the area known as 'New Nubia', 75 kilometres north of Aswan, while 70,000 Sudanese Nubians were sent to the 'New Halfa' Irrigation Scheme on the Sudanese border with Ethiopia (Dafalla and Nordiska afrikainstitutet c. 1975; Fahim 1980).

Ethnographic studies on the Nubian community both prior to and immediately following the resettlement were conducted by Scudder (1968), Fernea and Gerster (1971–1973), Adams (1977), Kennedy (1978), Hohenwart (1979), Rouchdy (1980) and Fahim (1972–1982) (all cited in Hopkins and Mehanna 2010) to assess the extent to which Egyptian Nubians had adapted to life in their new environment. While acknowledging a general decline in living standards and increase in multidimensional stresses in the years immediately post-displacement, these early studies suggested that, overall, there had been 'a positive resettlement outcome' (Scudder 2006, p. 74), particularly given that the younger generation appeared positively inclined towards the idea of building a 'modern Nubia' with greater employment opportunities that could prevent labour migration and keep families together.

However, despite initial indications that Egyptian Nubians would soon adapt to their new environment and feel 'at home' in the resettlement site, a longitudinal ethnographic study conducted by anthropologist Hussein Fahim from 1969 to 1982 (Fahim and Field 1972; Fahim 1980; Fahim 1983) found that over 15 years after resettlement there was severe social and psychological breakdowns and the prevalence of 'resettlement illness' among the oustees (Fahim 1983, p. 109). Among the reasons cited were inadequate community consultation; poor scheduling of moves; the breakdown of neighbourhood, family and kinship ties; widespread disappointment about unfulfilled government promises; feelings of cultural and environmental dislocation; and the limited economic resources and opportunities available in New Nubia (Fahim 1983, pp. 111–161).

Indeed, by the mid 1980s, many villagers had still not received formal title deeds to the land that formed part of their compensation package and lost their motivation to invest in the resettlement site, while many of those who remained, and had not migrated to the cities in search of work, became dependent on state aid or remittances from family members or were actively dreaming of departure (Shami and Center for Migration Studies (US) 1994, p. 157). It was this tendency to look beyond the resettlement site, both in terms of expanding existing patterns of secondary migration and returning, in limited numbers, to the shores of Lake Nasser to resettle their homeland that led Fahim to conclude that 'the Kom Ombo settlement failed, in the eyes of most Nubians, to become a viable community that could provide a promising future' (Fahim 1983, p. 111).

However, since 1983 no further longitudinal studies of resettlement dynamics in New Nubia have been published, save for a partially updated version of

Kennedy and Fernea's *Nubian Ceremonial Life: Studies in Islamic Syncretism and Cultural Change* (2005) which records the changing cultural traditions of Old Nubia in the 50 years leading up to construction of the Aswan High Dam. Because its main findings are based on fieldwork carried out by members of the Ethnological Survey of Egypt in the 1960s immediately prior to, and post, displacement, it is not clear to what extent these cultural traditions had continued to be observed in the resettlement site, although Fernea notes in the revised introduction that because many were linked to the topography and geography of old Nubia, it was likely they had changed or disappeared entirely over time (Kennedy and Fernea 2005, p. x).

Speaking through the silence, literary texts such as Muhammad Khalil Qasim's *The River Gauge* (2011 [1968]), Yahya Mukhtār's *Mountains of Kohl* (1975), Haggag Oddoul's *Nights of Musk* (1989) and Idris 'Ali's *Dongola: A Novel of Nubia* (1998) refocus critical attention on to marginalised Nubian voices, perspectives and experiences which, as Mukhtār observes, 'were only documented in literature, never in the history books' (Saad 2012). As well as helping fill this knowledge gap by providing an insider's perspective about the long-term impact of DIDR and the ways in which the community, historically, has sought to resist DIDR, contemporary Nubian literature also constitutes a powerful form of DIDR activism in its own right by intervening in the public sphere to provoke a political response to long-marginalised Nubian demands for social justice and cultural recognition.

By way of example, Muhammad Khalil Qasim's novel *The River Gauge* (Qasim 2011 [1968]), which was first published in 1968, is the first literary text to focus on the marginalised Nubian experience of dam-induced displacement and resettlement. In describing the long-term impacts of previous dam-induced displacements on Nubian culture and society and articulating the community's material and symbolic resistance to DIDR, it proffers an alternative reading of the social and environmental legacy of the Aswan Dam to that embedded in hegemonic discourses of the period and draws the reader's attention to the need to mitigate the economic, social and environmental injustices that stem from involuntary displacement.

Case study: Muhammad Khalil Qasim's *The River Gauge* (2011 [1968])

A long social realist novel describing life in the village of Qata in the years prior to, during and after the second raising of the Aswan Low Dam in 1933, *The River Gauge* is divided into two parts, the first of which is primarily ethnographic and documents the details of Nubian customary life, from birth, death and marriage rites to the harvest season and religious festivals, accompanied by detailed descriptions of the village architecture, landscape, dress and food. By contrast, the second half of the novel is much more deeply politicised, chronicling the community's material and symbolic resistance to the dam project; their hurried evacuation to the barren hills on the far bank of the Nile; and the multidimensional stresses and impoverishment risks they face in the resettlement site in the years that follow.

Although a work of fiction, the novel nevertheless contains clear autobiographical elements. Like Hamid, the child-narrator, Qasim was born in Qata in the 1920s and was 11 when the Aswan Barrage was raised in 1933, whereupon his father chose to send his son to primary school in Aneeba due to the widespread perception amongst the community that educating the youth was the key to escaping the poverty and denigration to which the Nubian community had often been subjected. However, *The River Gauge* not only derives from Qasim's subjective personal recollections and perspectives but is the product of sustained critical engagement with fellow Nubian detainees in Wāhāt prison such as Salah Hafez, Fareed Faraj, Hassan Fuad and Zahdi and Ali al-Shalqani who assisted in the elaboration of the narrative ('Aleywa 2011, p. 10), suggesting a more balanced, objective and representative narrative voice than one would expect to find in a purely autobiographical text.

Thus, although it is narrated primarily by Hamid through the prism of his lived experience, the novel not only expresses the unitary perspective of the first-person narrator towards displacement and resettlement but moves between characters and locations. This technique provides multiple lenses from across the spectrum of Nubian society from which to view the community's response to the proposed dam project and the major political developments taking place at both local and national levels, including the attempted assassination of Prime Minister Sidqi Pasha by Nubian separatist Hussein Taha and the imprisonment of Nubian political activists resisting DIDR.

Given the political censorship that prevailed when *The River Gauge* was written, whereby any overt criticism of the Aswan Dam was deemed subversive or even treacherous (Fahim 1980, p. 29; Kérisel 2001, pp. 120–142), couching his dissenting views in the medium of a fictional autobiography of childhood may have given Qasim a greater degree of discursive freedom and protective cover in articulating resistance to DIDR.

DIDR resistance is first justified in the novel as an existential imperative for the Nubian people on the basis that 'even sheep do something en route to the slaughter house!' (Qasim 2011 [1968], p. 71). This position is subsequently given religious backing when the Imam Sheikh Sabir endorses opposition to the dam in his Friday sermon and cites examples from the Qur'an and the hadith to legitimise the villagers' opposition to state policy both in the eyes of the villagers and, presumably, to vindicate this stance in the eyes of the reader (Qasim 2011 [1968], p. 365).

The first strategy employed by Nubian activists to mobilise people to resist DIDR is a lobbying campaign whereby local people were encouraged to add their signatures to petitions and open letters rejecting the proposed dam project, and complaining about the undervaluation of their lands and property by the compensation committee and the proposed resettlement site in Upper Egypt (Qasim 2011 [1968], p. 290). However, instead of being read, considered and acted upon by the authorities in Cairo, we learn that these complaints 'were thrown immediately upon arrival into the rubbish bin' (Qasim 2011 [1968], p. 397). Realising that the institutional complaints mechanism merely acted as a 'safety valve' for them to vent their anger rather than providing a meaningful platform for political redress, the villagers start to explore other avenues of resistance.

The reader is then invited to 'listen in' on the Nubian community's clandestine elaboration of strategies for blocking the dam project and rejecting the proposed compensation allowance that go beyond strategies of non-violence resistance to encompass violent insurrection, including the Nubian activist Taha Hussein's audacious plan to assassinate the Egyptian Prime Minister Ismail Sidqi. This attempt ultimately fails, resulting in the detention and imprisonment of many local activists. More successful, however, is the campaign to boycott the government's compensation scheme, which represented a significant undervaluation of their land and property, whereby militias staffed by local volunteers set up a permanent cordon around the *omda* (headman's) house with the aim of extracting a more advantageous compensation arrangement from the authorities.

However, despite their best efforts to create a unified front for DIDR resistance, grassroots morale quickly crumbles due to the effects of poverty, disease and famine on the local population and the lure of the 'crisp green guineas' that represented more money than the Nubian oustees had ever held in their hands at once (Qasim 2011 [1968], pp. 348–398). Thus, although it is structured as a resistance narrative, what *The River Gauge* ultimately depicts is the initial failure of local resistance movements to stop the raising of the Aswan Dam.

As the narrative moves to the barren West Bank of the Nile following displacement, it is clear that the losses endured as the oustees struggle to adjust to their new physical environment are emotional as well as material, causing the narrator to observe that although its inhabitants remained the same, 'the village was no longer our village' (Qasim 2011 [1968], p. 495). The text describes how, after a fire destroyed their makeshift dwellings and consumed their belongings, livestock, food supplies and the compensation money they had received, 'misery gripped the hearts of the people and they lived in the open air and didn't even think about erecting new tents', causing the community to sink into even greater poverty (Qasim 2011 [1968], pp. 463–498).

Consumed by listlessness, anger and despair, the community stops observing key cultural rites such as weddings and religious festivals in a spiral of 'cultural involution'. Thus, rather than preparing for Eid in the customary manner, with elaborate and time-consuming religious and culinary rituals, the villagers do nothing except for 'playing *sija* [gambling], lying on the ground or staring at the east bank of the Nile which had turned into a huge lake, grieving for their lost home' (Qasim 2011 [1968], p. 469), which aptly illustrates the extent to which social disarticulation had taken hold in the resettlement site.

The novel also makes clear that the sorrow and alienation caused by social disarticulation not only affected the oustees who had remained on the West Bank of the Nile at Karan Nawj opposite their ancestral village, but was a repeated pattern among the Nubian oustees who had resettled in Upper Egypt. Thus, when Hamid's father expresses a wish to move away in search of a better life there, Fadel tells him that Nubian oustees faced similar challenges in the other resettlement sites. Flourishing Sheikh Saber's letter from Tawd he states:

> '[I]t's all the same Amin. Here you have got nothing but stones but in Upper Egypt there is only barren land with no water', reading aloud an extract that warns them that they 'haven't seen the Nile since we arrived. The land in front of our eyes seems dead and people are not welcoming. They regard us as strangers', ending 'Eid al Fitr Mubarak from this strange country. We wish you a happier Eid in our country [ie. Nubia]'.
>
> (Qasim 2011 [1968], p. 470)

However, rather than descend into a chronic state of hopelessness, the text suggests that the principles of self-reliance and mutual help derived from the experience of DIDR resistance is an essential component of the community's efforts to improvise solutions to problems they encounter on the ground in the resettlement site. Thus, it narrates that following the fire that destroys their homes and possessions, the villagers became determined to rebuild their lives once again and 'turn the yellow land green' through irrigation and cultivation (Qasim 2011 [1968], p. 402). Despite the initial absence of government aid, they manage to replace their canvas tents with orderly rows of stone houses and devise novel irrigation techniques such as digging deep wells in the mountainside to access groundwater and constructing a system of waterwheels to lift the river water up the steep slope of the river bank to their fields (Qasim 2011 [1968], pp. 482, 507).

Thus, although the community failed to stop the dam project itself, the text emphasises how Nubian oustees reapplied the campaigning strategies learned in resisting DIDR to launch new petitions to the Egyptian authorities using the slogan: '*Nahnū mankubūn al-t'alīa al-thānia*' ('We are those afflicted by the second rising [of the barrage]') (Qasim 2011 [1968], p. 481). Centred around practical demands aimed at improving conditions in the resettlement site such as irrigation pumps, new hospitals and the removal of age barriers to education, the oustees partially achieve their objectives by the end of the novel. It concludes with Hamid leaving the village to attend primary school in the new administrative centre at Aneeba to gain the skills and knowledge he needs to succeed in wider Egyptian society, which, in the novel's symbolic economy, symbolises the importance of casting off the constraints of old ways of thinking in order to secure economic and social progress at both the individual and communal level.

The political outcomes of Nubian literary DIDR activism

This brief analysis of Qasim's early Nubian resistance novel *The River Gauge* suggests that literature not only provides a platform for the displaced to raise awareness among the public and decision makers about the long-term impacts of DIDR that might otherwise remain unvoiced, but enhances the visibility of their voices in situations where oustees are politically and socially marginalised to promote political change.

As the Nubian writer-activist Haggag Hassan Oddoul has observed, the affective power of storytelling lies both in its capacity to humanise experiences of displacement and generate an emotional reaction to injustice in order to 'influence professional politicians, no matter how much they would prefer to ignore it' (Aboul-Ela 2005). As such, literary displacement narratives are not simply 'tales' but politicised discourses that aim to influence public policy by drawing transnational attention to the issues at stake and thus pressurising those in power to listen more attentively to the views of oustees and, crucially, take action (Bennett and MacDowell 2012).

With this in mind, I would argue that the growing readership and increasing critical esteem in which Nubian literature has been held at both domestic and international level over the course of the last 20 years may help explain why long-standing demands for social and economic justice, cultural recognition and the 'right to return' to Nubia finally became matters of government concern after decades of inaction by Presidents Nasser, Sadat and Mubarak.

Not only were Oddoul, Mukhtār and 'Ali awarded a number of prestigious literary awards including the State Encouragement Prize for Fiction and the Sawiris Cultural Foundation prize between 1990 and 2005, which enhanced their cultural capital and authority within the Egyptian establishment, but Oddoul's play *People of the River* and 'Ali's *Nubia.com* were performed in Cairo to widespread popular acclaim in 2007. Their widespread appeal helped generate informed public discussion in the press and within the political establishment about the 'Nubian question' (Jacquemond 2008, pp. 183–184).

At an international level, the translation of a number of important contemporary Nubian literary texts, including Idris 'Ali's polemical novel *Dongola: A Novel of Nubia* (1998) calling for direct political action to reclaim Nubian rights, which received the University of Arkansas Press Award for Translation in 2003, made Nubian literature available to a global readership for the first time. In parallel, texts written by writers in solidarity with the Nubian cause, notably Anne Michaels' acclaimed novel *The Winter Vault* (Michaels 2010), both increased international awareness of the Nubian's history of displacement and comparatively situated this as part of the wider transnational critique of megadams, which may have further increased pressure on the Egyptian authorities to act.

Due to its transnational reach and growing public popularity, literature by Nubian writer-activists came to occupy a privileged position from which to advocate more effectively for political demands. This process is illustrated by the fact that the Cairo International Book Fair and Egyptian Ministry of Culture held seminars on the impact of Nubian literature on Egyptian culture for the first time in late 2011 (Masress 2011), while in April 2011 a major conference entitled 'The Problem of Nubian Rights before and after the January 25 Revolution' brought together prominent writers, intellectuals and political activists who reiterated long-standing political demands for compensation; cultural and language rights; guaranteed electoral representation; and the 'right of return' to their homeland which was widely reported in the press (Begg 2011).

Partly as a result of this growing public pressure, and partly as a result of the more democratic and pluralist aspirations unleashed by the January 25 Revolution, developments at the political level quickly followed. In July 2011 it was reported that the Egyptian authorities had announced their 'full support' for

Nubian calls to resettle the shores of Lake Nasser and were considering rebuilding some Nubian villages closer to Old Nubia in the Toshka Depression (Begg 2011). Little action was taken to implement this decree until July 2013, however, due to the political turmoil that culminated in the ousting of President Morsi, when the prominent Nubian writer-activist Haggag Hassan Oddoul was appointed to the 'Rights and Freedoms subcommittee' in the 50-member Assembly charged with amending the Egyptian Constitution.

Oddoul's role was to ensure not only that the amended constitution included suitable guarantees of minority culture and language rights but to negotiate long-standing Nubian political demands (Salah 2013). These aspirations were finally fulfilled in January 2014 when Article 236 of the new Egyptian constitution was signed into law, guaranteeing Nubian cultural, political and language rights for the first time as well as legally enshrining the Nubian people's 'right to return' to their original territories and develop settlements there 'within 10 years' (al-Nubi 2013).

Representing the fruition of hard-fought Nubian resistance and DIDR activism ever since construction of the Aswan High Dam in 1964, this I would argue could never have been achieved without the cumulative pressure of public voices such as those of Oddoul, 'Ali, Mukhtār and Qasim which helped change public perceptions of the legitimacy of Nubian demands and generate the political leverage necessary to pave the way for political reform.

Conclusion

As I have attempted to show, beyond the documental value that literary texts can provide about the strategies employed by oustee communities to resist DIDR and its long-term impacts on their social and cultural life, literature itself can play a vital role in DIDR activism by enhancing the visibility of oustees' voices and political demands. Literary displacement narratives such as Muhammad Khalil Qasim's *The River Gauge* and Idris 'Ali's *Dongola: A Novel of Nubia* spoke through the silence at the heart of the Egyptian establishment to raise public consciousness at national and international levels about the long-term costs of dam-related displacement and resettlement on the Nubian people which helped leverage political reform. By intervening directly in the public sphere to lend legitimacy and weight to oustee perspectives and demands, writer-activists and their oeuvres constitute an important, if under-studied, aspect of DIDR activism that merits further critical consideration.

References

Aboul-Ela, H., 2005. Haggag Hassan Adoul: Nubia's Human Aspirations: Interview conducted by H. Aboul-Ela in *The Nubian*, 23 January. Available at: thenubian.net/haggag/interview.doc [Accessed 5 April 2012].

'Aleywa, Q.M., 2011. Introduction to Al-Shamandoura. In M.K. Qasim, *Al-Shamandoura*. Cairo, Egypt: Al-haya al-'aāma lee quṣuwr al-thaqafa.

'Ali, I., 1998. *Dongola: A Novel of Nubia*. Fayetteville: University of Arkansas Press.

al-Nubi, M., 2013. Al-Ahram Publishes the Draft Egyptian Constitution in English, *Al-Ahram*, Cairo, issue 46410, 30 December. Available at: www.ahram.org.eg/NewsQ/250587.aspx [Accessed 30 April 2014].

Begg, T., 2011. What Next For Egypt's Forgotten Minority? *Think Africa Press*, 14 July 2011. Available at: http://thinkafricapress.com/egypt/what-next-egypts-forgotten-minority [Accessed 5 April 2012].

Bennett, O. and MacDowell, C., 2012. *Displaced: the human cost of development and resettlement*, New York: Palgrave Macmillan.

Carrigan, A., 2013. The Cultural Politics of Prevention: Postcolonial Disaster and the Environmental Humanities. In *11th ASNEL Postgraduate Summer School*. Just Politics? Postcolonial Ecocriticism between Imagination and Occupation. Universität Potsdam.

Cernea, M., 1999. *The Economics of Involuntary Resettlement: Questions and Challenges*, Washington, DC: World Bank.

Chaturvedi, V., 2000. *Mapping subaltern studies and the postcolonial*, London: Verso.

Dafalla, H. and Nordiska afrikainstitutet., c. 1975. *The Nubian exodus*, London: C. Hurst, in association with the Scandinavian Institute of African Studies, Uppsala.

Fahim, H.M., 1980. *Dams, people, and development: the Aswan High Dam case*, New York: Pergamon Press.

Fahim, H.M., 1983. *Egyptian Nubians: resettlement and years of coping*, Salt Lake City, UT: University of Utah Press.

Fahim, H.M. and Field, H., 1972. *Nubian resettlement in the Sudan*, Coconut Grove, FL: Field Research Projects.

Hopkins, N.S. and Mehanna, S.R., 2010. *Nubian encounters: the story of the Nubian ethnological survey 1961–1964*. Cairo: The American University of Cairo Press.

Jacquemond, R., 2008. *Conscience of the nation: writers, state, and society in modern Egypt*, Cairo; New York: American University in Cairo Press.

Kennedy, J.G. and Fernea, R.A., 2005. *Nubian ceremonial life: studies in Islamic syncretism and cultural change*, Cairo: American University in Cairo Press.

Kérisel, J., 2001. *The Nile and its masters: past, present, future: source of hope and anger*, Rotterdam; Brookfield, VT: A.A. Balkema.

Masress, 2011. Culture Minister to Host Nubian Literature Seminar, 23 September. Available at: www.masress.com/en/youm7en/345569 [Accessed 5 April 2012].

McCully, P., 2001. *Silenced rivers: the ecology and politics of large dams*, London: Zed Books.

Michaels, A., 2010. *The winter vault*, London: Bloomsbury.

Mukhtār, Y., 1975. *Mountains of Kohl* [*Jibāl Al-Koḥl: Riwāya Min Al-Nūba*], Cairo: Dar al-Hilal.

Nixon, R., 2011. *Slow violence and the environmentalism of the poor*, Cambridge, MA: Harvard University Press.

Oddoul, H.H., 1989. *Nights of Musk* [*Layālī al-Misk al-'Atīqa*], Cairo: Kotobarabia.

Oliver-Smith, A., 2011. *Defying displacement: grassroots resistance and the critique of development*, Austin, TX; Chesham: University of Texas Press; Combined Academic [distributor].

Qasim, M.K., 2011 [1968]. *The River Gauge* [*Al-Shamandoura*], 3rd edn, Cairo, Egypt: Al-Hay'a al-'Ama Lee Qusuwr al-Thaqafa.

Roy, A., 1999. The Greater Common Good. *www.narmada.org*. Available at: www.narmada.org/gcg/gcg.html [Accessed 10 September 2013].

Saad, M., 2012. Borders Writers: Decades of Marginalisation and the Quest of Justice – Books – Ahram Online. Available at: http://english.ahram.org.eg/NewsContentP/18/33294/Books/Borders-writers-Decades-of-marginalisation-and-the.aspx [Accessed 5 April 2012].

Said, E., 2002. The Public Role of Writers and Intellectuals. In Small, H. (ed.) *The Public Intellectual*. Oxford: Blackwell, pp. 19–39.

Salah, F., 2013. The Forgotten Minorities: Egypt's Nubians and Amazigh in the Amended Constitution. *EgyptSource*. Available at: www.atlanticcouncil.org/blogs/egyptsource/the-forgotten-minorities-egypt-s-nubians-and-amazigh-in-the-amended-constitution [Accessed 14 July 2014].

Scott, J.C., 1990. *Domination and the arts of resistance: hidden transcripts*, New Haven, CT; London: Yale University Press.

Scott, J.C., 1998. *Seeing like a state: how certain schemes to improve the human condition have failed*, New Haven, CT: Yale University Press.

Scudder, T. [Main author], 2006. *The future of large dams: dealing with social, environmental and political costs*, London: Earthscan.

Shami, S.K. and Center for Migration Studies (US), 1994. *Population displacement and resettlement: development and conflict in the Middle East*, New York: Center for Migration Studies.

World Bank, 2001. Ext Opmanual – OP 4.12 – Involuntary Resettlement. *World Bank*. Available at: http://web.worldbank.org/WBSITE/EXTERNAL/PROJECTS/EXTPOLICIES/EXTOPMANUAL/0,,contentMDK:20064610~menuPK:64701637~pagePK:64709096~piPK:64709108~theSitePK:502184,00.html#_ftn1 [Accessed 12 August 2014].

World Commission on Dams, 2000. *Dams and development: a new framework for decision-making. The report of the World Commission on Dams: an overview*, London; Sterling, VA: Earthscan.

14 Activists in urban forced resettlement

Dolores Koenig

Introduction

A major problem of existing approaches to development-induced displacement and resettlement (DIDR) is the neglect of its political aspects, including conflicts of interest and power differentials between resettled communities and larger political economic forces as well as within resettled groups (Koenig, 2006, p. 111). DIDR activism, political action that calls into question existing power relations, argues for greater inclusion of the affected, involving them in decisions about infrastructure and in formulating and implementing resettlement initiatives.

This chapter focuses on DIDR activism in urban areas to better understand the strategies that activists employ and to examine the extent to which they have changed the balance of power and outcomes of displacement and resettlement. The first two sections provide background information on the approach of DIDR analysts to activism and the role of activists in urban areas. The next section discusses the methodology of this chapter. The final two sections consider urban activism in the context of DIDR. One presents major activist strategies while the other discusses the success of activists in bringing about change. The conclusion outlines potential steps for research and practice.

DIDR and activism

DIDR activism, the organized efforts of the affected to achieve specific goals, is extremely common and includes attempts to stop infrastructure construction, to decrease numbers resettled, and to get better resettlement benefits and compensation. Scholars have outlined reasons for resistance to individual dams, such as the Narmada in India (Fisher, 2009), and carried out synthetic analyses of DIDR resistance (Oliver-Smith, 2006). Scholarly analysis has been complemented by the work of international non-governmental organizations (NGOs) to support resistance against forced resettlement because of human rights and environmental concerns (Clark, 2009). Most of the focus has been on resistance to dams, especially in rural areas. Urban activism within the context of DIDR has yet to receive full scholarly attention.

This chapter complements this work by looking specifically at urban DIDR. While exhibiting many similarities, rural and urban DIDR differ in three important ways. First, in many rural areas, infrastructure construction disrupts relative autonomy from centers of power. Consequently, rural resistance often emphasizes cultural preservation, especially for indigenous peoples, and avoids the power of centralized states (Oliver-Smith, 2006). This was not an issue in the urban DIDR I investigated; displaced urbanites more often wanted to conserve or increase the benefits from living within national cultures. Second, international NGOs have played an important role in rural resistance, offering financial and logistical support (Fisher, 2009). While some urban activists benefited from transnational links, most relied on domestic alliances. Third, the focus of rural and urban activism is different. Since most rural people subsist directly from their lands, by farming, fishing, or herding, reconstruction of land-based assets is vital. In contrast, urban residents are more likely to generate livelihoods from jobs that require assets other than land; land for housing is valued, but economic reconstruction needs attention to other assets (Koenig, 2009).

Resettlement policies generally do not mention activism or resistance and instead focus on delivering what is considered to be good resettlement. Generally, this includes minimizing the numbers displaced, planning development programs to improve or maintain livelihoods, consulting the affected about resettlement options, and encouraging their participation in planning and implementing resettlement programs (WB, 2001; ADB, 2009; IFC, 2012).

General development theorists argue that the participation of affected groups is crucial for sustainable development (Nolan, 2002). Notwithstanding, critics have argued that development practitioners often use participation instrumentally (Mosse, 2005), as consultation and participation are usually articulated through officially defined channels and activities designed top-down by implementing organizations. Evidence suggests that the situation is similar in DIDR projects. Although participation is emphasized in the major DIDR policies, the word remains undefined, consistent with Rew et al. (2006, p. 47) observation that policies and programs often use vague terms that can be interpreted in myriad ways. The experience of India's Mumbai Urban Transport Project (MUTP), which relocated some 20,000 households in the early 2000s, is indicative. Having received World Bank funding, this project was required to follow its guidelines on consultation and participation.[1] However, the World Bank Inspection Panel (2005, p. 91) noted that "when meetings with [project affected persons] took place, 'consultation' with them seemed to be more in the nature of telling them what was to occur than engaging them in meaningful discussion on alternative options."

Moreover, urban initiatives often displace people without much consultation or notice (UN Habitat, 2007, p. 236). When projects were funded primarily by national governments, eviction might take place abruptly and unilaterally. In the MUTP, at least 10,000 people were evicted with little consultation before 2002, when the funding agreement was signed by the World Bank and the government of India (World Band Inspection Panel, 2005, p. 21).

Project authorities are often reluctant to cede meaningful decision-making powers to the affected and displaced. Amid the complexities and contradictions of DIDR, the conflicting time frames of different actors and competing visions of development can turn shared decision making into open-ended political negotiation with unpredictable outcomes and costs (de Wet, 2006, pp. 187–188). Even those who strongly favor participation and inclusion admit that implementation remains challenging. The World Commission on Dams acknowledged that even in open-ended negotiations, all parties, working in good faith, may not be able to find consensus on how to proceed (WCD, 2000, p. 210). Scudder (2005, p. 303) noted that stakeholder representatives often need to be "instructed" about the nature and objectives of consultative decision making.

Urban activism and DIDR

Urban areas are well situated for activist efforts because they are densely populated and usually close to centers of power. New activists as well as those already working toward political change are primed to address DIDR when it threatens urban residents. Dense urban organization allows groups to multiply efforts to exert pressure on municipal and national governments on many issues, including DIDR. Moreover, high urban density expedites the communication of resettlement knowledge and rumors (Koenig, 2009, p. 135).

Despite these advantages, urban density also presents problems. Some 75 years ago, Louis Wirth (1938) remarked that cities offered people anonymity and freedom from traditional social bonds. Several activists I interviewed reiterated such sentiments, stating that urbanites often exhibited more individualism than their rural counterparts, making efforts to organize them consistently and collectively toward social change quite difficult. Indeed, activist groups themselves can have very different points of view about the problems they face and how to solve them. When they differ on priority goals, strategies, or tactics, it is difficult to act in solidarity.

Because cities are centers of power, they contain powerful elites, often living in class segregated neighborhoods. Nonetheless, poorer residents often live in close proximity and have economic and political contacts with the more affluent. They work for and with the better-off, collecting their garbage and selling them food and other goods (Koenig, 2009). In democratic societies, the less affluent are courted by elites during elections because of the large number of votes they represent. In both Senegal and India, activists that I interviewed mentioned the importance of the urban poor as a political bloc. To expand the poor's influence, community organizers, NGOs, and other activists, usually national, but sometimes international, worked with the less affluent to combat poverty and inequality and to improve daily life. As one Indian activist told me, the goals of his organization were to minimize displacement, get the state to recognize its obligations to its citizens, and protect property and human rights before, during, and after development.

The approach: a synthetic overview

This chapter offers an initial attempt at understanding the strategies and successes of urban DIDR activism. It remains largely exploratory because few readily available studies focus on the subject. Like the archives relied on by historians, information is patchy, varying greatly in detail. While many studies refer to displacement and resettlement in passing, rarely is information presented systematically. Each document serves as a kind of ethnographic snapshot from a particular place and time with little or no indication of later effects. Since complete data are often unavailable and ultimate outcomes remain unclear, my goal in this chapter is to synthesize many sources to create a basic framework for what is known about urban DIDR activism. The findings presented over subsequent pages should be considered hypotheses for further study.

Documentary evidence was collected from written sources, including scholarly studies, NGO, governmental, and private reports, and popular press accounts. I was able to complement the documentary study with several short field trips in 2008–2009, funded by an American University Presidential Fellowship. I targeted five cities demonstrating rapid growth and displacement: Mumbai and Delhi in India and Dakar, Bamako, and Ouagadougou in West Africa. I interviewed scholars, policy makers, NGO representatives, and others involved with DIDR. Comments from interviews are usually paraphrases from comprehensive notes rather than direct quotes. I also collected local scholarly and media accounts.

Five major cases

While a wide number of sources and examples are mentioned, I rely on five primary cases for this chapter because they offered the most detailed and applicable information on DIDR activism. They reflect a variety of different DIDR causes and political and economic contexts across diverse global milieus.

Expressway construction, Washington, D.C., U.S.A.

The 1950 Master Plan for the District of Columbia envisaged the construction of major new expressways as part of the interstate highway system proposed by President Eisenhower. One planned road would destroy some 4,000 homes in predominantly African American neighborhoods. In the mid 1960s, as formal planning began, a group of directly affected black Washingtonians joined with concerned white citizens to create the Emergency Committee on the Transportation Crisis to prevent construction. Building on the experience the different groups had in the Civil Rights movement, activists used demonstrations, public protest, and petition drives, collaborated with planning groups, and sued in the courts. By 1976, they had procured an agreement that road funds could be used to construct Washington's subway system. In 1980, work on the expressway system was definitively stopped. The source of this case is documentary (Levey and Levey, 2000).

Castanhão Dam and Pecem Industrial and Port Complex, Brazil

Poor urban residents in this community were working for social change with a local community organizer when plans for a dam and adjoining industrial complex were announced in 1985. Upon hearing about the new infrastructure project, the group quickly reoriented its social justice efforts to oppose dam construction. Despite securing support from the Brazilian anti-dam movement, several pro-poor organizations, and various other domestic groups, those vulnerable to displacement were unable to prevent construction. Between 1995, when work on the project began, and 2002, when the dam became operational, activists did convince the government to listen to their concerns. Among other things, they sought assurances that, should resettlement occur, they would be resettled together and could participate in the design of the relocation site. Although the government believed that some project opposition emerged because of inadequate information or "misinformation," it spearheaded Multiparticipatory Groups, which brought together government, project representatives, and affected residents at both the dam and industrial sites. Community members became active participants, using these groups as forums to discuss many issues, including public safety and environmental protection. However, as of 2009, many of the planned development projects remained unbuilt, and the resettled faced unemployment and economic problems. The source of this case is documentary (Tankha et al., 1998; Amorim, 2009).

Eviction from Senou airport zone, Bamako, Mali

In 1995, residents from the Senou neighborhood near the Bamako airport were summarily evicted and their houses razed without warning when the airport zone was expanded. After demolition, the affected organized an association to get indemnities and undertook a census of inhabitants and demolished buildings. They called upon the *Association Malienne des Droits de l'Homme* (Malian Association for Human Rights) and *L'Espace d'Interpellation Démocratique* (Space for Democratic Claims) to help publicize their plight to a wider audience. The group recounted its experiences on local radio and television. In 2000, the government allocated to the residents a substantial piece of land on which to construct a new neighborhood. In 2009, roads were being built and schools, markets, and public services were under construction. The source of this case is field research, complemented by a written account by an anthropologist from the neighborhood (Koné, 2009).

MUTP, Mumbai, India

Although metropolitan Mumbai, formerly Bombay, is one of India's major economic centers with a population of some 18 million, conditions remain far from what planners consider a world class city. Transport, water, and sewage infrastructure are all deficient. An estimated 40 percent of the population lives in substandard housing, and the government considers many Mumbaikars to be squatters in unrecognized neighborhoods (Koenig, 2014). Planners want to improve transportation, including better roads, rail, bridges, metro rail, and airports; they also want to upgrade housing and eliminate slums. Despite good intentions, these efforts displace large numbers of people. Evictions still occur, especially in unrecognized slums. For example, nearly 86,000 domiciles situated in and around Sanjay Gandhi National Park were destroyed in 2003. In late 2004 and early 2005, another 80,000 homes across Mumbai were demolished (UN Habitat, 2007, p. 158).

India's democratic traditions, based on Gandhi's mass activism, a free press, and regular elections, provide a context for the urban poor to press their causes. Many activist organizations work for the rights of the poor and disadvantaged, with some federating to enhance their impact. Mumbai's active free press commonly writes about urban development and displacement. Interviewees repeatedly reminded me that Mumbai's poor can and do vote. Politicians must promise them benefits such as better housing to be elected. Virtually no displacement and resettlement occurs without protest or commentary.

The MUTP, meant to improve Mumbai's road and rail traffic, resettled 20,000 displaced households in multiple sites. Two activist organizations, Society for the Promotion of Area Resource Centers (SPARC) and the Slum Rehabilitation Society, were hired to assist in project implementation. The affected were allocated new apartments at no cost. While the new accommodations were tiny (a standard 225 square feet), over 95 percent of households had more space than before (TISS, 2008, p. 9). The resettled also received assistance in creating cooperative housing societies and a fund whose interest was used to pay some required fees. The affected did not accept the resettlement conditions without protest. Affected shopkeepers, working with several NGOs, brought a complaint to the World Bank Inspection Panel in 2004, arguing that compensation did not conform to the Bank's Involuntary Resettlement Policy. With support from an NGO, YUVA, the residents at one Mumbai resettlement site, Vashi Naka, posted a YouTube video about the hunger strike they had undertaken to gain increased benefits (Yuvamedia, 2008). Material about the MUTP and other Mumbai displacement came from field research, supplemented by significant documentary information.

Development in the Muthurwa neighborhood, Nairobi, Kenya

In 2010, renters living in Nairobi's Muthurwa neighborhood were threatened with eviction when the landowners, two pension schemes, decided to sell the land for real estate development. The owners stopped repairing houses, evicted some people, destroyed sanitation systems, and disconnected water. Affected residents organized and went to court, arguing that these actions were counter to the human rights provisions in the Kenyan constitution. The judge temporarily stayed the neighborhood's destruction; residents were to pay their rent and the owners were to maintain the housing. Working with Habitat International

Coalition/Housing and Land Rights Network, the neighborhood carried out a survey to assess the probable losses of those facing displacement. In August 2013, the court ruled that the tenants' rights to adequate housing were violated; the final judgment set standards for their eviction in line with Kenyan law. The judge directed the government to create a legal framework for evictions that adhered to international standards and encouraged the development of a comprehensive urban housing program, but did not directly compensate the evictees for their losses. The land owners and evictees must directly negotiate an eviction program and any compensation, a process underway at the time of publication (Schechla, personal communication). Information on this case is documentary (Lenaola, 2013; Schechla, 2013).

Major forms of DIDR activism

The case studies suggest that urban DIDR activism often begins with attempts to stop displacement-causing projects (Washington, D.C., Castanhão, Muthurwa), but activists may refocus their aims when it becomes clear that the project is going forward. Activists may then try to reduce the numbers of people displaced, get better compensation and benefits, or change other aspects of resettlement. Improvements were also the goal when people were evicted without notice (Senou).

Even when activists realize that they cannot stop construction, they often propose it as an initial gambit to bring developers and policy makers to the negotiating table. As one activist in Mumbai's periphery told me, if a proposal emerged to create a Special Economic Zone in his district, his organization would begin by opposing it, using whatever means made most sense at the time. He believed that only an initial stance of opposition could make the more powerful listen and get the poor their due share of development, including higher compensation, a greater share of profits, and/or guarantees of more jobs.

Strategies to stop or change DIDR build on existing traditions of urban activism and organization, especially notable in Washington, D.C., Castanhão, and Mumbai. Even when new anti-displacement organizations were formed, they often used skills gained by individuals working for other kinds of social change. In Mumbai, for example, housing was one focus of activism, and, for some, served as an element of democratic social change (Das, 2003). Since 1984, SPARC (2014) has worked with Mumbai pavement dwellers to improve their lives and livelihoods and to address the housing crisis of the many that live in informal housing and slums. Moreover, urban activists learned from rural precedents. The movement Gar Bachao Gar Banao Andolan, which assisted urban poor threatened by or subjected to slum demolition, was inspired by Medha Patkar's resistance to the Narmada dams (Fisher, 2009, p. 166). This internationally known activist met with some of those resettled by the MUTP to discuss strategies.

Because its goals and strategies evolve over time, urban DIDR activism is difficult to typologize in a static manner. This section considers six major strategies, used cumulatively where possible.

Negotiating with decision makers

Fieldwork showed that many activist groups started by addressing decision makers about infrastructure development and its effects. Although this proved impossible in cases of sudden eviction, many infrastructure projects are planned well in advance, giving people time to address policy makers and project heads. The only place where this strategy was at least partly effective was Castanhão, where it led to the creation of the Multiparticipatory Groups that facilitated negotiation between the affected and others. This case suggests that if decision makers had the political will to respond to the concerns of the affected and integrate their representatives into decision making, the latter would often accept these invitations. Most case study groups, however, did not meet an open ear from officials and turned to alternative strategies.

Using alliances to build influence and support

Often the voices of the affected are insufficient in themselves to impact proceedings effectively. In these circumstances, activists may create coalitions with other groups to bring their concerns to a wider audience and enhance pressure upon governments. Domestic alliances, common in the cases here, were organized horizontally with other groups in similar situations or vertically with more influential and powerful groups. Alliance building was used in Washington, D.C., Castanhão, Senou, the MUTP, and elsewhere in Mumbai.

Urban and peri-urban activists have also created transnational vertical alliances, partnering with international organizations, often NGOs, with greater resources or influence. Organizations such as the Habitat International Coalition/Housing and Land Rights Network, which assisted the Muthurwa residents, and the International Accountability Project have targeted DIDR. Although many groups found external allies valuable, others believed that their assistance was limited as it was subject to global competition. Several activists in Mumbai pointed out that the 2003–2005 evictions got little international attention despite their attempts to publicize them. They believed that this was due to competition from DIDR elsewhere as well as natural disasters. They said that urban organizations paid more attention to the 700,000 Zimbabweans evicted by President Mugabe's 2005 program of slum clearance, while humanitarian organizations were preoccupied by the December 2004 tsunami that devastated Southeast Asia.

Using media

To enhance the efficacy of DIDR activism, even that supported by coalitions, activists often gained public support for their cause through the local media. Urban areas usually have active radio, television, written press, and new social media based around text messages and the Internet. Activists at Senou used local media outlets to publicize their case; there is much information in the Mumbai press about displacement and resettlement, including the MUTP. One MUTP group posted a YouTube video. Gar Bachao Gar Banao Andolan uses an international listserve to notify people about potential grievances and actions. Use of the media is not limited to those directly affected. In Mumbai, PUKAR's (Partners for Urban Knowledge, Action and Research) publications and exhibits have alerted a large audience to the threat of demolition in deteriorating older neighborhoods (PUKAR Editors' Collective, 2008).

Using national courts

Another common strategy is to file court cases, either before or after displacement, using any available laws, to stop displacement or improve resettlement benefits. Among the five cases studied, the use of domestic courts was most crucial in Washington, D.C., where a decision of the U.S. District Court stopped construction, and Nairobi, Kenya, where petitioners won the right to legal eviction.

Recourse to the policies of international institutions

When international institutions have DIDR or human rights policies, aggrieved residents, often working with activists, have brought information about contraventions of their policies to their attention. In the cases here, shopkeepers from the MUTP received improved benefits after their complaint to the World Bank Inspection Panel. Elsewhere, those affected by Cambodian airport construction, funded by the International Finance Corporation (IFC), brought a case concerning inadequate compensation and resettlement plans to its compliance advisor (CAO, 2010), and Nairobi residents affected by a road project complained to the European Commission that their displacement was contrary to provisions on sustainable development and human rights in the Lome Conventions governing European foreign assistance (Oxfam, 1996).

Mass demonstrations

Other strategies of DIDR activism are sometimes complemented by demonstrations to reinforce media attention, broaden public support, and increase pressure on politicians. Activist organizations marched against the Washington, D.C., freeway, the planned Mumbai metro, and other Mumbai initiatives.

Achievements of DIDR activism

"It is enormously difficult for local populations adversely affected by DIDR to influence their own situation," claimed William Fisher (2009, p. 176) in his discussion of global DIDR activism. Arguably, the urban activists discussed here were not convinced by such sentiments. Even though their commitment to activism was clear, what were the effects of their actions? Tracking outcomes over time is crucial to understand the efficacy of DIDR activism, but it does pose a challenge.

First, it is nearly impossible to know what outcomes would have occurred without the activism. Given DIDR's complexity, many factors play a role. Political negotiation is always highly contingent, and attempts to change DIDR are fundamentally about altering the distribution of power. Since the path of change is neither linear nor unidirectional, DIDR outcomes may take several years to emerge. Second, change takes place gradually: 15 years to stop freeway construction in Washington, D.C.; five years to get a new neighborhood in Senou, but almost 15 to lay it out and get services; about three years from the filing of the Muthurwa court case until the court's ruling. Third, DIDR change is incremental. Although efforts to stop one particular project may prove unsuccessful, they may reshape the landscape for the next project and others to follow. The final section outlines several broad trends discernible in the examples used in this chapter, supplemented by additional information when necessary.

Stopping infrastructure construction

In only one of the examples did activism prevent construction. In contrast to the Washington, D.C., campaign, most local efforts proved unable effectively to block projects. One task for future research is to see whether this pattern is supported over a larger sample of projects.

Activism has sometimes been successful at reducing the overall footprint of urban infrastructure, subjecting fewer people to displacement. In none of the five case studies was the footprint decreased. However, fieldwork showed that the resettlement expert on a Senegalese project to finance roads, municipal buildings, and market places for newly elected communal governments convinced some mayors and communal councils to consider the political repercussions of displacing their constituents. As he noted, those displaced might well organize to eject those politicians from office. Thus, to avoid future activism against them, officials were sometimes persuaded to build in areas where displacement was avoided or decreased.

Carrying out resettlement

Activists have also succeeded in improving resettlement benefits. In two of the four examples where displacement occurred, activism brought better benefits to at least some displaced. In Senou, the displaced got a new neighborhood and official building lots, while MUTP shopkeepers received a better benefit package. Elsewhere, as well, public organizations and private companies were willing to increase compensation so they could begin work, and, in the Philippines, one people's organization negotiated rights to new lots in an urban renewal area (Koenig, 2009, p. 136).

Changing policy

Activism has played a crucial role in efforts to improve DIDR policies. While the bulldozing of so-called slum areas appears to have been relatively common in the decades following World War II, new legal barriers have been instituted in many countries (UN Habitat, 2007, p. 15). Indeed, all four research countries had adopted policies against mass evictions, especially in the context of urban redevelopment. One of the most important policy changes spurred by activists occurred in September 2013, when India adopted The Right to Fair Compensation and Transparency in Land Acquisition, Rehabilitation and Resettlement Act to replace the 1894 Land Acquisition Act. Although it took many years, much pressure and negotiation, and several separate attempts to craft successful legislation, the law eventually passed. Despite some shortcomings, scholars (Cernea, 2013) have found the law a credible improvement because it obliges projects to resettle the displaced and facilitate their recovery. It also provides some human rights protections, new economic entitlements, and increased access to information. Even some activists who fought until the last moment for more changes have characterized it as a "tool for struggle" for more equitable development planning (NAPM, 2013).

Another important change in policy is the definition of the Maharashtra "cut-off date"; residents officially counted before this date benefit from resettlement if displaced, whatever their tenure status and the legal status of their neighborhood. There has been pressure to extend the date, initially 1976, then 1985, then January 1995 (Das, 2003, p. 214). In July 2014, a government resolution extended the cut-off date until 2000 (*Times of India*, 2014).

Activism has also promoted selectivity in the ways that governments implement current policies; of particular interest is the provision of enhanced benefits. Even before Mumbai's cut-off date was recently changed, some large projects, such as the redevelopment of the Dharavi slum, used 2000. Mumbai also enacted several slum development initiatives that offered residents benefits beyond the strict framework of India's 1894 Land Acquisition Act. Activists attributed these changes to the pressure put on elected officials by Mumbai's poorer residents.

Conclusion

Clearly, the issue of DIDR activism warrants more considered and systematic analysis of a larger sample to verify these patterns and better understand how activism has affected DIDR outcomes. At what phases of displacement and resettlement have activists been most successful? Do some combinations of strategies work better than others? How much difference do formal policies make? In addressing these questions, it is important to consider the similarities and the differences between urban and rural DIDR activism and how they can learn from one another.

Findings presented here suggest that DIDR activists have often been quite effective in gaining better compensation and resettlement conditions for affected individuals and households. They have also played an important role in pressuring governments to enact more humane policies on displacement and resettlement. Resettlement policy makers and project personnel trying to create more equitable programs and address conflicts of interest among the different DIDR participants could learn much from the political struggles of activists already working with affected populations.

Finding ways to partner with activists to create better resettlement programs that are more responsive to local conditions is surely a step in the right direction.

Note

1 This project followed the 1990 version of the World Bank Involuntary Resettlement policy. Requirements for consultation are similar, but the 2001 guidelines enhance the emphasis on participation.

References

ADB (Asian Development Bank), 2009. *Safeguard policy statement.* Manila: Asian Development Bank.

Amorim, I., 2009. Resettlement of communities: The case study of Jaguariba, a resilient community (northeast of Brazil). *JAMBÁ: Journal of Disaster Risk Studies*, 2(3), pp. 216–234.

CAO (Compliance Advisor/Ombudsman, IFC), 2010. Ombudsman assessment report: Complaint regarding IFC's Cambodia Airport II Project. Available at: www.cao-ombudsman.org/cases/document-links/documents/CambodiaAirportAssessmentReportFINALWebsite.pdf [Accessed January 19, 2014].

Cernea, M., 2013. Progress in India: New legislation to protect persons internally displaced by development projects. *Brookings Up Front.* Available at: www.brookings.edu/blogs/up-front/posts/2013/10/21-india-displacement-cernea [Accessed October 28, 2013].

Clark, D., 2009. Power to the people: Moving towards a rights-respecting resettlement framework. In: A. Oliver-Smith, ed. *Development and dispossession: The crisis of forced displacement and resettlement.* Santa Fe, NM: School for Advanced Research Press, pp. 181–199.

Das, P.K., 2003. Slums: The continuing struggle for housing. In: S. Patel and J. Masselos, eds. *Bombay and Mumbai: The city in transition.* New Delhi: Oxford University Press, pp. 207–234.

de Wet, C., 2006. Risk, complexity and local initiative in forced resettlement. In: C. de Wet, ed. *Development-induced displacement: Problems, policies and people.* Oxford: Berghahn, pp. 180–202.

Fisher, W., 2009. Local displacement, global activism: DFDR and transnational advocacy. In: A. Oliver-Smith, ed. *Development and dispossession: The crisis of forced displacement and resettlement.* Santa Fe, NM: School for Advanced Research Press, pp. 163–179.

IFC (International Finance Corporation), 2012. *Performance Standard 5: Land acquisition and involuntary resettlement.* Washington, DC: International Finance Corporation.

Koenig, D., 2006. Enhancing local development in development-induced displacement and resettlement projects. In: C. de Wet, ed. *Development-induced displacement: Problems, policies and people.* Oxford: Berghahn, pp. 105–140.

Koenig, D., 2009. Urban relocation and resettlement: Distinctive problems, distinctive opportunities. In: A. Oliver-Smith, ed. *Development and dispossession: The crisis of forced displacement and resettlement.* Santa Fe, NM: School for Advanced Research Press, pp. 119–139.

Koenig, D., 2014. Reconstructing and improving livelihoods among the urban displaced: Lessons from Mumbai. In: J. Perera, ed. *Lose to gain: Is involuntary resettlement a development opportunity?* Manila: Asian Development Bank, pp. 126–150.

Koné, Y.F., 2009. *Settlement, demolition, and resettlement in the Senou neighborhood*. Bamako. Report to American University.

Lenaola, I., 2013. Judgment, Petition No. 65 of 2010. Available at: http://kenyalaw.org/caselaw/cases/view/90359/ [Accessed January 21, 2014].

Levey, B. and Levey, J.F., 2000. End of the roads. *Washington Post Magazine*, November 26, pp. 10–26.

Mosse, D., 2005. *Cultivating development: An ethnography of aid policy and practice*. London: Pluto Press.

NAPM (National Alliance of People's Movements), 2013. An invitation: Two day meeting on new Land Acquisition Act, people's movements and its political implications. Available at: http://napm-india.org/content/invitation-two-day-meeting-new-land-acquisition-act-peoples-movements-and-its-political-impl [Accessed November 5, 2013].

Nolan, R., 2002. *Development anthropology: Encounters in the real world*. Boulder, CO: Westview Press.

Oliver-Smith, A., 2006. Displacement, resistance and the critique of development: From the grass roots to the global. In: C. de Wet, ed. *Development-induced displacement: Problems, policies and people*. Oxford: Berghahn, pp. 141–179.

Oxfam, 1996. *A profile of European aid II: Northern corridor transport project, Adverse social and environmental impacts caused by the rehabilitation of the Westlands-St. Austins and Kabete-Limuru roads, Kenya*. Oxford: Oxfam UK/I Policy Department.

PUKAR Editors' Collective, 2008. *Mumbai's barefoot researchers*. Mumbai: PUKAR (Partners for Urban Knowledge, Action and Research).

Rew, A., Fisher, E., and Pandey, B., 2006. Policy practices in development-induced displacement and rehabilitation. In: C. de Wet, ed. *Development-induced displacement: Problems, policies and people*. Oxford: Berghahn, pp. 38–70.

Schechla, J., 2013. A reparations framework for urban forced evictions: Cases from the Middle East and East Africa. Paper presented at conference *Urban displacement and development: Moving the debate forward*, Copenhagen, February 7–8.

Scudder, T., 2005. *The future of large dams: Dealing with social, environmental, institutional and political costs*. London: Earthscan.

SPARC (Society for the Promotion of Area Resource Centers), 2014. Home. Available at: www.sparcindia.org [Accessed July 2, 2014].

Tankha, S., Burtner J., and Schmandt J., 1998. Relocation and resettlement in Ceará: Second interim report on findings to the Secretary of Water Resources, State of Ceará. The Woodlands, TX: Center for Global Studies, Houston Advanced Research Center.

Times of India, 2014. Govt extends cut-off date for slum regularization to January 2000, *The Times of India*, 23 July. Available at: http://timesofindia.indiatimes.com/city/mumbai/Govt-extends-cut-off-date-for-slum-regularization-to-January-2000/articleshow/38884035.cms [Accessed August 2, 2014].

TISS (Tata Institute of Social Sciences), 2008. *Impact assessment of resettlement implementations under Mumbai Urban Transport Project*. Mumbai: TISS.

UN Habitat (United Nations Human Settlements Programme), 2007. *Enhancing urban safety and security: Global report on human settlements 2007*. London: Earthscan.

WB (World Bank), 2001. *OP 4.12 Involuntary resettlement*. Washington, DC: World Bank.

WCD (World Commission on Dams), 2000. *Dams and development: A new framework for decision-making*. The report of the World Commission on Dams. London: Earthscan.

Wirth, L., 1938. Urbanism as a way of life. *American Journal of Sociology*, 44, pp. 1–24.

World Bank Inspection Panel, 2005. *Investigation report, India: Mumbai Urban Transport Project* (IBRD Loan No. 4665-IN; IDA Credit No. 3662-IN). Washington, DC: World Bank Inspection Panel.

Yuvamedia, 2008. Vashi Naka hunger strike. Available at: www.youtube.com/watch?v=lbiGyeWgD08 [Accessed January 20, 2014].

Conclusion

A step forward in theory, methodology and practice in development-induced displacement and resettlement

Narae Choi and Irge Satiroglu

The current book emerged as a response to a long overdue call for a focused discussion on DIDR, particularly the kind that brings a range of perspectives and promotes cross-fertilisation. The papers included in this volume deliver a collective message with regard to where development-induced displacement and resettlement (DIDR) research and practice stand and where it should head towards.

What do we know about DIDR?

Is DIDR losing its stake in the wider development arena? Is it now being treated as the same old problem? Despite being a long-standing challenge in the history of development, DIDR has remained largely unresolved. The concern is amplified when we consider both persisting and fresh challenges in a changing landscape of development aid and investments, increasingly shaped by private entities, which has hitherto blurred the accountability issue. This requires us to revisit what we think we know about DIDR; or perhaps we should return to the fundamental methodological, ethical and political questions; or it may be a time to bring in new perspectives to the 'same old problem'.

Thought-provoking questions on the existing body of knowledge and the mode of practice are running through the volume. Satiroglu starts by highlighting the dilemma that there is no consensus on what success is in DIDR, neither on how to assess it. Over a case study that was not a successful resettlement per se but arguably resulted with improved conditions for some of the displaced groups, she questions the completeness and comprehensiveness of our understanding on the long-term consequences of DIDR and germane factors and opportunities that may impact upon these consequences.

In fact, despite a strong belief that effective management of DIDR would prevent associated risks, identification of impacts, precise definition of desired outcomes and measurement methodologies await further refinement. It is still questionable whether we understand the adverse impacts of DIDR comprehensively, when considering indirect impacts experienced by those who did not move but were nonetheless impacted in the process (Choi). Underlined by both researches (Satiroglu and Choi) is the complexity of DIDR whereby differential impacts cannot be easily aggregated into a clear-cut conclusion. Such complexity arises from the embedded nature of settlements within a specific locality (or 'emplacement') and the consequent socio-spatial changes involved in DIDR ('de-emplacement' and 're-emplacement') which cannot be easily managed by the logic of rational planning (de Wet). This raises a pressing need for contextualised understanding of DIDR, which is underlined and exemplified by many case studies in the book (e.g. Gouws, Narayan, Satiroglu and Serje). Shortfalls in understanding the complexity of DIDR have practical implications for the capacity of both affected people and practitioners to address the challenges. DIDR research and practice is largely focused on planners' evaluation and mitigation of risks, while this information is not sufficiently shared with the displaced people. Xi *et al.* raise a poignant question of 'risk assessment for whom and by whom?' and demonstrate that the risk perception of the displaced influence their actual experiences of resettlement in such a way that those who are aware of the risks awaiting them are much more prepared and remain resilient. On the other hand, when excluded from risk information, they are less capable of coping and more exposed to unexpected difficulties without adequate preparation. By engaging with such a basic question of 'what a household is', Gouws also illustrates the complexities inherent to resettlement. While a household is a common unit of entitlement that typically forms the base on which resettlement is planned, he notes that the very definition of what constitutes a household is fraught with social, legislative, perceptual and semantic influences. This often leads to disputes over the meaning of a household in project implementation as its definition can have real impacts on livelihoods and social relationships. At the centre of the shortfalls of, and contestations over, knowledge is the imbalance in access to information and the power to legitimise certain information over others, which relates to ethical and political questions that are fundamental to the field.

Empowerment: the power of people in a structurally unjust situation

That population movement is considered and included as part of a planned change has raised a series of critical questions such as whether displacement by development is inevitable in the first place (Choi), under what conditions it can be justified (Drydyk) and who has the power to make such decision (Serje), and whether we are aware of what we are up against (de Wet). The concern with the high risk of injustice involved in DIDR has been the prime driver behind most papers in this volume and empowerment has surfaced as a keyword, acknowledged in the way that the power imbalance inherent in the decision of population displacement and often unjust processes and outcomes emanating from it needs to be addressed; and that affected people, despite the incredible challenges imposed on them, have demonstrated resilience, power and agency over and over again (Kavanagh, Koenig and Gilmore).

Having a clear framework to identify values with which we can distinguish worthwhile development from maldevelopment has proved to be crucial for advancing the ethical discussions in DIDR. Based on the development ethics values framework, Drydyk defines the entitlements of displaced people as appropriate means of achieving worthwhile development. The entitlement to empowerment is particularly instrumental for both procedural and consequential justice, which in turn requires information dissemination, space for negotiation, facilitation and management, and good governance and compliance protection. Likewise, focusing on the international rights and policies that are relevant to DIDR, Morel proposes that establishing an explicit 'right not to be displaced' would be a powerful conceptual tool for protecting people from arbitrary displacement.

However, these ethical concerns unfold within locally specific political economies whereby the power to justify and impose forced population movement prevails. While it is important to have a legal framework protecting the rights of displaced people and compensating them for the harm inflicted on them (Price and Morel), the governance system for DIDR translated from the international to the local level is never straightforward. The realisation of rights- and risks-based approaches towards DIDR has depended on state regulation and corporate self-regulation (Price). Particularly, in the changing environment of global project financing, the international financial institutions' standards on DIDR cover only a fraction of cases and their capacity to monitor and evaluate DIDR outcomes is further limited. As an acute illustration, Serje demonstrates through the narratives of the displaced how the state creates a space of 'exception' in Colombia whereby urban informal settlers are seen as communities to be 'normalized' and resettlement features as a process of formalising the informal way of living.

As compared to the world of policies and implementations, DIDR activism creates a space where the existing power relations are called into question and the conventional models of development are challenged. It is also a claim and action of affected people for greater inclusion in development and resettlement decision making, which counteracts a common perception of the displacees as 'passive victims', who are oppressed, disarticulated and impoverished. While the structural injustice needs to be addressed, the power and agency of people in defining their own future is reaffirmed by many chapters in this volume. A fine balance needs to be struck, however. So-called DIDR experts may not know better than people and thus are not qualified to decide 'the best' for people, but unless the aforementioned knowledge deficit on the part of people is not addressed, it may not be possible for people to make the right decision for themselves either.

Empowerment plays a critical role at this crossroad. The centrality of empowerment to equity is evidenced by the acts of people challenging power imbalance (Koenig), filling the regulatory and protection gap (Kavanagh) and creating a space for voicing their experience and views (Gilmore). In particular, knowledge (more than project information) features as a powerful means of empowerment to promote people's resilience/strength, for which knowledge sharing down the system to the local level becomes critical (de Wet and Price). In addition to the range of strategies that DIDR activists and affected people resort to, more creative means of activism and intellectual inputs for empowerment are also proposed. Notably, the potential of literature is discovered to be an influential means for agency, activism and resistance in a situation of radical power imbalances between governments, development agencies and corporate interests, and the displaced (Gilmore). The research by Xi *et al.* is evidence in itself demonstrating that the transparency of risk information, which is currently confined to the circle of project proprietors, is an indispensable component of successful resettlement outcomes.

Multidisciplinary approach and methodological advancement

Coming out of the volume are two clear directions for advancing DIDR studies, namely, cross-fertilisation with multiple disciplines and methodological diversification. To begin with, Choi argues that the separation of DIDR research from broader development discussions may weaken our ability to question some of the assumptions in the field. Satiroglu underlines the global scarcity of comparable quantitative pre- and post-project data and advocates the integrated use of quantitative and qualitative tools in research to avoid possible biases that are not unlikely given the complex, political, and sensitive nature of DIDR.

Many chapters are illustrative of the potential ways to enrich the field on both fronts. In engaging with pertinent ethical issues around the justification (or the justifiability) of DIDR, Drydyk and de Wet borrow insights from development ethics and complexity theory, respectively, demonstrating how theorisation in DIDR studies can be deepened with the aide of meta-theories. Likewise, Morel draws on the international law and well-established human rights in systematically exploring the legal basis for protecting people against arbitrary forms of development-induced displacement (DID).

Gilmore and Xi *et al.* expand the boundary of DIDR studies by tapping into other disciplines and introduce fresh perspectives that can complement/strengthen the conventional methodologies in the field. Coming from the literary background, Gilmore finds a new methodological potential whereby literature can provide rich materials for better understanding the reasons behind people's resistance and the strategies to achieve their political objectives. Xi *et al.* make an invaluable contribution not only by engaging with one of the least studied issues, namely, the impacts of DIDR on mental health, but also by creating a link with the field of psychology and utilising its refined methodologies for measuring risk perception, preparedness and psychological well-being. Conducted with the same respondents over a long period of time, their research also reveals the advantages and importance of a longitudinal approach in DIDR.

Using comparable data across cases has availed researchers to extract invaluable information for DIDR. The tradition has continued with this volume. Koenig identifies common strategies of urban activists by cross-examining multiple DIDR cases and likewise Kavanagh delineates from different cases in Myanmar how DIDR-affected people resist, negotiate and claim rights in the absence of proper governance and legal protection. In exploring diverse ways in which a household is understood, Gouws utilises his project experiences in a few countries in Africa. Using rich data documenting the experiences of eviction and relocation in 14 slum communities in Chennai, Narayan compares them at various stages in order to verify any consistency across cases. These studies demonstrate the possibility of a more rigorous comparative study at the global/regional, national and local (e.g. city-wide) levels.

Final remarks

DIDR is an inherently complex phenomenon involving socio-spatial changes, time-consuming processes with long-lasting implications and multiple stakeholders of varying interests and power. Yet, despite all the complexity and challenges it poses, emerging studies suggest that the long-term consequences may not necessarily be negative upon all the displaced people. Is there any chance that DIDR may also encompass hidden opportunities for the displaced people such as increased freedom and mobility when backed up with adequate land resettlement and cash compensation options?

While decades of research and practice have seen progress on this front, it is still questionable whether we have developed and promoted sufficient theories, methods and policies to facilitate justice in DIDR situations. Research suggests that projects are frequently 'rushed into' and denied the necessary time and resources to investigate and mitigate the displacement impacts. The norms, dynamics and needs of the displaced communities are not always well-understood and people are not fully informed of potential risks involved in displacement and resettlement, which can allow them to prepare accordingly and thus have better control over their lives, resources and futures. We still lack data to systematically compare pre- and post-project conditions and to refine our understanding on what works to mitigate the impacts of DIDR. Neither is there a consensus on what 'success' is and how to assess it. Filling the gaps in terms of such guiding data, agreeing upon resettlement targets and methods of assessment will be one solid step towards identifying and materialising potential 'hidden' opportunities in the process of DIDR.

With this book, we attempt to suggest new perspectives that question assumptions in the field, and engage with ethics of DIDR, policy discourses and DIDR activism. By presenting some of the most stimulating discussions of the International Conference on DIDR, we hope to share the theoretical and methodological dynamism created through the dialogue of different disciplines and perspectives and make our contribution to the knowledge and data produced over the past 50 years. Yet, we acknowledge that there remains much to be explored and examined in the field and we should continue working towards advancement of the policies and practices through questioning, researching and collaborating across disciplines and sectors.

Index